INTO THE AMAZON

An Incredible Story of Survival in the Jungle

JOHN HARRISON

INTO THE AMAZON

First published in 2001 as *Off the Map: The Call of the Amazonian Wild*

This edition published 2011

Summersdale Publishers Ltd
46 West Street
Chichester
West Sussex
PO19 1RP
UK

www.summersdale.com

Printed and bound in Great Britain

ISBN: 978-1-84953-147-4

To Heather and our children, Lewis and Ella

After seven canoeing expeditions to the Amazon, John Harrison is regarded as one of the world's experts on independent jungle exploration. His first book *Up the Creek: An Amazon Adventure* was described as *'an admirable book by an admirable man'* in *The Daily Telegraph*.

He was profiled by National Geographic TV in 1991, and has chaired tropical forest workshops at the Royal Geographical Society. He lives in Bristol.

Praise for *Into the Amazon*:

'A tightly-drawn narrative, full of adventure and excitement'
TRAVELLER magazine

'John Harrison is one of an increasingly rare breed of true explorers whose motive is neither science nor sensationalism... This is a genuine traveller's tale, realistic both in its description of extreme jungle life and also of the stresses to which even the best relationships are prone to in such an environment'
Robin Hanbury-Tenison, THE FIELD

'This is the real thing: the excitement, delight, hardship, beauty and danger of paddling into unexplored Amazon forests, and told with charm and knowledge'
Dr John Hemming, former Director of
the Royal Geographical Society

CONTENTS

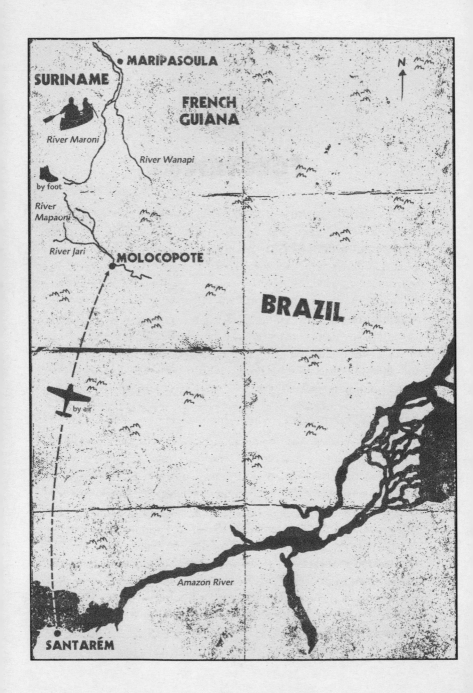

Foreword

In 1985 I had the pleasure of writing the foreword to John Harrison's *Up the Creek*, a memorable account of a gallant failure to paddle from Monte Dourado up the Jari and Mapaoni rivers to French Guiana. Since then John has remained closely involved with his beloved Amazonia, and some years later – middle-aged and with an abdominal hernia – he decided to try again, starting from Molocopote, crossing into Surinam and descending a few more unheard of rivers to the former French penal colony. Meanwhile he had acquired a suitable wife; so suitable that she was his companion on this journey and probably one of the reasons why it ended successfully after months of unimaginable hardship. As has often been proved over the centuries, what women lack in muscle-power is compensated for by their stamina and stoicism.

Not that marital bliss prevailed all the way – that would be unnatural – and its waning during the later stages gives yet another dimension to this polymathic adventure story. It took the couple thirty-six days to find a way across the pathless Tumucumaque Hills and then to transport their folding canoe and camping gear to the banks of the Ouaremapaan River in Surinam. This was an unexpected delay and by then their food supply was running out and their tolerance of each other's idiosyncrasies had almost evaporated.

By contemporary standards, John and Heather Harrison are daft masochists. The invention of the outboard engine means that you no longer have to paddle your own canoe. The development of sophisticated communications systems means that you no longer have to be cut off for months from the rest of humanity. However, if you relish the challenge of travelling through uninhabited territory in a style that unites you with your forbidding but very beautiful surroundings, then you prefer to depend on wo/ man-power and trust to luck. John Harrison notes that when using an outboard engine, 'Drums of gasoline fill half the canoe under a halo of stinking fumes, and the engine leaves a trail of blue exhaust, emitting a din that obliterates the birdsong or the rustlings and calls that betray the presence of an animal nearby.'

In times past, travellers in remote regions had no choice but to cut themselves off from the outside world for many months – sometimes years. To me that (increasingly elusive) feeling of isolation is an essential ingredient of a real journey, as distinct from a mere trip. Yet the modern traveller is often condemned as 'irresponsible' if s/he fails to keep in touch, or at least carry the means to do so in an emergency. Even thirty-three years ago this was the case, when I disappeared into the High Andes for four months with a nine-year-old daughter, a mule and no radio.

Now, as John Harrison notes, numerous gizmos are available, including HF radio transceivers, car-battery-powered and equipped with 30-foot aerials, which enable the user to contact any telephone number anywhere. As for the satellite phone, John succinctly explains that it would 'make a wilderness experience seem pretty 'erness to me.' (Hear, hear!) Another gadget can send an SOS to jet planes way up there in the stratosphere but John dreaded an accidental switch-on and the arrival of rescue aircraft, marine commandos and the British press. Here I reckon he is flattering the British press: their twenty-first century representatives have little in common with Henry Morton Stanley.

Some readers of this superb narrative will ask, 'What's the point? Why endure so many months of deprivation, exertion, isolation and danger? Why undertake a journey that taxes one – physically, mentally and emotionally – to the limit?' Part of the answer must be that the Harrisons wanted to remain in touch with the realities of life as it was lived for hundreds of generations before technology rendered our survival skills redundant. They wanted to use their bodies to get from Point A to Point B, which inevitably makes them seem eccentric in an age that has devalued the human body's potential.

Another clue to the motives of such eccentric travellers is offered by C. D. Darlington, whose magnum opus was *The Evolution of Man and Society*. He wrote:

> Man has been brought to the point where, tightly packed in numbers and partly fixed in character, in beliefs and in institutions, he has come near to being deprived of his initiative. He is no longer completely the master of his destiny that he once imagined himself to be.

A remedy for this is to paddle your own canoe hundreds of miles up fast-flowing Amazonian tributaries through uninhabited primary forest.

What mutations await us if we continue to not use our bodies for the purposes for which nature designed them? This is no frivolous question. Already motor-dependent societies have produced millions of children and young adults to whom walking more than 10 yards seems an unfamiliar, unnecessary and distasteful activity. Some privileged children are regularly exercised in structured, expensive ways – driven to swimming pools, ballet classes, football grounds and junior gyms by conscientious, exhausted parents. Most underprivileged children watch TV or play computer games to the detriment of their physical development. Mutations sound long-term but in fact can happen quite quickly, over generations rather than centuries. I would like to see this book on the syllabus of all schools in the UK and Ireland as an inspiration to the young, an example of what the human body and mind can achieve when functioning independently of engines.

In my view 'mind' is the key word. The average man or woman could do what John and Heather did without any special training if so minded. John admits that at the start of their journey he was overweight and neither he nor Heather were in top condition. The Harrisons are not 'professionals' who make a big thing of physical fitness. It seems they share my attitude: one starts out carrying a deplorable surplus of fat, knowing that soon one's exertions en route will have eliminated it. Indeed, it can be very useful – even essential – in certain circumstances. If one finds oneself in an area where supplies cannot be found the camel principle may be applied and those extra pounds can enable one to walk 25 miles a day on a tin of sardines.

During the early stages of their journey, Heather and John met a few impoverished Brazilian gold prospectors operating in small teams that are flown to their base camps in the interior by light aircraft. When scattered all over the vastness of Amazonia such small teams add up and shortly before the Harrisons' journey 50,000 *garimpeiros* had been expelled from the Yanomani territory near the Venezuelan border. In November 2000 twelve *garimpeiros* were killed by Indians on the upper Jari where they had been illegally mining within a reserve and had started a fire which killed an Indian woman and her child. John and Heather found the *garimpeiros* congenial folk but because of their activities it is by now extremely difficult to find pristine rivers or streams anywhere in Amazonia.

Canoes, like bicycles, impose wholesome anti-consumerism limitations. You cannot load them with all those superfluous camping comforts, gadgets and goodies offered to 4x4 travellers and backpackers who use trains and motor vehicles. Instead, you must think hard about what is truly necessary for your survival in a particular area – which is very little, especially in Amazonia where the climate allowed Heather and John to go naked once they had said goodbye to the *garimpeiros*. Food made up by far the greatest part of their gear so every day the canoe became lighter.

This book is much more than an exciting adventure story. Casually – never deserting the narrative to go off on wordy tangents – John Harrison makes us reflect on several of those issues that confront and confuse citizens of our overdeveloped world. He doesn't enjoy killing his fellow creatures but of course if you're hungry enough you do kill them, as some of them kill other species for food. At the end of a sombre recollection of monkey hunts John writes: 'Such is all hunting, in my opinion. There is no joy in it – only an occasional thrill when the quarry is being stalked – but that turns to sadness and guilt when the bloody pile of fur or feathers is retrieved.'

Inevitably, a melancholy undercurrent flows through this book. As corporate interests (logging, mining, damming, ranching, soya bean growing) speedily intrude into almost every corner of our planet, untouched regions such as the Harrisons travelled through are doomed. In the last chapter John writes: 'The last hours of paddling had passed us through a shocking hinterland of devastation. The reality of rainforest destruction had been forgotten in the months travelling through unsullied primary forest but now suddenly it was all around...' What makes this destruction so extra-enraging – and simultaneously so despair-inducing – is the sheer futility of many projects. As John points out, most of the grandiose schemes don't work, yet their failures go unheeded. Another profit-hungry corporation comes along with another crazy notion and another vast area is ravaged, then abandoned because it is not profitable after all, leaving 'the bequest of useless desert to future generations'. By the year 2020, if the Brazilian government's $40 billion Avança Brasil plan succeeds, scarcely 10 per cent of Amazonia's primary forest will remain standing. This is very frightening.

Such developments spell disaster not only for the populations – human and otherwise – of the regions concerned but for the whole planet. Avança Brasil, backed by the Japanese government and God knows who else, is a vicious example of globalisation as that word is now understood; it will improve trading links between the Pacific Ring and the south of South America. And it neatly fits on the same shelf as America's spurning of the Kyoto Agreement. To quote C. D. Darlington again: 'Every invention of man has made his environment more favourable for his short-term multiplication. But it has made his environment less favourable for his long-term survival.' It may well be that this book is seen, some years hence, as the last authentic account of a journey through the incomparable wonders of the Amazonian world as it has existed for countless millennia before human technological ingenuity enabled human greed to destroy it.

Dervla Murphy

PROLOGUE

December 1983

'How deep should a grave be anyway?' Peter asked, scuffing the patch of rough ground with the toe of his sandal.

I thought back to a blustery winter long before, and the burial of a friend who hadn't survived the heady exhilaration of a new driving licence. I remembered the cold wind whipping the yews, the devastated parents clutching each other to keep from falling apart and the group of pasty-faced friends staring into the dark trench of the grave. It had seemed bottomless. All our assumptions of immortality lay in that conker-coloured coffin whose lid echoed under the hard rain of clay.

'I don't know,' I answered now. 'At least five feet I guess.'

'Bloody hell,' he muttered. 'Deep as that? We'd better get started then.'

The layer of topsoil was only 3 inches deep, then we were through to a glutinous clay which the axe sliced into chunks. Large rocks and sinewy roots from long-dead trees made us fight for every shovel scoop, and under the full glare of the tropical sun we were soon running with sweat that stung our eyes and darkened the waistband of our shorts. After forty-five minutes, and still barely a foot down, we stopped for a rest in some nearby shade.

Our food supplies had run out ten days earlier and since then we'd eaten almost nothing. The pangs of hunger had diminished a little, to be replaced with an overwhelming feebleness and lethargy. I gulped from a water bottle and could feel the cool liquid splashing down on the empty floor of my stomach.

'Is that a ripe cashew I can see up there?' Peter asked suddenly, raising himself on one elbow to tilt his gaunt whiskery chin and peer at the branches above his head.

'I believe it is. Give us a leg up will you?'

He descended with an apple-shaped fruit devoid of any blush of ripeness, but we shared its tough pulp, feeling our mouths go furry from the acidity. Peter pocketed the crescent nut to roast later. We then visited the other three fruit trees, but with no further luck.

'Lunch break over.' he announced, before adding, 'When I think of all those times I moaned about my dull sandwiches at work, and threw them away uneaten!'

We smiled wearily. Four months alone together in the jungle had forged a good friendship; we'd been through a lot together. A Swiss landscape gardener, Peter was also a lover of fine food, but he'd come to the wrong place here. In recent weeks we'd eaten just about anything that swam, slithered, swung, flew or hopped. I'd learnt that he was invariably generous, reliable and good-natured, and didn't have an ounce of malice or unpleasantness in his body. Regretfully in our time together he'd have learnt some less palatable insights about me.

Four hours later we sat down, exhausted, on the pile of earth by the grave and looked into its depths. It was a fine job. The neat perpendicular sides were pleasing to the eye and Fernando could be laid to rest 5 feet down with ample room to stretch out. It just seemed a bit of a shame to fill it in so soon.

A small dark-skinned man came ambling up the trail from camp.

'Trust Epileptic to turn up when the work's done,' I muttered. He was a shifty, light-fingered, unsavoury man in his early thirties who thought himself wily and cunning. He was now our only companion. He approached the grave while we watched him in hostile silence, and scrutinised our work without comment.

'Did you find any cashews today?' he asked innocently.

'Just one,' Peter replied.

'Where's my share? I thought we'd agreed to share out any food between us?' His mouth turned down in a wounded pout of betrayal.

'It wasn't big enough, an—'

I butted in. 'Anyway, we were working while you've been lying in your hammock all morning, so we needed it more.'

'I had malaria last night,' he whined. 'I was so weak this morning that I couldn't even stand up.'

I remembered his theatrical groans in the darkness. Once he'd whimpered, 'Oh my dear God, I'm dying!' and I had called out, 'Well hurry up then, for pity's sake!' Maybe I could get a job at the local hospice.

'Oh you poor thing,' I snapped. 'We *all* had malaria last night, but we don't use it as an excuse every time there's some work to be done!'

My self-control seemed to evaporate when I had dealings with Epileptic, and I detested the little weasel with an irrational hatred way beyond anything I'd felt before. Peter, being Swiss, adopted that comfortable neutral stance that has kept his country out of Europe's messy wars. I can't remember Epileptic's real name; in fact I doubt if we were ever interested enough to find it out. Epileptic was the cruel label that we'd given him because, after running out of tablets, his attacks now came daily, making the poor man terrified to go too near the river or the fire. We should have been more sympathetic.

I could see that he felt just as much hatred for me. His face was contorted now, and his arms began windmilling about.

'Shout, shout, shout! You're always shouting! Three days ago you shouted at me for not sharing a bit of food, and now you two eat behind my back!'

He was right, but Peter and I had caught him eating all fifty cashew nuts that we'd roasted to eat communally, so there was a difference in scale.

'Anyway,' he went on, adopting a laughable expression of unctuous piety, 'you should lower your voice and show some respect for the dead man lying over there.'

'I wish it was you who was dead,' I said venomously, and the conviction in my voice shook all three of us. 'I wouldn't bother digging a grave though – just toss you in the river for the piranhas – if they could face eating you, that is.' I put my face near his, and added with a leer. 'Maybe I'll do that anyway next time you have one of your fits.'

'For Christ's sake, that's enough!' Peter appealed, seizing my shoulder.

It was enough. The stricken look that had flitted across the man's face made me feel horribly ashamed of myself. Shaking off Peter's hand I turned and walked away down to the river, stripping off my shorts and sprawling in the shallows. The mossy green water of the Jari flowed around me, and I stared morosely at the jungle on the far bank while little fish pecked experimentally at my skin, occasionally nibbling an infected scab and making me wince. Reminded of the toothpick-thin candiru fish that likes to dart up human orifices from where they can only be removed by surgery, I wriggled my bottom deeper into the sand, and kept a protective hand over other important bits.

Would we ever get out of this place?

We'd had sixteen days of waiting already – sixteen days of hunger, sickness and mind-numbing boredom. A plane might never come. We could wait day after day until we were too weak to paddle the 300 miles downstream to the nearest habitation. If the pilot didn't return soon we'd join Fernando, dying senselessly in the middle of nowhere.

We'd had no choice but to return to this airstrip of Molocopote after we'd failed in our goal to portage the canoe over the hills that form the border between Brazil and Surinam. It was the only place we'd met people in the last four months.

Peter and I had come the hard way to get here, paddling against the current. At 500 miles in length, the Jari is a modest river in that part of the world where seventeen of the Amazon's tributaries are more than a thousand miles long. It's tiny compared to the mighty Rio Negro which, at 2,400 miles, is the second largest river in the world with a discharge slightly greater than the Congo and three times that of the Mississippi. The Jari is a mere creek when compared with the giant Madeira, Tapajós, Purus, Juruá, Xingu or Araguaia. It's the last major northern tributary of the Amazon, spilling its waters almost into the delta itself.

Huge it isn't, but there's something wild and untameable about the Jari that sets it apart from other Amazon rivers I know. Rising in the Tumucumaque Hills a couple of miles from the border with Surinam, it tinkles over some small rapids near the source and then settles down to meander along sedately for the next 250 miles, giving every impression of being a mature river; calm and unexcitable. Then it suddenly recaptures its youthful vigour, dropping over two 60-foot waterfalls and seventy rapids in the next 200 miles, only calming down in the last 50 miles before it joins the Amazon.

This natural barrier of white water is impressive indeed. Peter and I had been in the rapids for weeks, wading day after day, roping up, carrying sacks, and portaging the canoe, with the roar of the river a constant accompaniment. Jagged rocks threatened to rip us to pieces if we made a mistake, and black boulders shone through rainbow-tinged spray. The whole river poured down chutes with barely a ripple but with the power of a dam sluiceway, or fell over sheer cliffs with a thunder that we could hear for twenty-four hours before we got there. And this was the dry season with the river 20 feet lower than it would be in the rains. Eighty-foot tree trunks lay bleaching in the sun where they had been tossed at high water; debris and flotsam hung in the bushes high above our heads; rocky platforms sometimes 100 yards wide separated the reduced river from its jungle banks, polished to a shine by tumbling pebbles, or with deep blow holes now full of stagnant water that the current had reamed out with spinning boulders.

Malaria had been with us all the way, often forcing us to camp, racked with shakes and sweats and aching bones until high doses of quinine revived some of our strength. When we'd passed Molocopote six weeks before, the place had been free of malaria. The boss of the gold workings had done his best to keep it healthy; giving all his men blood tests to ensure that they were free of the disease. How could he have predicted that two ague-ridden Europeans would arrive out of nowhere, stay for three days and leave anopheles mosquitoes ready to regurgitate their tainted blood into their next victim?

Our difficulties hadn't ended in the quieter water above the rapids. It was approaching the end of the dry season and hundreds of fallen trees had littered the shallows of the little creek that was to take us into the hills. Each one forced us to lift out our sacks, haul the canoe over and reload. Ten yards later we'd do it again, and again and again – forty or fifty times a day to advance a mile at most.

Yet it hadn't all been grim and joyless. When malaria left us alone we felt stronger, fitter and healthier than at any other time in our lives. We'd fought epic battles with giant catfish and seen most of the Amazon animals, even ones that were nearing extinction elsewhere. We'd seen places that came as near to paradise as any and set off each day into the unknown, curious and excited because our useless maps gave us no idea what to expect around the corner. We'd joked and laughed a surprising amount, and we wouldn't have missed it for the world.

The decision to quit had been postponed until our food and quinine were almost gone, until our bodies began to fail us in a demand for rest. Peter was complaining of heart palpitations and showing the early signs of mucosal leishmaniasis, a disease spread by sand flies, where the infection begins as a skin nodule at the site of the bite before progressing to severe ulceration of the mucus membranes around the nose and mouth. Severe facial disfigurement can occur if it's left untreated. We both had vivax and falciparum strains of malaria that would kill us once the quinine ran out.

Our expedition failed because we hadn't been able to find the starting point for the 15-mile portage through hilly jungle to Surinam, using the route of an old Indian trail. By carrying the canoe and gear across the watershed we could reach a river on the other side and avoid returning down the Jari. But our maps weren't accurate enough to be sure of our position, the terrain lacked any distinguishing features that might have aided us, and the Indians had left the region many years before so there was no one around to help.

So we'd given up and paddled for ten days back to Molocopote, the only place for hundreds of miles where we knew we'd find people. This was the site of a Wayaná Indian village that had been abandoned in the late 1970s. The Brazilian Indian protection agency, The National Foundation for the Indians, had cleared an airstrip to bring in supplies and personnel, and for many years the upper Jari was closed to outsiders. The ban was only lifted in 1981. The Indians had gone, but the airstrip remained and the gold prospectors had assured us that in an emergency we could fly out from there in one of their supply planes.

We retraced our steps with a sense of failure and disappointment at first, but before long we were desperate to escape. Stripped of our goal to cross the mountains, our motivation had gone. The daily routine of physical effort and monotonous chores now seemed so unbearably tedious that we couldn't understand how we'd endured it for so long.

So, sixteen days earlier, we'd run the bow of the canoe up on the sandy foreshore and whooped with relief. No more paddling. In a day or two we could be in the city, getting our malaria treated, enjoying the bustle of the streets in the week before Christmas, gorging on varied, tasty food, getting news from home, receiving more mental stimulation in one day than in a month out in the jungle.

But Christmas had been and gone – just one more endless day that had passed with ears cocked for the drone of our salvation. One plane had arrived ten days before, but there'd been no room onboard for Peter, Epileptic, Fernando and me.

And now Fernando was dead.

I heard Peter calling and dragged myself reluctantly out of the river. A wave of dizziness hit, turning my vision to monochrome, knocking me to my knees where I squatted with my head down until it passed. Time to bury our dead. It was New Year's Eve by our calculations. We couldn't be certain without a watch or calendar, but it must have been within a day or two of that. There wouldn't be much celebration that night.

Fernando was still in the hammock where he'd died. We pulled back the blanket and glanced squeamishly at his deathly visage, strangely yellow from the malaria that had killed him. Some little black ants had formed a column that ran from the struts of the shelter, down the hammock ropes and onto his skin where a few were disappearing between his parted lips. We brushed them off the cold face with a shudder before we pulled the cloth around him again.

Epileptic was impatient with the reluctant way we handled the body, and pushed us aside muttering, 'For heaven's sake, haven't you seen a dead person before?'

Peter and I shook our heads.

'How the hell can you get to your age and not have seen someone dead?' he asked in amazement. All the differences between the life experience of affluent Europeans and poor Brazilians were held in that question, and Epileptic seemed chuffed that he'd beaten the fancy foreigners at something.

It was a scruffy funeral procession, the three of us in shorts, barefoot, unshaven and uncombed as we carried the burdened hammock up the slope and laid twenty-year-old Fernando to rest. He'd died quite unnecessarily. The pilot should have given him priority, but none of the other prospectors had been willing to give up their place. Most of them were seriously ill too. Another pilot failed to return and we had no radio to call for help. So the amiable young man who'd hoped to find enough gold to pay for his wedding had died a prospector's death in a jungle clearing far from home, a victim of the mosquito. In my pocket was the phial of gold dust that I would hand over to his fiancée one day. It seemed a paltry amount to die for.

We began to fill in the red clay and a rather macabre scene took place that had Peter and me giggling hysterically, much to Epileptic's disgust. He'd done nothing to help when Fernando was alive but was a stickler for protocol now he was dead. After cooling in the hammock, Fernando's body had adopted a stiffened banana shape that wouldn't lie quite flat as we placed him face up in the bottom of the trench. As we began to shovel the soil over his feet, the weight pushed them down, causing the head and torso to rear up by a corresponding amount at the other end. Only when we shovelled earth over the head did we keep him down. When all the earth was replaced we each muttered a prayer, and Peter picked some wild flowers to lay on the top.

I looked around at the grassy clearing, with its fruit trees and bushes that the Indians had planted – some for gourds, some for decorative berries, some for arrow shafts – at the river that curved around in a large loop below, at the blue sky with the constant progression of fluffy cumulus that rolled in from the east, at the yellow and black oropendolas that flew around their basket nests in a nearby tree uttering a repertoire of cheeps, whistles, bubbling song and merriment. It could be worse. A smoke-blackened urban cemetery in England would certainly be worse than this.

'One down, three to go,' I joked as we walked back to camp, and Peter scowled at my poor taste.

We were finally rescued five days later. I doubt if we'd have been able to stand much more. Lethargic from hunger and sickness and with our quinine gone, we'd have died within two weeks anyhow, but worst of all was our mental deterioration. After months of constant activity and movement, with a high degree of excitement and motivation, we were bound to feel a sense of restlessness and loss. An end followed by three weeks of total and absolute nothingness had driven us to the edge of insanity. With nothing to do, nothing to read, and nothing to keep us remotely occupied, each day had seemed like ten.

Our saviour was a taciturn individual who believed in collecting his fares in advance. Peter and I had no money, but the pilot seemed satisfied with the two shotguns that we offered, even though one had a broken stock. Epileptic had no gold and nothing of any value, so the pilot refused to allow him on board.

'I'm not a charity,' he said. 'You wouldn't expect to get on a bus or train without paying so why should my plane be different?'

Epileptic's face crumpled in tears, and for a moment we felt the compassion and sense of solidarity that our joint predicament should have forged long before.

'I'll be getting some money sent from Switzerland in a few days,' said Peter. 'I could pay you his fare then.'

I glanced at my saintly companion in awe. Feeling sorry for Epileptic was one thing, but I couldn't switch from loathing to such charity in the space of a few minutes. I thought I'd better offer something nonetheless.

'We've got some medical equipment that you'd be able to sell to prospectors, some knives, hammocks, cooking pots, blankets, fishing tackle...' It didn't sound a very enticing package, and the pilot stared at me through his mirrored sunglasses, unimpressed.

'What about that gold dust?' Epileptic remembered suddenly, eagerly turning to me. 'That gold that Fernando gave you!'

'He asked me to give it to his fiancée,' I protested. 'It was one of his last requests.'

'I need it more than she does,' he argued. 'Fernando was my friend, he'd want me to have it.'

I doubted that somehow.

'What do you think?' I asked Peter, keen not to make this decision alone.

'I think you've really got to follow Fernando's wishes,' he said. 'He entrusted you with that task, didn't he?'

'His fiancée need never know! Don't tell me you were actually going to seek her out!' protested Epileptic, unerringly choosing the one argument that hardened our hearts against him.

The pilot was growing impatient. 'Come on or we won't make it to Santarém before dark.'

'You can't leave this guy here all alone with nothing to eat!' Peter protested.

'Oh yes I can,' he replied. 'Some of his mates are coming back in a week or so to continue prospecting, and they'll bring supplies. When he's earned his fare like everyone else he can leave. I know this son of a bitch. He's always broke and always begging favours. I don't like him.'

Before we had time to think up a solution he signalled us to get in, slammed the door, started the engine and began taxiing over the grass.

As the plane climbed away and headed south-west towards the real world, we looked back at the insignificant little clearing, and the lonely figure of Epileptic trudging dejectedly down the red smear of the trail. At last we were free, but the elation was soured by a sense of guilt that we hadn't done enough.

As for Molocopote, I never wanted to see the damn place ever again.

CHAPTER ONE

EIGHT YEARS LATER

Engines are mysterious things. They overheat, electrical systems short circuit, oil pressures soar or plummet, belts and fuel lines rupture, and pistons and big ends can shatter and be thrown like shrapnel clear through crankcases. Sometimes they just stop for no apparent reason at all. Given all the frenzied movement, with parts whizzing round at 5,000 revolutions a minute, 83 revolutions a second, it's hardly surprising. We all expect our cars to fail us occasionally. What's strange is that they're as reliable as they are.

The fallibility of the internal combustion engine makes it difficult to relax when flying in a single-engine plane. I gazed at the hilly jungle below, parted only by a few wild rivers. Hundreds and hundreds of miles with nowhere to land, and countless unyielding, rock-hard tree trunks to scrunch up the aluminium aircraft like some recyclable drinks can. Listening anxiously for the slightest hiccup or change in the dull, vibrating roar, I scanned the bewildering array of dials for one with a needle in the red.

Turning to our pilot I asked whether he'd ever had to make a forced landing or crashed. He frowned slightly at my bad taste in mentioning the C-word.

'I've crashed twice on landing,' he admitted, dipping the plane a fraction to avoid a bunch of heavy grey cloud. He shrugged philosophically. 'It happens out here – bad weather, muddy airstrips, and there's always the temptation to stuff too much weight on board.'

'Were you hurt?'

'I broke three ribs and an arm on the first one, and escaped without a scratch on the second. I also crash-landed once when I got lost in bad weather and ran out of fuel. The rain was so heavy I had to fly solely on instruments; I couldn't see any landmarks, rivers, nothing. All was grey, and those little airstrips are hard enough to see even on a fine day.' He was silent for a while. 'I landed in the treetops. I'd have probably chosen a river if I could have seen one, but they aren't always much good – too many rocks and driftwood. Anyway, you don't get that long to make up your mind when the engine stops. If you find an expanse of water you can skim the plane down smoothly and it stays afloat for a long time. Or so they say.'

'Oh good,' I muttered.

A mischievous glint appeared in his eye. 'To land in the trees you have to stall the plane deliberately just as you get a few feet above the trees. Like this.'

Before I could protest that I really wasn't that interested and stop him, he reduced power and pulled the nose up. The stall alarm bleated in protest and the plane seemed to hang stationary for a while before falling vertically, tail first, with a sickening uplift of the guts. My hands flew up and I swear my eyeballs left sticky marks on the back of my dark glasses. A little squeak escaped my lips; perhaps it was a scream. I heard Heather cry out from behind me. Unable to hear the conversation from her seat in the back she must have thought the plane was falling to bits.

Cesar chuckled, kicked a rudder, moved the stick, increased power and pointed the nose down. Soon we were back at our cruising speed.

'I landed in the crown of a tree as lightly as a feather, barely denting the plane. The radio was still working so I could call for a helicopter rescue, but it took five hours for them to find me, and every now and then the wind caused the plane to give a little lurch and slip a little. I thought it safer to climb out and stand in the branches. It was a long, long way to the ground.'

Cesar hadn't flown to Molocopote airstrip for many years but he propped a map on the dashboard and consulted it when his memory failed him. We crossed several rivers, including the Paru, the Paru de Oueste and the Ipitinga, whose rapids showed like creases on aluminium foil. The gold camp of Flechão on the Ipitinga was a large scar of smashed trees with dozens of miners' shelters covered with blue tarpaulins, pits full of muddy water and a stained river downstream. Down there the fever for gold was almost certainly being replaced by that more humdrum version spread by mosquitoes.

All these rivers had their source in the Tumucumaque Hills that form the eastern end of the Guiana Shield – the northern watershed of the Amazon basin. This is one of the oldest mountain ranges in the world, dating back 4,600 million years to the Archean period, and it has played an important role in the shaping of Amazonia.

The Amazon used to flow westwards and into the Pacific until the rise of the Andes about 40 million years ago robbed the river of its only outlet to an ocean. The Guiana Shield and the more southerly Brazilian Highlands were still joined in the east, preventing any access to the Atlantic, so the Amazon basin became an enormous area of lake and swamp. It only succeeded in breaking eastwards ten million years ago through a low-lying valley separating the two areas of highlands. As sea level was much lower during the Ice Age, with much of the earth's water frozen at the Poles, the fast-flowing Amazon ate into its sediments and deepened its channel to 300 feet in places.

The once mighty peaks of the Tumucumaque have now been whittled down to a confusion of rounded hills, seldom higher than 4,000 feet. Even these tough igneous rocks with high proportions of iron and magnesium haven't been able to withstand more than 4.5 billion years of attack by torrential rain and pitiless sun.

On the Brazilian side of the watershed the eroded particles and sediments were carried through the churning foam of the cataracts and deposited on that 30,000-foot mound of alluvial debris in the depths of the Atlantic beyond the Amazon's mouth.

The French explorer and geographer Jean Hurault described the remnants of the Tumucumaque as 'an infinity of hills, as anonymous as the waves on the sea'. He should know; being one of the first to survey part of it while working on the demarcation of the border between French Guiana and Brazil in the 1950s. Until the advent of aerial surveys in the last forty years, the Guiana Highlands were one of the least-known regions on earth. El Dorado was thought to be hidden in this mysterious wilderness, along with the fabled tribe of Amazon warrior women. Fortune-seekers felt that these hills must contain, at the very least, a fabulous wealth of gold and diamonds, and went off searching, some never to return.

Even today this region is totally uninhabited and largely unexplored, making it one of the last truly wild regions of Amazonia. The barrier of rapids on all the rivers that flow from these hills has kept it that way.

1990 had been a catastrophic year for our pilot, Cesar. He made national news when one of his larger planes was hijacked while on its daily run around the goldfields near the town of Itaituba. The demand had been for 20 kilos of gold. There were no passengers on board – only a pilot and the two hijackers – and they circled around while Cesar and the police in Santarém decided what to do. The police refused to consider any compromise.

'I wasn't keen to pay up,' Cesar explained, 'but they wouldn't have let me anyway. They told me the hijackers had to die to discourage others from trying this sort of thing.'

The Brazilian Federal Police Force is one of the most trigger-happy in the world. In the city of São Paulo they shot dead 1,470 people in 1992, roughly one every six hours. Their shootings accounted for 12 per cent of Rio's homicides in 2000.

Even prison overcrowding can be rectified in this manner, as they showed by killing 111 prisoners during a riot at the Carandiru detention centre in October 1992.

They handled Cesar's hijack with their usual finesse. Over the radio the pilot was instructed that after landing at Santarém he should bring the plane to a halt at a certain angle to the control tower. He should also sit forward in his seat. One can only imagine what he thought when he received this message from the Federal Police, and I'm sure he sat very far forward indeed. As soon as the plane came to a standstill the police sprayed the centre and rear of the fuselage with bullets for more than a minute, killing the two hijackers. Not a subtle negotiating tactic, but effective.

'Made a hell of a mess of the plane, and my pilot was lucky it didn't catch fire,' said Cesar. 'I'll never get any compensation, but I suppose repairs cost me a lot less than twenty kilos of gold.'

Five months later Cesar had another disaster. His new ten-seater aircraft crashed into the forest, killing seven and seriously wounding three. The pilot had forgotten to fill up with fuel. First one engine stopped, and although they were directly over an airstrip, a rainstorm hid it from view. Three minutes later the second engine coughed and died.

'Good job that pilot died,' muttered Cesar, hands clenching on the controls, 'because I'd have killed the careless son of a bitch myself if he hadn't.'

You couldn't imagine solid, dependable Cesar forgetting to top up the tank, being lax about servicing his planes or not carrying out pre-flight checks, but when we were doing some filming in the Amazon the previous year, our pilot had been very different. Paulo always looked as if he'd had a sleepless night, coming straight from some bar perhaps, unshaven, red-eyed and wincing at the noise of the engine. His plane didn't inspire much confidence either. The back was awash with spilt diesel from the drums he carried to the gold camps, the bodywork was dented, and the doors were held closed with twists of wire. Seat belts? You were lucky if you got a seat. The counter said the plane had flown more than 20,000 hours, but it was broken, so that was probably just for starters.

Paulo would start the engine and take off after the most cursory of checks. Once airborne he turned to talk to those behind him, hardly ever looking ahead or making those fussy little adjustments to the controls that Cesar was always engaged in. At times he grew quiet, his chin down, eyes invisible behind his dark glasses and in a panic we'd talk to him, fishing for consciousness. I wasn't surprised to find out that he too had crashed one day after forgetting to check his fuel.

It's not a part of the world where pilots, sloppy or otherwise, live forever. Most of them are excellent at their job, but the weather's unpredictable, the planes beyond their best, the airstrips short and slippery, and there's no radar to help. But the rewards are high, particularly for those servicing the gold camps, and a successful pilot can soon afford more planes and pilots to fly them. Cesar had five planes and probably earned over half a million dollars a year. In Santarém that's a fortune, but I still doubt if Cesar manages to have a good time in that dull little town that we'd left with few regrets an hour before.

I probably hold the record for being a foreign tourist in Santarém twenty-three times, for stays of up to three weeks at a stretch. It's one of those crossroads towns that a traveller passes through, but rarely stays for long through choice. I have got on and off riverboats here, taking the road south to the Mato Grosso, or spending time assembling canoes and hiring planes to fly me into the bush.

It's not all bad. It's suffocatingly hot, but it has a pleasant position where the Tapajós meets the Amazon, and there's a modest meeting of the two different coloured waters to admire. The fish market at dawn has some fabulous whiskery catfish. It also has a busy commercial sector with rows of shops selling identical produce, where browsing is actively discouraged. Seated on a raised podium, the boss, usually Syrian or Japanese, signals the assistants to go and harass anyone who crosses the threshold, so a tiresome teenager follows a foot behind you, repeatedly inquiring how he can help. Touch an item, and he practically has it wrapped for you. Walk out without buying anything and you expect to see the kid's body floating in the river later.

Santarém seems lively during the day with lots of bustle at the waterfront, and one can find most items to equip a jungle expedition here. It's at night that the place is excruciatingly dull. Travellers on their way to the deep forest wish to sample some last pleasures and carousing. Those just out of the forest are even more desperate for a good time. But in Santarém there's little to stay awake for.

Topping up your glass at the Bar Mascote, you watch the flashes of electrical storms far away in the Tumucumaque Hills, the swarms of insects around the street lights, or prostitutes fleecing the gold prospectors of their hard-earned nuggets. Three-quarters of the tables are empty, and from ten o'clock onwards the waiter makes it clear that you're keeping him from his bed. The traveller grows depressed, especially one spending time here alone, and as the empty beer bottles accumulate on the table he decides to go home, even though it's January and he hates cold weather.

I've since learned that Santarém is about to be thrust very brusquely into the twenty-first century. With enormous areas of former savannah and forest turned over to soya bean production in the Mato Grosso, it is planned to open a new deep-water port in the town to allow the grain producers to export their crop to Europe more cheaply. It could mean 15 million tons of soya being freighted 600 miles up the improved BR-163 highway every year, and end Santarém's isolation forever.

Anyway, I feel better after that therapeutic purging of the ennui suffered in the town. Actually, I guess I'm blaming the whole place for one act of cruelty I witnessed years ago. I'd just stepped off a riverboat early one morning, arriving in Santarém for the very first time, and paused to cross the road that runs down the waterfront. A few yards in front of me an amiable-looking street dog hauled himself up from where he'd obviously spent the night, shook off a cloud of dust and then bent his spine in one of those ecstatic stretches with his hindquarters high in the air and his front legs extended, chin on the ground.

He was a yard from the curb, actually in the roadway, but traffic was very scarce and the road was wide. I'd paused to let a pick-up pass, and then things all happened very fast. The vehicle made a sudden swerve to take it from the centre of the road to the verge, and I glimpsed three laughing faces as it caught the dog with the front fender, knocking it down with a yelp of pain and then riding right over it with a rear wheel. A whoop of success came from the front seat and they carried on their way leaving the dying dog at my feet, twirling round its crushed hindquarters howling in agony. After a numb moment of disbelief I grabbed a tyre lever from a truck driver who was changing a wheel nearby and quickly killed the dog with one swing. Call me a sentimental old fool but that incident really put me off the whole town.

Cesar must be saving a lot of money by living in such a dull place, but hopefully he'll retire before his luck runs out. His friend Alizio had seven planes by the time he was twenty-nine and seemed to have his life all mapped out. A devout Seventh-Day Adventist, he was slightly humourless company, but the Protestant work ethic had helped him prosper. We'd flown a couple of times with him the previous year and had arranged to do so again, but he crashed one day on landing.

'No drinking, no smoking, no women; just church and work, work, work!' sneered his replacement, the red-eyed Paulo, puffing on a cigarette and scratching his crotch. 'And where did it get him? Dead, that's where! Dead, like the rest of us. Earlier than the rest of us! All that money and dead at twenty-nine, after a life of no fun. Poor sad bastard.'

The jungle viewed from 4,000 feet looked like a green tufted carpet flawed with a few coloured bits of fluff that were the flowering trees. It was hilly, but only the shadows on the flanks told you so. The sky was blue with clumps of large cumulus and the clouds' shadows were scattered over the carpet below like stains. Frankly it wasn't a very exciting view. Reassuring, certainly, to see so much pristine rainforest, unsullied and unbroken for two and a half hours' flying time, but the eye grew tired of such uniformity and seized upon any clearing or break with relief. These, apart from two goldfields, were natural – large treeless swampy areas with glinting pools, or scars on the hillsides from recent landslides.

Soon the Jari was below us, twisting and turning in those large meanders that mercifully the canoeist is usually ignorant of as he paddles along. Sometimes the river writhed in a huge circle of 2 miles or more, only to advance 200 yards. Cloud was forcing us low and Cesar asked for our help to spot the little shaved patch of Molocopote.

This was a nervous time, worrying whether the grass on the airstrip had grown too long, or if someone had deliberately blocked it. There could be dozens of gold prospectors, or a platoon of soldiers on an exercise who might demand some authorisation for being so far off the tourist trail. Alternatively, the place could be deserted, with giant otters in the river and capybara and deer coming out to graze at night. You never knew.

Cesar pointed ahead to a tiny patch of lighter green on a river bend, insignificant in that infinite sea of forest. You could imagine the dread of a pilot peering through the drumming droplets on his windshield at a world turned grey, the only colour the red of his fuel gauge. Dropping down to look it over, the plane bouncing in the thermals, Cesar banked round in a tight turn to examine the short strip of bumpy grass.

'The grass is long but it should still be OK,' he said. I would have preferred more certainty in his voice. I could see no sign of smoke, or canoes moored on the riverbank, and though the two shelters had tarpaulins covering them, they looked deserted.

Cesar circled round and across the river to line up his approach, and then we were coming in. Heather reached forward and squeezed my shoulder as we skimmed the treetops, the plane seeming to stop dead in the air as the power was reduced, making our stomachs flutter. Then I was only aware of the rush of approaching greenery and the frenzied beep of the stall warning, then the bump and shake and swerve as the plane pitched and yawed down the strip. The propeller scythed the longest grass, throwing back a green mush of clippings onto the windscreen. Would we stop before that line of trees, or would this be the day in strange aviators' slang when Cesar 'bought the farm'?

The brakes worked. The nose didn't pitch forward, smashing the whirling propeller against the ground and sending the blades spinning through the cockpit. We didn't somersault along in a fireball of burning fuel. We just came to a halt with 60 yards to spare. I removed my hands from where they had been braced on the dashboard, leaving a damp smear behind.

After turning and taxiing back, Cesar switched off the motor and we sat for a moment with ears still ringing from its roar. Gradually we became aware of birdsong and the hum of insects, and stepped out into a midday sun that produced an immediate sheen of sweat. The dry season had hardly begun but the grass was already browning.

We could hardly restrain our impatience to go and explore. Cesar was keen to go with us, but first pulled a pistol from his briefcase.

'You never know who could be here,' he argued, when he saw our apprehensive glances. 'This would be a great place for drug smugglers to rendezvous – so near the border and no radar around.' He was right, and we hoped that any drug traffickers hiding in the bushes would show themselves so that Cesar could shoot them before he flew away and left us there alone.

Inevitably Molocopote had changed. Two new shelters had been erected and someone had planted five more cashew nut saplings and several lime trees. In the past, the camp area had been piled high with old plastic sheeting, tin cans, engine parts, rusting oil drums and other rubbish. Now it was spotless.

Cesar was sleuthing over in the cookhouse. 'Someone was here yesterday, or even early this morning,' he called. 'The ashes are still warm and look what's here!' He held up the charred remains of a small piranha. Were people hiding in the shrubbery, sighting down their rifle barrels at my sweaty back? Would those super-rich dope dealers really grill a bony piranha for breakfast? We felt a flicker of apprehension as we returned to the plane to start unloading.

Ten large waterproof sacks full of food and equipment, the folding canoe, paddles, axe, machetes, fishing rod, cameras, watertight drums, hammocks, blankets and the numerous bits and pieces needed for a five-month trip were soon piled at the side of the plane. Then Cesar passed out our illegal shotgun that he'd hidden to avoid having it confiscated by the controls at Santarém airport.

Heather handed over a thick wad of notes that he put in his briefcase without counting. He seemed reluctant to go. 'Are you sure you don't want to fix a date for me to come and pick you up? I don't like the idea of leaving you here with no radio and nobody around to help.'

'We'll be OK,' I answered. Soon our only link with the outside world would be severed, and we either succeeded in crossing the hills or we'd have to canoe the three hundred miles down the Jari to civilisation. Our morale was a little shaky as it sometimes is at these moments, but Heather got us laughing by asking Cesar whether he was offering to come back free of charge.

'Oh no. I'm not that worried about you!'

'The only reason we're crossing the hills to Surinam is to escape your exorbitant rates you know. Better to leave the country on foot than pay another eight hundred dollars.'

We shook hands, and Cesar clambered across the wing and into his seat.

'Rather you than me,' he said. 'All those jaguars and snakes and creepy crawlies. Indians too I bet. You're very brave.'

'Or crazy?'

'That too of course, but I was brought up to be polite.'

We pushed on a wing tip to help turn him around, shouted goodbye, and watched as he taxied up to the end of the strip, turned and roared past us and into the air. It's at moments like this that you suddenly remember that you've left the canoe frame in the forward locker of the departing aircraft. We stood for a while amid our brightly-coloured pile of worldly goods listening to the engine fade away, and then we got to work.

A decrepit wheelbarrow that was lying near one of the huts helped get the sacks the 400 yards to the waterfront. There wasn't anything left of the Indian village that had existed there until the late 1970s, occupying some high ground overlooking the bend in the river. In 1983 the area between the river and the airstrip had been fairly open, but to reach the four cashew trees that Peter, Epileptic and I had squabbled over it would now be necessary to push through shoulder-high grass. Until as late as the 1950s the Jari had a large Indian population, but disease and a certain amount of warfare had caused the survivors to leave, some to the river Paru in the west and some to French Guiana and Surinam.

When Peter and I first visited Molocopote, one of the gold prospectors had been digging around in some Indian graves with the enthusiasm of the amateur archaeologist. He found that one had been buried with a Coca-Cola bottle, another with a tube of Colgate, and close examination of some bones told him that one had died from shotgun wounds. Everyone had been nervous about this desecration of Indian burial sites, and urged him to put everything back in the ground quickly, before a party of Wayana braves appeared to put some flowers on Mum's grave.

I pushed the squeaking wheelbarrow down the hill, stopping to reload the sacks when the wheel hit a rut and catapulted them on to the ground. Over to the left was the place where Peter and I had buried Fernando.

Molocopote has many ghosts and bad memories, but one can't deny that it's a marvellous place. Its name is evocative when pronounced in the Brazilian way with the 't' softened: *Molocopochee*. It is a corruption of *Molocco-Pata* which means 'the village of chief Molocco' in Wayana. These days it would make a superb spot for a research station, right in the middle of a massive area of undisturbed primary rainforest. It just needs a few buildings to accommodate the scientists and their collections and perhaps some rooms for tourists to come and help finance the centre. It is wasted on a bunch of gold prospectors or foreign adventurers in search of an unusual holiday.

Instead, the proposed BR-210 Northern Perimeter Highway will pass 10 miles to the south, and Molocopote will become part of someone's cattle ranch, or another infertile plot for the landless. At the moment the jungle is creeping back to reclaim the site; in many places the grass is head-high and the secondary growth of light-loving trees is nearly as tall as the uncut forest behind it. The area is small enough to be reseeded by the wind and in twenty years few parts will be penetrable.

I was making my third trip with some lighter sacks when I looked up and saw two men walking towards me. I jerked to a stop and watched them warily. It was a relief to see that they were unarmed and wearing faded T-shirts and grubby shorts: not the sort of designer clothing that one associates with spivs from the Medellin cartel.

I'm always impressed by the self-possession of the humble Brazilian. He can be hoeing his vegetable plot in his homestead beside a river, 25 miles from his nearest neighbour, when he glances up to see outlandish figures stepping towards him across his bean patch. Tall, fair, burnt, grizzled, unshaven, half-naked weirdos with sun-dazzled, startlingly blue, deranged eyes. The equivalent would be for us to look up from washing the Mondeo on a quiet Sunday morning and see a bunch of naked savages in warpaint coming up the drive. However, instead of running screaming indoors, these courageous characters don't even blink in surprise. Their faces remain impassive, they even manage to smile and look courteous and welcoming, and they speak with no trace of fear or suspicion.

These two prospectors were typical. Faced with a white-bodied, red-faced extraterrestrial with a bandage wound around his stomach (I was worried my hernia might pop out with all the lifting), they held their ground and didn't even collapse in a giggling heap.

We moved to the shade of one of the shelters where I learnt that they'd been waiting for a planeload of supplies. Six of their companions were working upstream on the Paruzinho creek.

'The plane should have come six days ago,' explained Oscar. He was quite a handsome young man when he kept his mouth shut, but appalling dental decay ruined his smile. One felt a wave of relief when his lips closed over the wreckage.

We sat down on some sawn sections of tree trunk, and they stared in astonishment as Heather came panting down the trail wearing a backpack and holding three paddles and the shotgun. They gallantly stood up to greet her and fetched a log from the other shelter.

'Very beautiful,' said Pedro appreciatively. 'The prettiest girl I've seen in six months.' He paused. 'In fact, the only girl I've seen in six months, but no less beautiful for all that.'

We shared the last of my factory-made cigarettes. From now on I'd be smoking hand-rolling tobacco that is more practical for expedition life.

'How long are you going to wait for this plane?' I asked.

'No longer. In fact this morning we set off to paddle upstream and explain to our boss what's happened. He must be wondering what's become of us. We'd got two miles when we heard your plane and rushed back.'

They asked if they could have a bit of our *farinha* (manioc flour) and rice. Expecting to be away from camp for only one night, they were hungry. We gave them a kilo of each and they presented us with a couple of smelly grilled piranhas which we hadn't been in the jungle long enough to appreciate. Standing nearby I was conscious of the pungent smell of wood smoke, sweat, tobacco, unwashed clothing and fish that emanated from the men. It wasn't particularly unpleasant and I knew we'd be smelling like that within a week or two.

'When are you going to take a break in town?' asked Heather.

Both had already been there six months, but felt they hadn't earned enough to justify the expense of the journey.

'This area is really crap for gold,' said Pedro. He was in his mid twenties with a musculature honed by paddle, pick and shovel to a level that would be the envy of gym enthusiasts in the wealthy nations. He was a bit of a dandy despite his rags – a small straw hat, almost useless for providing shade, perched on his head and he had a neat little moustache, shaped with painstaking shaving. His urbane sophisticate's face seemed small and incongruous on that boxer's physique.

'I've worked in Roraima, Rondônia and Acre states and on the rivers Tapajós, Trombetas and Roosevelt, but I've never seen a poorer area than this. Some of those were pretty disappointing too, but this is the worst. It's also the furthest away from town, so it costs much more to get here and fly in supplies.' He scratched some red swellings on his forearms and added, 'The mosquitoes are terrible too.'

'It was so bloody good in Roraima where we were before,' added Oscar. 'Why the hell didn't they leave us alone?'

I guessed he was referring to the recent expulsion of gold prospectors from Yanomami Indian territory near the border with Venezuela. Over the course of several years, with the authorities looking the other way, more than 50,000 miners had invaded the Indians' land, opening up dozens of airstrips and polluting the pristine rivers and streams. Skirmishes had taken place between the Indians and the prospectors, leading to several deaths, but the real damage was probably more insidious. Indians began to congregate around the airstrips waiting for hand-outs, contracting diseases like malaria, measles and influenza that their immune systems couldn't handle, the men offered alcohol and the women encouraged into prostitution. An international outcry had finally forced the government to act.

Spend any time with *garimpeiros*, as the Brazilian gold prospectors are called, and one is awed by their toughness, generosity, good nature and resourcefulness. The best of them have the Indian skills for fishing, hunting, boatmanship and making shelters, baskets or anything else from forest materials, but they handle modern equipment equally efficiently. It's brutally hard work, especially for those whose workings are far from an airstrip. Heavy machinery and drums of fuel are manhandled past rapids and along muddy forest trails through the appliance of rollers, levers and brute strength. Despite all these qualities, the *garimpeiros* are just not temperamentally suited for contact with isolated Indian tribes whose lands must seem the last few tempting areas not explored with shovel and gold pan.

Eventually Oscar and Pedro stood up and prepared to leave. They were returning to camp to try and rouse the pilot on the radio. We shook hands and wished each other luck before Pedro pushed the canoe off the sand, muscles rippling under his dark skin like rats in a sack, and we watched them paddle strongly away, hugging the margin of the river to escape the worst of the current.

We lit a fire, put the kettle on for a cup of tea and started to assemble the canoe, eager to escape Molocopote before the mosquitoes came out to play. We preferred to pitch our camp under the trees in the forest. At least with the folding canoe we had the choice to move on within an hour. On previous expeditions our plywood canoe kits had taken at least eight days to put together, and when we'd assembled one at a goldfield in 1987 an audience watched our every move. Most of the *garimpeiros* only stayed a day or two while they waited for a plane or a canoe to take them to the gold workings, but five men were always there, ogling at Heather, whispering amongst themselves, staring belligerently at me. They all carried pistols, stuck amid the blubber that hung over their waistbands or in fancy holsters with full ammunition belts. They came from the south of the country where there is a large population of German descent, and they assumed we'd share the view that the other prospectors were a bunch of *'Indios'* or *'macacos'* (monkeys).

On our first evening the friendly storekeeper asked us if we were armed, and I lied that we had a couple of revolvers.

'Good,' he said. 'It's the only thing some of these guys understand.'

But as the days went by the story lost credibility. Our waists were the only ones unadorned with weaponry, and the attitude of the group was becoming increasingly abusive. When one of our friends warned us to sleep with the guns loaded in our hammocks I confessed we only had a 20-gauge single-barrelled shotgun.

'That's no good if they all rush you at once, is it? You'd better borrow mine,' he said, offering one of those long barrel 45s that I thought had died out with Billy the Kid.

'Any trouble and just shoot. A lot of people will help you out if it comes to a fight.'

This was the life. Any dispute, minor irritation, noisy neighbour, man leering at your wife, and you just shot them. No messing about with noise abatement officers, arbitration services, neighbourhood policemen. It was a heady feeling to hold the gun's oily heaviness, roll its cylinder against my palm, tip out the squat bullets and slide them in again. I was ready to clean up the neighbourhood and there wasn't a policeman for hundreds of miles. I could get away with it too. When those slobs began smacking their lips as Heather bent over to glue a section on to the canoe, or giggled when I hammered my thumb instead of a nail, or made monkey noises when one of the darker men walked by, I was tempted to walk up and blow all five of them away. All I'd have got was a hell of a reputation and a bit of respect. In the bars of Amazonia they'd be talking of me still.

It was almost disappointing to hand the gun back, unused, three days later.

With practice, the folding canoe takes about half an hour to assemble and can be dismantled in half that time. It's a simple design; interlocking aluminium poles run along its length, meshing with eight ribs that stretch the fabric outwards. This Norwegian 'Ally' is the only folding canoe that I know of on the market. Quite a few companies produce large folding kayaks, but they don't have the carrying capacity of a Canadian canoe, and have to be loaded more carefully with items stuffed under the decks. All my Amazon canoeing has been done in canoes, not kayaks, starting with dugouts that I bought for a few pounds, or plank-built ones I made myself.

The 'Ally' does look a little flimsy for the harsh Amazon conditions, but for a trip that entails flying in bush planes, hauling up rapids, clambering over dozens of fallen trees, and then portaging across a watershed for 15 miles, no other canoe will do. It has its design faults and irritations: the most tiresome being the way the seats are mounted. These aren't clipped securely, merely notched over the poles, so as you backpaddle they can pop off, throwing you into the bilges. This ceases to be funny very quickly. Also the poles and frames aren't clipped firmly together, so that when you walk around in the boat or haul heavy sacks in and out they slowly separate and the canoe falls to pieces. We overcame this by wiring each section to the other, a long fiddly job that is only worth contemplating when the canoe is going to be left assembled for several weeks.

There are two thicknesses of fabric: the heaviest for the bottom, which is exceptionally tough, and a thinner material for the sides. We'd have liked the whole canoe to be made of the heavier stuff but this would have meant a custom-made model, and the basic craft is expensive enough. If the canoe disintegrated hundreds of miles from help I'm sure the matter of a few hundred pounds would seem pretty trivial, but in the month before departure when thousands of pounds haemorrhaged out of our bank account at alarming speed, it was easy to panic and make false economies.

We chose the scant shade of a sparsely leafed tree for the assembly of the canoe and the wiring together of all the joints. Above us, oropendolas flew back and forth to their basket nests, receiving a chirruping welcome from the chicks within. In a fork at the very top of the tree I could see the papier mâché cylinder of the wasps' nest that nearly always shares the nesting site of these birds. Quite what the wasps gain from this relationship isn't clear – perhaps the oropendolas secrete a chemical odour that repels the insects that prey on wasp grubs – but the benefit to the birds is considerable. The wasps chase off other insects, thus protecting the oropendola chicks from being parasitised by botflies. Where oropendolas nest away from wasps, scientists have discovered that they're more likely to tolerate the cowbird dropping an egg into their nests. The cowbird chick snaps instinctively at all flying insects and so protects the defenceless young oropendolas from the botflies. They don't seem to heave the other chicks over the side of the nest like other cuckoos do, so the only price to the adult oropendolas is another mouth to feed.

Back in the hotel room at Santarém we'd separated all the food into packages of a kilo or less, wrapped in three layers of plastic and stashed in watertight sacks. We tried to keep these sacks to a manageable weight because they were going to be hauled in and out of the canoe countless times over the next weeks. Luxuries like the 5 kilos of fresh onions, and 3 kilos each of limes and garlic were kept in the coolest positions. The tins of cooking oil and tomato purée were loaded first, being the only items that could get wet in the bilges without any harm being done.

The canoe sank lower and lower in the water until it seemed likely that our weight would push it under, but when we climbed in the level rose to within an inch of the gunwales and stopped. We wouldn't be able to wriggle around too much or tackle choppy water, but we'd soon eat our way through much of the food, and it could only get lighter.

'Well, off we go!' said Heather, wriggling into the front seat, having to shove water containers, a machete and 30 yards of rope aside to stretch out her legs.

'Let's hope we don't come slinking back here in a few months after another heroic failure,' I said, taking a farewell glance at the familiar landmarks of Molocopote behind me.

'No way. Things are going to be so different this time. You've got me instead of that weakling Peter, for a start! We're also in good health and we haven't exhausted ourselves coming up against the current through all those rapids.'

I seized the paddle, feeling the smooth warm wood in my hands, eager to move but apprehensive about the journey ahead.

'It does seem a daft idea to me sometimes.'

'Only *sometimes*?' She laughed. 'One attempt at this caper might have been enough for most people. But not you.'

'Unfinished business. It'll niggle at me unless I give it another go.'

'Well let's get on with it then, instead of just sitting here.'

So freeing the canoe from the grip of the sand, we slowly paddled off towards the Tumucumaque hills.

In 1950 a young French explorer, Raymond Maufrais, set off into these same hills and was never seen again. An Indian found his last camp in the forest and among the abandoned possessions was a diary that described his struggle for survival and his physical decline from hunger, malaria and dysentery. On the last page he wrote that he no longer had the strength to build a raft or canoe and was going to swim downstream for help:

I'll soon be seeing you, my dearest parents! Trust in me! This notebook is yours; I thought of you as I wrote it, and soon I shall put it into your hands. I promised to come back; and come back I will, God willing.

I'd come across the diaries (published in book form) while preparing for my first trip to the Jari, and Peter and I had read passages to each other at stages of our journey. Whether we were lost, sick, stung by wasps and hornets, shocked by electric eels, afraid and hungry, we could always be sure that Raymond had experienced the same, and worse, before us.

Raymond's rather reckless disregard for his own safety had prompted some criticism after his disappearance: 'That unhappy, deluded young Frenchman, who in order apparently to prove to himself that he was not a coward, persisted in adventuring on various expeditions, virtually without equipment, into the most inaccessible South American jungles,' wrote one. 'Raymond set off into the heart of the unknown forests of Guiana [...] It was magnificent, but it was reckless and it appalled those of us who know the forest, for it was courting disaster,' wrote a more sympathetic Eduardo Barros Prado.

It is difficult to be a wholehearted fan of Raymond Maufrais. His arrogance stopped him from ever listening to advice, and his naivety inevitably led him into trouble. Of course, had he succeeded in his plan and survived, his critics would have praised his audacity and wisdom in ignoring the advice of the faint-hearted. But he failed, and he disappeared, and in a very public way. *'L'affaire Maufrais'* filled the European papers for months, especially when his father, Edgar, left his job in Toulon and began searching for his son in the Amazon forest, making some extraordinary journeys over the next sixteen years.

For my part, I can see the glaring errors that he made and the over-ambitious goals he set himself, but I still admire his spirit and enthusiasm. But then I suppose I would, as I've also dismissed the counsel of wiser men and set off on Amazon journeys with little thought of the risks. Hardly surprising when the so-called experts reply to one's petitions for advice as one did to me in 1979 before my first expedition. This gentleman, a veteran of numerous jungle campaigns, and a wizard no doubt at moving troops and howitzers through rainforest terrain, wrote back the following: 'Only two pieces of advice: keep your boots polished and your crotch powdered.' Or was it the other way round?

Sitting beside campfires on the upper Jari river, with the shadows flickering over our malarial gauntness, forced to kill monkeys and anything else for food, wandering lost around the foothills of the Tumucumaque, Peter and I had pitied Raymond above all for his loneliness. We shared many of his privations but at least we had companionship; this would be a terrible place to be alone. Raymond only had a little terrier called Bobby that he'd adopted in a village in French Guiana:

Close-cropped dirty white hair, pink belly, black patches on that indecent, sickly pink, a lively eye, but a nondescript face and weak little teeth. Yesterday you let a cat take all your bread and milk. You were howling like a baby. You shake with fright at the sight of another dog. When we're out hunting you're terrified of the forest, and if you meet a stranger you jump up and lick his hand.

You shall be my only companion. You'll see the Tumuc Humacs; if I die, you'll die with me; you'll sleep in my hammock and we'll pick the same bones together. So let's get going, Bobby. And please help me to find our daily steak, and give me a friendly nuzzle when you see that I'm feeling low. I'm counting on you, d'you see?

This expedition to the Tumucumaque (or Tumuc Humacs as they are known in French Guiana) was Raymond's second visit to the South American jungles. Three years before, he'd accompanied a Brazilian party that was searching for eight men who had disappeared in the Mato Grosso. They found their remains; killed, it appeared, by Chavante Indians. Raymond learnt much about the forest from travelling in the company of these experts, but then seemed to think that he'd served his apprenticeship, knew everything there was to know, and could now go anywhere and go alone.

Ever since I first read his diary I'd considered doing a trip in his footsteps, reaching the banks of the Tamouri where he disappeared, even pushing on with his proposed route. The same sector of the Tumucumaque had appealed to us both, and I'd concocted the plan of ascending the Jari and crossing the hills before I came across his book and learnt that he'd died approaching them from the other side. Here was a kindred spirit who, significantly I felt, had disappeared a month or two before I was born in 1950.

The sun's rays reflected off the water, causing my head to hum and vision to wobble, and squinting from under our wide-brimmed straw hats we zigzagged along the margin of the river in the lee of bushes and fallen trees, the canoe feeling heavy and sluggish. Efficient jungle travellers would have prepared themselves for this moment with punishing training schedules, but I looked down with shame at the little roll of fat that flopped over my shorts, and Heather could only manage ten consecutive paddle strokes before she had to rest. Canoeing's great for giving you a six-pack stomach and a torso to die for – all supported on spindly, unused legs – but that would come later. The vegetation crawled by and those upper body muscles, so cruelly yanked from atrophy, whinged, complained, rebelled and finally forced a halt when we'd only gone 4 miles.

Shoulders, arms, back and stomach ached with weariness, our skin smarted from mild sunburn, but whilst sipping the first cocktail of rum and limes we felt content. Supper was bubbling on the fire and the hammocks, wrapped in mosquito netting, were comfortably strung between trees and protected from rain under a plastic sheet. This little patch of jungle, cleared by sweeps of our machetes, had probably never been trodden upon by human feet.

The forest was alive with sound as day turned to dusk. Whoops, trills, squeaks, whistles and whirrings, nearly all of them as familiar as old friends, welcomed us back. Fireflies winked their twin green headlamps and made kamikaze descents into the fire unless we knocked them away. Several dozen mosquitoes hovered around trying to settle but were thwarted by thick clothing and powerful insect repellents. Malaria had ruined trips in the past and we would do everything we could to avoid it this time.

Howler monkeys called from somewhere a mile away on the far bank 'like the roaring of a wind through the portals of Hades' as one writer described it rather melodramatically. Another said they make 'a most fearful and harrowing noise, under which it is difficult to keep up one's buoyancy of spirit. The feeling of inhospitable wildness, which the forest is calculated to inspire, is increased tenfold under this fearful uproar'. Steady on. It's a marvellous sound, only frightening if you didn't know it was produced by monkeys, because such a deep, growling roar would seem more likely from the jaws of a pride of man-eating big cats.

Weighing up to 15 kilos and standing a metre tall, howlers are the largest of the South American monkeys (although the gangly spider monkeys look bigger), with a rich ginger-red coat that glows regally in sunlight. They have a slightly moronic-looking face, with low foreheads and huge jaws, and they move slowly through the trees with none of the agility of most monkey species. It's not surprising to learn that their brains are relatively small for their body weight, that the social interactions within the troupe are low-key, or that they are one of the few species that don't adapt to life as a pet. However, they live in relatively permanent groups of up to twenty individuals, with one dominant male. Occasionally we've seen immature males alone so there must be battles to assume dominance in a troupe. Researchers say that when a new male takes over, he may begin his reign by killing all the infants in a bloody purge of his predecessor's offspring.

The purpose of the howling is to demarcate territory and to notify other groups of their position. Territories overlap, but they can space themselves out and avoid competition. Calling is most common at dawn or dusk, or after rain or a disturbance, but really the male seems to crank up a good group shout whenever he feels like it. He starts the proceedings by uttering long, rasping, vibrating exhalations, followed by almost equally powerful inhalations, and after ten or so of these he attains a crescendo that becomes a sustained roar. When this falters slightly, presumably when he's drawing breath, you become aware of an almost falsetto trilling and layers of descant. The chorus ends after four or five minutes with a last few coughs from the male. This is supposed to halt the rest of the troupe, but they often carry on yelling, ignoring the rather peevish coughs of the master. I've always found their performances both wonderful and comforting, but C. W. Beebe thought differently. 'It touched some secret chord of long lost fear, when speech was yet unformed... the calmness and silence of the jungle gave place to a hidden portent of evil.'

This distant calling seemed to have gone on longer than usual and sounded more than ever like a strong wind. Then I noticed that the flames were billowing and dancing, leaves and debris were pattering down from the canopy, and the stars had gone.

This was a real wind that had us glancing nervously at the trees that groaned and whipped around our tiny little clearing. We just had time to get our equipment under cover before the rain came hammering down. Solid sheets of water cascaded off the tarpaulin, reducing the fire to a steaming pile of charcoal with our supper still uncooked. To bed. Only 7 p.m. and off to bed with empty stomachs. Our feeling of well-being had been washed away too.

I heard Heather say something from her hammock that almost touched mine.

'What?' I yelled.

She raised the flap of her mosquito net, leant over the gap and shone her torch into my cocoon. Her wet hair was plastered to her cheeks, but she was smiling.

'I was just saying that one day we should have a real holiday for a change. You know – hotels, restaurants, beaches, beds, that sort of thing.'

'Don't be ridiculous.'

We kissed goodnight and I lay back listening to the storm, staring into the blackness, damp creeping down the ropes. I was fully clothed in jeans and a sweatshirt but still needed a blanket to keep out the chill.

It all seemed faintly absurd. Hanging there in the pitch-blackness, feeling the hammock rock from the trees' sway, with debris plopping on to the plastic above, senses numbed by the drumming deluge and the crack of thunder.

What on earth were we doing?

CHAPTER TWO

We'd camped on a high patch of jungle that was now an island in the flood, the trees dripping steadily into our gloomy compost-smelling little underworld. I crouched in the spongy leaf-mould trying to coax fire from soaking firewood while Heather took down the hammocks and tarpaulin and bailed several inches of rainwater from the canoe.

I chuntered and swore to myself as the fire went out again, and cut a very large piece of bicycle tyre inner tube to start all over again. We'd scrounged a bundle of these from a repair shop in Santarém as pieces usually burn slowly enough to dry and ignite the kindling, but the wood around here had lain saturated for months. I peeled the wet bark off twigs to expose a drier core, huffed and puffed life into unpromising smouldering glows and wafted vigorously with a pan lid until my wrist ached. Nostalgia was growing for high-speed electric kettles and boxes of breakfast cereal as I disappeared from view in dense clouds of choking smoke and steam before finally producing a pot of coffee and a bowl of porridge in an hour and a half.

Even so much thick smoke hadn't driven away the winged tormentors that bent their proboscises trying to penetrate the heavy weave of our clothing, and exposed areas of skin were smothered with repellent so corrosive that it melted plastic and welded ballpoint pens to our fingers. Once camp was broken and everything loaded in the canoe, we rushed to strip off our nighttime clothing and don shorts and T-shirts, all the while performing a leaping, thigh-slapping dance like demented Tyroleans.

Out on the river the cloud hung low over the treetops in a grey murk, and a chilling fine drizzle plastered our hair to our scalps. The swollen Jari surged by with that unstoppable power of a river in spate; whirlpools suddenly boiling up to the surface and bubbly foam wheeling in eddies near the bank. A tree trunk floated past, suddenly stood on end and sank vertically like a giant fisherman's float before rising again. The forest was flooded in places for several hundred yards inland and trees stood marooned in water as they had for the past five months. Most species of plant would die without a supply of oxygen to the roots, yet the majority of Amazonian species don't even lose their leaves, and smaller saplings spend much of their immature lives completely submerged.

Two macaws flew overhead, screeching and swearing at the sight of us. Jungle-dwellers can apparently tell what colour they are without looking up, just from subtle differences in the racket they make, but these were close enough for us to see the blue and yellow of their plumage; colours seemingly designed to make them as conspicuous as possible in a world of green.

The rhythmic splash of our paddles and the little pattering of droplets from the blades were sounds that blended into this watery world. The current gurgled around obstacles, and the flexible tip of a sunken tree jigged up and down, up and down. We kept to the margins, ducking under bushes, brushing past creepers that hung down to the water, adjusting our direction with sweeps of the paddles. Heather and I had shared a canoe enough to know what we each had to do, the exercise warmed us, and it felt good to be on the move.

There is no such pleasure or sense of achievement when using an outboard motor. Drums of gasoline fill half the canoe under a halo of stinking fumes, and the engine leaves a trail of blue exhaust, emitting a din that obliterates the birdsong or the rustlings and calls that betray the presence of an animal nearby. Passengers sit in bored inactivity, hoping to see something interesting, rushing forward in pointless haste.

The previous year, Heather, Peter and I had spent ten days at a deserted airstrip making a large plywood canoe to carry a film crew of three and several hundred kilos of filming equipment. In the weeks of chaos before leaving home there'd been no time to learn how to operate an outboard motor so we screwed the new Brazilian 18-h.p. motor on the stern and set off on the maiden voyage. We planned to potter a couple of miles upstream, each get some practice, and then return to camp. Peter pulled on the cord until it grudgingly spluttered into life, vibrating violently in an ugly clatter. There'd been no other motors for sale in Santarém, and it hadn't been nearly as cheap as it looked. Brazilians generally preferred to pay extra and get a Japanese import.

Peter took us upstream at a sedate pace, and the light craft cut through the current with ease. Heather then took her turn and, after an erratic start, got the hang of it quickly. I then settled confidently in the stern and grasped the tiller. Beginning cautiously I chugged upstream, turned around and headed gently homewards. However, as we rounded a bend and I saw our camp ahead, a little demon whispered in my ear and I decided to roar up to it in style. I opened the throttle, the bow lifted and we sped forward with a jolt. Peter and Heather turned and looked at me in alarm, but I gave them a cocky smile. Having spent five minutes in charge of an outboard motor I'd decided it was child's play and that I knew everything there was to know about the subject. However, for a second there I'd taken my eyes off the river. I looked up to see that we were veering towards the bank.

I yanked the lever sharply, causing the canoe to heel over, throwing Heather and Peter against the side. I tried to correct the damage by moving the tiller in the other direction, again too brusquely. We careered to the right, the boat still speeding forward at full throttle as my hand seemed to have seized and frozen. In panic I decided to release hold of the tiller altogether, in the hope that the throttle had a spring on it like a motorbike's, and that it would close off the acceleration. On the contrary; the outboard swung free into full lock, forcing the canoe to try and execute an impossibly tight turn, and it flipped over, tossing us into the green waters. The revolving propeller crashed down a foot from my face and all went quiet.

I surfaced to an overwhelming feeling of embarrassment. A show-off who had fallen flat on his face and made a right prat of himself.

'What the hell were you doing?' Heather asked, getting one arm on to the upturned hull.

'I was trying to be a smart-arse,' I admitted. Peter and Heather exchanged looks, no doubt thinking that I was a natural and didn't have to try so hard.

There followed a long and grim struggle to get the waterlogged canoe to shore, the current sweeping us 2 miles past our camp, while a storm lashed the surface of the water into a sheet of bouncing droplets. Only a fallen tree that stuck out 80 feet into the river stopped us from being swept all the way down the river and out into the Atlantic.

We pulled the canoe through 100 yards of drowned forest, creepers snagging and hauling us back, until we found a muddy islet of higher ground. In utter exhaustion we lay panting with our skins puckered and pale from our ninety-minute immersion; Heather and Peter had no breath left to berate me for my stupidity. That would come later. For the moment we had to tie up the canoe, pull the outboard on to dry land and then splash back to camp through 2 miles of dense, flooded jungle. All before it got dark.

The memory of that afternoon (and the next morning when we had to go and retrieve everything) seems to have left a profound impression on my companions. It's extraordinary how often it surfaces in conversation even to this day. And I still know nothing about handling an outboard engine because I've never been allowed to take control of one again.

By midday we knew that the mouth of the Mapaoni tributary couldn't be far away, so we moved over to the right bank. It would be the Mapaoni that would take us to the Tumucumaque hills. There is a huge boulder at least 20 feet tall where the Jari and Mapaoni meet. This eroded mass of stone sits on a sandbank that is also several feet above the low water mark. I knew this as I'd seen it in the past. Yet as we reached the confluence there was no sign of it, not the merest hint of a ripple; just a huge expanse of water where the two streams met.

We were resting there, letting the canoe spin around lazily, when we heard the buzz of an outboard motor coming down the Jari. It seemed that the area around Molocopote wasn't quite as empty of people as we'd thought. If we moved quickly there was time to hide ourselves in the bushes, which is the cowardly way we sometimes behave. Not because *garimpeiros* are likely to be a threat, but because we obviously arouse a lot of curiosity, and in a world without women the men's ocular re-acquaintance with the female anatomy could be discomforting for Heather.

A canoe came round the bend and swung over to check us out, the noise of the motor dropping a note and the bow wave diminishing. I counted three men and we could hear the excitement in their voices as they discussed this strange apparition.

We greeted them as they came alongside and they smiled warmly. We now noticed that there were three more lying stretched out and wrapped in blankets, too ill even to stir themselves and gawp at a woman after all these months.

'Oscar and Pedro told us about you,' the helmsman said. 'Said you'd be a way up the Mapaoni by now.'

'We're taking it easy,' I answered. 'The canoe's heavy and we feel a bit out of shape.' I often find myself making excuses to prospectors, daunted by their physical achievements.

'Quite a load you've got there,' he agreed kindly. 'You're doing pretty well I reckon. I used to paddle everywhere, but ever since I met Mr Yamaha here,' he patted his outboard, 'I've got lazy and fat.'

Fat he was not. Probably in his late forties, he was lean and muscular, with greying hair and a neat moustache. He looked very much in charge, and so far the others had said nothing but sat there nodding and smiling amiably enough.

'Are you all from Paruzinho creek?'

'That's right. We've radioed for a plane to take these guys to hospital. As you see, they're no good to anyone, lying down asleep all the time.' He smiled. 'When their malaria is cured I may let them back.'

'How far is it to your *garimpo*?' I asked.

'Oh, not far. Three, four hours' paddling, something like that. You want to come and stay with us for a day or two? We'd like that. Zezinho here,' he pointed at a small man with a mangled straw hat, 'shot a tapir last night so there's tons of meat to eat.'

Heather and I looked at each other, and she shrugged slightly.

'Why not?' I accepted.

'Great! Look, the plane's arriving in an hour. We'll get rid of these slackers, load up the supplies the plane is bringing, and we'll be back in three to four hours. You can't miss the Paruzinho because our machinery has made it a muddy red. Anyway, we'll be able to give you a tow later.'

They waved and whizzed off downstream, and knowing that a tow was coming, we paddled half-heartedly up the wide and featureless Jari.

We'd just noticed a discolouration of the river beginning over on the left bank when the three remaining *garimpeiros* caught us up in a canoe now laden with drums of fuel and sacks of rice and *farinha.* We tossed them our line and I held a paddle astern as a rudder to follow their course as closely as I could as they entered the Paruzinho, swerving around fallen trees or through little gaps left by encroaching bushes. The current was now faster and the motor rose an octave as it strained to propel the two heavy canoes, our bow wave occasionally swamping over the sides.

Half an hour took us to their camp where we found Pedro, Oscar and another man working in a large pit 30 yards inland. A pump was fighting a losing battle trying to keep the hole dry and the men waded in a foot of water. Oscar held a high-pressure hose that writhed in his hands, directing a blast of water at the wall of the pit that dislodged gravel, sand and large pebbles. Pedro controlled a larger diameter hose that he held in the area where the loosened material was landing, and a powerful pump hoovered the mix up to a grader on the dry ground above. The men were covered in mud and spray and were shivering violently when they left their work to come and greet us.

After the boss, Abel, had taken us to their shelter and made room for our hammocks, large slabs of dark red tapir meat were chosen from a drum of brine, and appetites whetted with little skewers of kebab before steaks were placed over the barbecue.

'You're quite a skilled butcher,' I joked to a blond southerner called Edison who was carefully selecting cuts and slicing them neatly with a sharp knife.

'It used to be my job,' he replied.

Abel laughed. 'We've got all sorts of skills here – butchers, factory workers, clerks, farmers, carpenters. One of those sick men who left today is a doctor of chemistry, but he'd be a lot more use if he was a doctor of medicine. I used to be a postman in Recife, but that's not very handy here.'

The pilot had brought them two bottles of *cachaça* and we drank *caipirinhas* of rum, lime and sugar while the tapir steaks sizzled on the grill and pots of rice and beans were prepared. I could feel the strong alcohol sluice through my almost empty stomach and pour through my veins in a warming rush, and the atmosphere became jovial and noisy as we stood around our tropical barbeque. Despite their sociability I sensed a reluctance to down tools and take an evening off. The men would normally take it in turns to work all night.

'We're not here to mess about,' Abel reasoned. 'The quicker we get a good profit, the quicker we can go home. There's not much romance in all this, and while this pit is producing reasonable quantities of gold we're eager to get it out.'

So after eating and drinking with us and taking an after-dinner coffee, some of them donned oilskins, made flaming torches from winding diesel-soaked cloth around sticks, and went back to work. Heather and I stood on the lip of the crater and watched the jets of clay-coloured water and the moving figures glistening in the spray, all lit in the orange glow. The machines thumped in a rhythm as regular and constant as a heartbeat. Feeling rather guilty at our sloth and tiredness we crawled into our hammocks and were soon asleep.

We had a go at the gold prospector's life ourselves the next day. After protesting that we were not expected to help out, and that it was work that was hard and uncomfortable, Abel allotted us our duties. I went down into the pit, and Heather stood beside the grader raking the pebbles about as they tumbled over the baffles, keeping them moving when they threatened to pile up. Oscar worked with her, shovelling the waste away as it rolled out of the bottom, or picking out the small rocks that were too heavy or misshapen to roll down the incline.

The grader was a Z-shaped arrangement of three boxes that had a series of baffles down their length. The hose from the pit poured a mixture of water, pebbles, mud and gravel into the top, and the mixture shuffled its way down the slope. On the floor of each box was a wire mesh, and underneath that was a piece of carpet to trap the gold.

Seeing the spray from the hoses I'd started work wearing an oilskin, but I soon found out why Antonio beside me was stripped to his shorts. The sweat was trapped by the clothing and chaffed my armpits and neck, so I stripped it off. I held the high-pressure hose, that the men called the *cobra fumando* (smoking snake), and directed its blast at the sides of the trench.

I could now see we were attacking what had once been the bed of a small creek. Over the course of millions of years, the rain had exposed the gold deposits of the Tumucumaque Hills, broken them down and carried them away in streams and rivers. The men dug and blasted until they reached a stratum of large pebbles, golf-ball-sized and above, that would have been laid down in ancient torrents and among which the heavy particles of gold might have settled. Over the centuries, waterways change course, silt up or return to forest, so some gold deposits will be a long way from any running water today. Even if these could be found, the absence of water would make the prospectors' task too difficult, so most work stream beds or their margins. The beds of deeper, navigable rivers are tackled with rafts and dredgers.

The band of pebbles stood out clearly in the clay bank, and I directed the squirming hose to blast them, shining and tumbling into the red water below. It was important to stand a few yards back to avoid the worst of the spray and grit, and because the undermined bank would periodically collapse with a crash.

Antonio controlled the pump that propelled the pebbles, mud and debris up to the grader. It seemed that there was little to be gained from deepening the trench as the band of pebbles ended just above the water that permanently covered the bottom of the pit and which the other pump could never suck away. So we were enlarging the hole outwards into the forest, ripping into the banks and the bed of old meanders. Sometimes the hose alone would not dislodge the lode bed, and Antonio attacked and loosened it with pick and shovel.

I won't say that I found it particularly hard work. Wet, muddy, uncomfortable and surprisingly cold, but the high-pressure hose was doing most of the work. Heather had the hotter job, away from the spray, blistering her hands on the rough handle of the rake. The noise of the machinery made conversation impossible, and we sloshed and shivered in our watery existence, oblivious to the world outside the trench. When we stopped for lunch it seemed strange to realise there was a blue sky above and a strong sun; that this wasn't some drizzly January day on an English building site.

Over the banter around the tapir stew at lunch, Abel was faced with a mock rebellion as we joked that we were going on strike unless working conditions were improved.

'I've got a *cabanagem* on my hands,' he moaned. 'I've heard about you English and your love of strikes. I'll have a word with my friends in the police and get you troublemakers deported.'

The term *'cabanagem'* had entered the vocabulary of the Amazon after the popular rebellion of the 1830s. Not that it started out as such: originally it was a dispute between the elites of the state of Pará after Brazilian Independence in 1822. On one side was the landed, mercantile elite who remained loyal to Portugal; on the other the native-born *nativistas* or *filantrópicos*. However, once fighting started, the oligarchs were unable to control the passions of their conscript armies, inflamed by the stories of the French Revolution and slave uprisings in the Caribbean.

The rebellion was also caused by heavy-handed attempts to cope with a labour shortage in Amazonia after Independence, when pro-Indian legislation was ignored, and Indians, mestizos and blacks were increasingly coerced and exploited. The *cabanagem* was named after the *cabanos*, the destitute migrants who lived in huts on the floodplains and riverbanks of the state of Pará.

It's estimated that this upheaval caused the death of 30,000 people: a fifth of the population of the province. The rebel forces occupied Belém in January 1835, killing the President of Pará, and the rebellion spread over most of Amazonia, taking Manaus the following year. However, the rebels seemed uncertain what to do with their success; they never formulated a set of aims and demands. They never even abolished slavery in the area they controlled.

It took the government until 1838 to totally repress the revolt, and while modern historians regard the *cabanagem* as the most profound rebellion against the injustices of nineteenth-century Brazil, it is doubtful that it changed much, judging by a decree issued by the President of Pará immediately afterwards. 'All coloured men who appear in any district without any known motive will immediately be arrested and sent for the government to dispose of them [...] Any individual living in a district who is not regularly employed in useful work will be sent to government factories or hired out to any private individual who needs him.'

That evening the men removed the pieces of carpet from the base of the grader and washed the sediments into a barrel. I'm not sure whether it would normally have been done that evening, or whether they wanted us to see the fruit of our labour before we left the next morning. Oscar stood in the stream, carefully washing the contents of the barrel in a gold pan. He swirled the muddy water, sweeping out the lighter stones and grit before washing the heavier fragments back into the barrel. All the men stood around puffing on chunky roll-ups, strangely unexcited as the result of their hard work was slowly revealed. The last time they had done this, four days before, they'd extracted 129 grams, and today would tell them if the tally was declining, and if the best days of this particular strike were over.

This wasn't really a Klondike-type of gold rush where barbers, clerks, lawyers, managers and teachers left the security and routine of their lives and answered the call of adventure and gold fever. A small percentage of the prospectors in Amazonia fit this mould, including one or two in Abel's crew, but the majority come because there's no alternative well-paid work available. They drift up from the increasingly mechanised agricultural world of southern Brazil where soya and coffee production is in larger and larger units and small farms are swallowed up. They leave little holdings in the arid north-east where the yield from the poor soil has dropped year by year, or where larger landowners have expelled them. Some of them have passed through interim periods in the shanty towns of Belém, Fortaleza or Recife, where the expectations of a better life were never realised.

Poverty had pushed them here, and poverty was probably awaiting them again, because few expect to find the amounts of gold that will secure their futures and provide a permanent escape. Most of them will enjoy a period of exceptionally good wages, but there won't be much surplus.

This is not to deny that the *garimpeiros* seem a different breed from the Brazilians who opt to stay at home. They are sharper, harder working, more adventurous and less tolerant of hierarchies and bureaucrats. They have a curiosity about the world and, though they love their country, are openly scornful of the mess it has become. They are a loss to Brazil, having talents that education, work and opportunity could have nurtured, and they are wasted out here in a jungle clearing, watching the success or failure of their venture appear in a golden sheen on the sides of Oscar's pan.

After many separations, only gold was left in the barrel, mixed with an equal quantity of black cassiterite, the ore of tin. Being almost as heavy as gold, this is hard to separate, so Abel took a bottle from his pocket and poured a few tablespoonfuls of gleaming mercury into the pan. As it was stirred around the mixture it picked up the gold into an amalgam of bigger, denser particles that could then be panned out from under the cassiterite.

The amalgam was then heated with a gas cartridge blow torch, the mercury departing in a white smoke that Heather and I stepped back to avoid. Edison sat stirring the mixture with his head near the deadly vapour. The Mad Hatter in *Alice's Adventures* was not a totally fictional creation: mercury poisoning was an occupational hazard of the hatter's trade.

Abel took out a set of jewellers' scales and weighed the handful of gold dust: 182 grams. Everyone smiled with relief. The amount was increasing and they wouldn't have to move on yet. Abel would take 65 per cent of this and the other men would share the rest. Abel paid for the machinery, fuel, food and other equipment. He paid the men's airfares to the *garimpo*, but not their fares out. It seemed an arrangement that the men were happy with. They knew how much Abel had to invest in pumps and equipment and we all knew how expensive the bush flights were. Of all the characters involved in gold prospecting, the pilots are probably the luckiest of all. They earn a fortune but can still be at home with their families every night.

The men each had 10 grams for four days work, and that was the equivalent of several weeks' manual work in the rest of Brazil where the minimum wage is less than £50 a month. Yet by the time they had paid for their flights back to town, had the inevitable celebrations and returned to their home states to see their families, there wouldn't be a lot left over. Many would have to pay for medical treatment for malaria or leishmaniasis, and the health of some would be permanently ruined. So they generally stayed as long as they could bear before flying to town; usually for six months or more if malaria didn't force an evacuation before then.

More tapir meat was thrown on the griddle, and there was even a first course of catfish that Pedro had caught after boating downstream to the Jari. Most fish had vacated the opaque waters of the Paruzinho for the time being.

This time nobody was going to work a night shift because the grader would have to be reassembled first, and everyone was in a party mood. We sat around the fire as night fell, swatting at mosquitoes and making sure that exposed skin was saturated with repellent. Any bite here could carry a little souvenir from those evacuated men.

We got our container of rum from the canoe and soon songs were sung, many beautifully, but our renditions of 'Yesterday' and 'Maxwell's Silver Hammer' were received with muted courtesy. A cassette recorder played tinny tunes and we took it in turns to dance with Heather. The men twirled her around in lusty lambadas, but were careful to keep their bodies a millimetre away from hers. They knew that nothing provoked violence and caused more shootings and knifings in gold camps than drunken disputes over women. That blond gringo might be sitting there on a section of tree trunk laughing happily at one of Zezinho's hunting stories, but mess with his wife and you never know what might happen. He might suddenly appear in front of you, waving a ridiculous little shotgun that some Santarém shopkeeper had cheated him for, and blow you away. Jealousy and *caipirinhas* didn't mix.

Actually, my chat with Zezinho had been marred by his prolific spitting. Every six or seven words would be punctuated by pauses to eject more sputum; the man was in danger of dehydration.

'I could see this huge dark shape through the trees, *splot*, and sneaked up, silent as a little breeze, *splat*, until I was within range, *splodge*, and eased around a tree trunk to get the heart shot. *Splat.*'

And so it went on until I had to lift my bare feet to escape the puddles of spittle. I wouldn't have minded if he was ejecting the usual by-products of strong Brazilian tobacco whose enormous tar levels make a smoker start the day in paroxysms of coughing and the expulsion of enough gunge to resurface the average driveway. Zezinho was just releasing globs of bubbly saliva that he didn't even fire away in long-distance salvos; just lowering his face until it was parallel to the ground and letting the threads hang there, swinging gently, until gravity broke them free and splashed them into the little lake at our feet.

The next morning, tired and hungover, we said goodbye and got ready to push off downstream. We'd told them of our plans to cross the Tumucumaque into French Guiana, and they knew that we didn't intend returning to Molocopote. However, I'd asked Abel if he expected to be up there for a few more months, because while they remained in the area planes would arrive at Molocopote, and they had a radio for emergencies. Once they were gone we'd have to paddle down the Jari, past some rapids and waterfalls that I had no wish to see again.

Abel didn't seem at all certain about his plans. 'Next week I'm going to Macapá to meet my partner who's working up the Rio Paru d'Oueste with another team. If I hear that he's doing well I may move this operation to join him. This lode's doing OK but may not last, and we had a hard time finding as much as we're getting now. I can't see us being here for that long.'

We shook hands with everyone, and just before we stepped into the canoe Abel handed me a spent brass shotgun case with its open end plugged with paper.

'What's this?' I asked.

'Four grams,' he replied. 'Your share for the work you did yesterday.'

'Don't be silly.'

'No, we want you to take it.'

The argument went on a long time as we stood in the smashed ruins of the jungle stream while little yellow butterflies danced around our feet. The men seemed genuinely hurt that we were rejecting their gift, however hard we tried to explain how wealthy we were, how they needed the money far more, how we were going to a place where we wouldn't need money for many months, how we had enjoyed our stay and had eaten them out of food.

Reluctantly they took it back, but it spoilt our departure. The gift had been freely offered as a token of friendship and we had spurned it. It made us feel sad and guilty for the rest of the day.

Within an hour and a half we were back at the confluence with the Mapaoni, and turned the bow towards the Tumucumaque. We'd enjoyed our time with the prospectors but now there was work to be done, paddles to be leant on and muscles to whip into line.

The Mapaoni was still as wide as the Thames at Henley but considerably more interesting than the swollen Jari had been. Eight years before, Peter and I had found the Mapaoni to be a rainforest paradise where we saw wildlife every day in a dry season idyll of yellow sandbanks and rocky margins. Unfortunately, a capsize on the Jari had ruined our camera several weeks before and we could only seethe in frustration as glorious photographic opportunities passed us by. I remember the fat anaconda that lay sunbathing on a fallen tree, its 20-foot length arranged in a perfectly symmetrical succession of patterned curves. Giant otters, deer, tapir, capybara, a jaguar, a puma, three ocelots and monkeys by the hundred watched us paddle by. Here was a river remote enough to escape the depredations of man.

Not so, it seemed. Abel had told us that forty *garimpeiros* had been working on the Mapaoni in recent months, though he thought they'd all left now, except for one team that might still be somewhere on the middle reaches of the river. It didn't take long to find traces of their activities. Strips of blue tarpaulin hung in the bushes, empty fuel drums bobbed in eddies, and we climbed ashore five times to explore abandoned camps. These were littered with cans, plastic bags, torch batteries, old clothing, abandoned machinery and a surprising number of empty deodorant roll-ons and cologne sprays. It seemed incongruous to imagine all those swarthy men so preoccupied with underarm odour.

We chose one to camp in, replacing a shelter's rotten, vermin-riddled thatch with our tarpaulin. In these open clearings firewood had a better chance of drying between the cloudbursts, and we hacked up the other structures for suitable logs.

I'd been growing sulkier all day, comparing this Mapaoni with the one I remembered, and regretting coming back at all. If we'd wanted a river devoid of wildlife and full of rubbish we needn't

have come as far as this. I took some of my frustration out on
the logs, swinging the axe so that splinters flew, piling up enough
firewood for a month. Heather took one irritated glance at my
scowls and busied herself preparing supper.

When I'd demolished every shelter except the one that was
supporting our hammocks, I stripped off and splashed in the river,
soaping my body and shampooing my hair. When I ducked down
deep to rinse it, I almost knocked myself out on a sunken piece of
machinery, and my mood soured again.

'It's like swimming in the Grand Union Canal!' I shouted,
fingering a bloody cut on my scalp. 'Probably find a supermarket
trolley next!'

I grabbed a towel and dried myself by the fire. 'I've been thinking
that we should change our plans – maybe go up to the top of the
Jari instead,' I announced.

'What are you talking about?' Heather asked with a frown.

'I don't think the prospectors have ever been up the Jari near its
source, and I haven't,' I argued. 'It's one of the few places around
here that I don't know already, and if I saw the Mapaoni when it
was undisturbed, what's the point of coming here again now it's
buggered up?'

Heather wasn't sympathetic.

'How do you know what's been happening up the top of the
Jari? There could be another airstrip up there, more gold workings.
And what do we do when we get up there – paddle all the way
down again? I've heard you go on and on about having another
go at crossing these hills, but now, six miles up the Mapaoni, you
decide that because you haven't seen a jaguar yet, you don't want
to carry on with that plan.' She stirred the rice furiously. 'Well I
do. I'm disappointed too, but it's very early days and anyway, I bet
we find that the prospectors never went further than the middle
reaches of the Mapaoni. Up at the top it'll be as good as ever.
You'll see.'

I hoped she was right. If the gold workings had been abandoned a couple of years before there wouldn't have been a problem. Disturbance and hunting on this scale doesn't wipe species out; it drives some deeper into the forest and makes others more secretive in their behaviour. But when peace returns, so do the animals, and surprisingly quickly.

Sitting on the watertight drums that doubled as our camp chairs, having a couple of calming drinks before supper, I let her persuade me to stick to our original plan of crossing the Tumucumaque hills, at least for a week or two.

At that moment though, I wished that we'd opted for a different objective on another river. The Amazon has more than a thousand tributaries that wriggle across a map of Amazonia like veins on a dried leaf. We could have explored something new, something unknown, instead of returning here to the scene of past failure. Places rarely seem so magical the second time round, even when they haven't been ripped apart by gangs of men in their search for fortune.

We had considered other options, but it's not that easy finding a wild, undisturbed river in Amazonia these days. Back in 1979 when I made my first canoe trip, almost any tributary would have been a winner, but the pace of deforestation and development has ruined huge areas and made it difficult to find a pristine creek. The states of Northern Mato Grosso, Rondônia, southern Pará and Acre have seen much of their forest cover removed for ill-fated cattle ranches, logging concessions or settlement programmes in the last twenty years. Some rivers on the border with Brazil and Peru, Colombia or Bolivia have clandestine activities at night where one wouldn't want to be an unwitting spectator. Huge quantities of cocaine are moved across these jungle frontiers and the price for being in the wrong place at the wrong time would surely be a bullet in the head.

The last really wild remnant of the Amazon rainforest – whose name still evokes an image of untamed savagery in the minds of most – is the area between the Amazon River and Brazil's northern neighbours of Guyana, Surinam and French Guiana. There are no roads, and every river has a barrier of rapids and falls similar to those on the Jari. Even here there are no-go areas. The Trombetas has huge bauxite mines, and iron ore is being extracted on the Jatapu. The upper Paru has a 3 million hectare Indian reserve where we'd be refused entry.

We'd been considering either the Curuapanema or the Maiouro rivers for our expedition when I received a letter. A young English guy had read the account of my previous attempt at crossing the Tumucumaque [*Up the Creek*], and was planning to give it a try himself. Would I mind giving him some advice?

I immediately felt a strange wave of pique and possessiveness. My patch was going to be trespassed upon! Some upstart was threatening to mount a big expedition, well-funded, free of disease, with the benefit of youth and vigour. They'd probably sweep effortlessly over the Tumucumaque and make my attempt with Peter look pretty pathetic.

Sure I had some advice for him. *Go and find a river of your own!* Before I'd really considered the implications, I'd penned him a reply saying that actually we were off to have another attempt at crossing the hills ourselves, leaving in August. That was eleven months before his intended departure, and as expected I never heard from him again.

All I had to do now was sell the idea to Heather. This would be her third expedition to the Amazon, and maybe the excitement of following her partner to these obscure places was beginning to pall? She probably regretted pressuring me to take her in the first place. It had all come to a head one November night four years before, after a boozy dinner party.

'That went well, didn't it?' I said to Heather, closing the door behind the last of the guests. A noncommittal grunt came from the sofa where she sat, legs tucked under her.

'What's the matter?'

'It was all right. For a while anyway.' She sighed, her face sulky. 'But it's hard for me when you all start your great Amazon reminiscences and your tall tales from the bush – all trying to outdo each other. What can I contribute, if I'm the only person in the room who's never been there?'

'I'm sorry if we go on a bit.'

'A bit! We had hours of it tonight. And you egg everyone on. I must have heard some of your stories twenty times, and I have to pretend that they're still exciting and fresh!'

'I expect everybody's heard my stories at least as many times as that,' I laughed. 'If you find I'm getting boring you should steer the conversation around to topics that interest you more.'

'Huh! Small chance when you collect five Amazon nutters in the room at the same time. Tanis goes on about Surinamese Indian tribes, Roger about some damn unpronounceable tributary near Itiquos—'

'Iquitos,' I corrected her.

'Thank you. And then you drone on about your great malaria attacks, or the parasites in your feet that have to be dug out with a needle, or the number of worms in a monkey's guts – usually when everyone's got a forkful of spaghetti halfway to their mouths. It goes on and on and on!'

I sat down on the arm of a chair.

'I guess we talk about it so much because it was great fun,' I said lamely. 'Simple as that.'

'Seems a strange sort of fun to me – malaria, biting bugs, torrential rain, endless rice and beans...'

'Ah, but that's only part of the story,' I said wistfully. 'Sure our memories get a bit selective after we've been home for a few months – you know how horrible events become transformed into amusing anecdotes.' I slumped into the chair, suddenly feeling queasy and unwell. I just wanted to crawl into the softness of our bed. 'Not only bad things either,' I continued with an effort, stifling an acidic burp. 'I can remember details of animals I saw, camps I made, fish I caught, all from jungle trips three, five, seven years ago.' I lit a cigarette and my body gave a shudder of outrage at the first puff before settling into a sullen acquiescence. 'We had a great two weeks in Greece last summer but I can't remember a thing about it. Can you? I know we had a good time but it's all faded.' I yawned. The hangover was starting and I slopped some wine in a glass to fend it off.

Heather held out her glass. 'I suppose it pisses me off because I never see you so animated or excited about things you do now. You just drift between one expedition and another with no real master plan, but always to the Amazon. It's like it's the only place you're interested in, and the most important thing you've ever done.' Her voice had quietened and she looked sad.

I woozily contemplated my limited life achievements. I'd travelled a lot, studied something obscure at university, lived for a while in Spain and Portugal and now I earned a living as a carpenter with occasional stints as a tour leader in South America. I'd left university twelve years before but was still behaving as if I were in my gap year. She wasn't going to give me some career advice, was she? Fighting off a little wave of depression I attempted a defence.

'Well, compared with my rich and varied life on London building sites those adventures do seem pretty marvellous. Work's just a means to an end – it pays for the next expedition, and those jaunts make it all worthwhile. If you'd done one of the trips you'd understand.'

'Exactly. But I haven't, and you don't want to take me, and I just have to put up with everyone droning on and on about it. I used to be interested but I can't contribute anything to the conversation, so I've grown bored.'

I'd resisted her accompanying me in the past, mainly because I was reluctant to take responsibility for her safety. While I'd come to regard the perils of the Amazon as rather overplayed, it would be a different matter to take a novice, guide her through it all and have to reassure her family that I intended bringing her back safely.

We hadn't talked about it for a long time, and sprawled in an armchair, tired and drunk, it no longer seemed such a big deal. Heather was physically tough and more spirited than many of the men that I'd travelled with, and most of them had been novices too. What she lacked in muscle she might make up for in determination, and perhaps I'd exaggerated my responsibilities in the past. She knew the risks, and was old enough to make her own decisions. We'd look after each other as best we could.

'Well let's go there this summer,' I offered suddenly.

'Where?'

'The Amazon of course.' There. I'd done it now. Would I regret this in the morning?

'I thought you didn't want to go with me. What about my new job?'

'You'll find another when we get back,' said the man least qualified to offer career advice.

Heather sat there, stunned at my sudden change of heart.

'You know I've never paddled a canoe before or spent a night in a tent,' she reminded me.

Oh God, bewailed a little sober voice in my head, *what the hell have I done?*

'Maybe you've been put off by all the stories you've heard,' I teased, part of me hoping that she'd agree. 'Might sound a bit risky, and if you decide it would be too much for you I'd quite understand.'

She roused herself. 'You must be joking! You're all a bunch of Walter Mittys anyway so I expect it's mostly bullshit. Instead of entering the jungle you probably all sit on Copacabana beach in Rio and work on your anecdotes.'

'Do you want to go?'

'Of course I do.'

'Good. That's settled. Can we go to bed now?'

When I hit her with my plans for this, our third expedition together, she'd argued quite persuasively that the journey entailed a rather unappealing combination of activities.

'Let's get this straight. First we have to paddle against the current for a hundred and fifty miles or so up a little creek with lots of rapids in its lower reaches, and thousands of fallen trees and log jams in the headwaters. Right?' I nodded. 'We then take the canoe out of the water and cut a fifteen-mile trail though thick jungle up and down mountains to reach the other side. Then we carry the canoe and a dozen sacks of stuff along the trail.' She smiled mirthlessly. 'And what's there on the other side? Something new? Not a chance. More fallen trees! More rapids!'

'Well every trip has a bit of hardshi—' I started to argue, but she cut me off.

'Of course it does, I've been on two of your twisted versions of what a holiday should be, remember? They were tough and exhausting, but they had rare interludes where a few moments of relaxation were permitted. This plan seems particularly masochistic and joyless, that's all I'm saying.'

She was right. I was struggling to think of a new marketing angle for this unsaleable idea when she walked up to me and gave me a hug.

'Don't look so forlorn. We obviously can't let that whipper-snapper of an adventurer steal your grand plan, so we'll give it a go.'

I squeezed her with gratitude. She really was more than I deserved. She gave a quiet sigh, and I looked into her face inquiringly.

'But you really do have a warped idea of how to show a girl a good time!'

And here we were, camped beside the Mapaoni, sitting amid litter and despoliation that we could have found much nearer home.

We'd just spent $800 flying up here; such expense and such a remote spot on the map should have guaranteed better than this. Now all we needed was to fail again in our objective. Would the starting point for the trail be any easier to find than last time? Would we remain in good health? Would this rather silly and masochistic enterprise enthuse and motivate us as much as it had in the past, or would we return home with another failure, to face our empty bank accounts with nothing to show for it?

A movement on the ground drew my attention away from these morose thoughts. A large spider was heading towards Heather's bare feet, and she lifted them out of the way. It was probably harmless, but you could never be sure.

Suddenly there was a loud buzz and a 2-inch black and orange wasp swooped down and stung the spider to death. We cautiously eased ourselves backwards as the wasp strolled over its victim, wings vibrating gently, its segmented body a picture of menace. It then bit off the eight legs, clutched the heavy remains to its belly, and blundered along the ground to get airborne. It was probably on its way to stuff the victim in a hole and lay eggs in it, assuring its larvae had plenty of meat for the first days of life. I hoped the spider was dead and not just paralysed. We watched it go.

'Bloody hell,' Heather muttered. 'This place is a jungle.'

Although the Tumucumaque Indian Reserve is centred on the upper Paru, its eastern boundary includes the headwaters of the Jari. The reserve is home to 2,700 Indians, mainly Wayana and Aparai, but also smaller groups of Tirio, Kaxuyana and Hixkaryana who tend to stay away from the missionary station on the Paru.

In November 2000, twelve *garimpeiros* were killed by Indians on the upper Jari. After arriving at Molocopote they had begun mining illegally within the reserve and their deaths were in retaliation for an incident where an Indian woman and a child were killed by a fire caused by the prospectors. According to the press report, the Indian tribe concerned was thought to be an uncontacted group of Kaxuyana.

Such incidents produce inevitable calls for efforts at 'pacification' and teams of experts will be sent to try and coax these groups into the centre of the reserve where they can be worked on by the missionaries and seduced by the free handouts that are available near the park headquarters. Through little fault of their own an independent, nomadic and unfettered way of life is going to be under assault. While it's encouraging that the Amazon Basin can still harbour uncontacted tribes, this incident shows all too clearly the value of keeping gold prospectors away from Indian reserves.

There seemed little point in rushing forward to the many rapids upstream that might be impassable with the river so full, so we took it easy and had a couple of days off in that first week. Every night we monitored the water level with sticks thrust into the margins; sometimes they showed an encouraging fall of 6 inches in twelve hours, but more frequently heavy downpours either kept the level constant or raised it back up again.

As we approached the headwaters we knew that the diversity and size of the fish was going to diminish, but the lower Mapaoni should hold some large catfish if the prospectors hadn't dynamited, netted or poisoned them all. Paddling away from camp at dusk I tied up to bushes or fallen trees and fished the deeper pools, out of the main current. Pestered by mosquitoes I sweated in heavy clothing, and as darkness fell the frogs began to thump and tweet and eerie rustlings came from the bank-side vegetation. Two hundred yards away the flickering warmth of our campfire enticed me to leave my lonely vigil, but the bait lay on the bottom, and the rod rested against the gunwale of the canoe. As I couldn't see its tip I had stripped 20 feet of line off the reel and coiled it on to a sheet of notebook paper to act as a bite indicator.

I puffed on a roll-up and sipped from a cup of rum. The stars reflected in the pale strip of midstream but it was black as tar near the banks. A large splash shattered the calm and the ripples rocked the canoe. Fish? Caiman? Swimming jaguar or anaconda heading my way? I resisted the temptation to flash the torch about.

There was a sudden rustling near my feet and the coils of line began leaving the sheet of paper, running smoothly up the rod rings and into the water. I picked up the rod and held it as the last of the slack disappeared, striking as I felt the weight of the moving fish.

There was no immediate drama; the fish continued heading calmly away, seemingly unaware that a hook had been planted in its jaw, and that a puny human was applying pressure to halt it. Gripping the butt of the rod firmly I tightened the drag on the reel, wedged myself in the seat, and heaved back as hard as I dared. There was a surge of muscled power and the fish was off, wrenching the rod tip into the water, threatening to break the 60-pound line unless I loosened off the pressure, pulling the canoe around in an arc and breaking free the loop of rope that I had loosely tied in the bushes. I was now adrift, being pulled around the dark river by a fish that was still swimming at full speed. Groping down for the torch I shone it on the reel – and saw that most of the line had gone.

Tightening the drag on the reel, I leaned back, raised the rod and heaved, promptly falling into the bottom of the canoe as the seat unclipped. Floundering in the bilges, I kept the line taut and felt the fish come to a halt. Vibrations strummed up the line as it shook its head or rubbed its jaw against something to dislodge the hook.

Little by little I wound line back on to the reel, not by moving the fish but because the canoe was pulled nearer. After five minutes I was directly above it. I was sweating heavily from the struggle and my arms and shoulders, already weary from a long day of paddling, were calling out for a rest. I slackened off and had a short break, but the fish moved off again. This time the fight had gone out of it. I stopped it quickly and slowly hauled it to the surface; it was now displaying all the fight of a sack of potatoes. The Amazon catfish were often like this: one mad unstoppable run and then a slightly disappointing surrender.

As the first swirls and splashes broke the surface, I switched the torch on and examined my catch. A huge, squat brown back rolled over and I saw a gleam of cream and orange flank. A *pirarara* catfish, 3 feet long and 50 pounds or a bit more. I ran my hand down the line until I reached the metal trace, and held on to that as I put the rod aside. The huge mouth, bewhiskered with foot-long barbels, broke the surface, gaped and emitted bubbly farting noises. It was big enough to take a football. The hook was embedded in the rubbery lips and I prised it out with a knife. The tired fish lay there for a moment not realising that it was free, and then wagged its tail and sank slowly out of sight. It had been too big for two people to eat.

Local people fear this fish because it apparently has a tendency to fasten tenaciously on the arms or legs of swimmers. John Hemming, the former director of the Royal Geographical Society and an authority on Amazonian tribes, visited a village of Carajá Indians on the Araguaia River in 1980 where one such fish had recently drowned a ten-year-old boy by seizing his arm and dragging him down. It was probably done as an instinctive reaction to the boy's splashing – the fish lacks the teeth to tear flesh off such a large victim – but the villagers believe they store their prey in lairs on the riverbed until it decomposes, much as crocodiles do.

The following day I fished some more and caught a *cachorro*, a dog-toothed characin. A pair of fangs in the lower jaw were so large that they couldn't be fitted in the closed mouth, and protruded by more than an inch through two holes in the upper jaw. They use these canines to attack relatively large fish, sometimes more than one and a half times their own length, stabbing them and rendering them helpless by puncturing the air-bladder.

Fishing, in addition to being exciting, varied our diet and supplemented the rather boring jungle staples. The menu was still based around rice, beans, spaghetti, porridge oats and wheat flour. We cultivated bean sprouts, made cinnamon oatcakes, prepared pancakes and chapattis and smothered everything with an assortment of spices, but the choice was inevitably limited. We'd found lentils in a Santarém supermarket but only bought 3 kilos, as they seemed a bit expensive. That's typical of the stinginess that we came to regret later: after having rice for the tenth meal in a row, the price of $5 for a kilo of lentils seemed an absolute bargain.

We paddled between walls of greenery where plants were gradually emerging from months of submersion, the scenery monotonous and unvaried. Large creatures were absent, but the birds were still there. Large green and rust-coloured kingfishers sat on their diving boards glaring down their beaks, and after a successful dive they bashed the catch against the perch before tossing it up to swallow head first. Failure to spear a fish was cursed with a chatter of frustration and a short flight to new hunting grounds. Cormorant-like 'snake birds' swam just under the water with only their long thin necks appearing from time to time to look around, and wading birds gravely paced through the shallows like thoughtful professors with their hands behind their backs. We disturbed clusters of tiny bats that would scatter from the shade of a tree trunk, flit as silently as windblown leaves and settle on another log, disappearing from view against the bark.

Once our bodies adjusted we could propel the canoe along for several hours without fatigue, even though the strong current prevented that effort being rewarded with much progress. Sometimes we could barely make any headway against the flow, despite whipping the water to froth. A pause for a rest or to scratch a bite and ten minutes' progress would be erased in a flash.

After portaging the canoe around a couple of small rapids we reached a major tributary coming in from the right, and at the confluence was a large shelter, covered with a newish blue tarpaulin.

'Better put your shorts on,' Heather warned me, covering her nakedness with T-shirt and shorts. 'Looks like we're going to have to be sociable.'

'When are we going to get this bloody river to ourselves?' I grumbled, a touch unreasonably as we hadn't seen anyone for more than a week. Once decent and presentable we paddled over only to find that there was nobody there. The owners had departed several months earlier judging by the weeds and new jungle growth, and the camp was littered with the usual debris. But hanging in the rafters, eye-catching even in the gloom, was a perfect jaguar skin. We took it out into the sunlight and the warmth of the golden sheen, the black rosettes and the bib of white on the chest took our breath away. It was hard to stop running our fingers through the dense softness and only a jagged hole from the fatal shotgun blast spoiled its perfection. Someone had made a fine job of the complicated business of drying and curing, and the pelt was soft and clean with just the faintest smell. We couldn't understand why it had been left behind. We replaced it in the rafters, not wanting to be accused of having killed it ourselves when we left the forest.

The hunting of jaguars for their fur has declined in the last decade since the introduction of controls set by the International Convention on the Trade of Endangered Species, but they are still threatened. It's estimated that each jaguar might need up to 100 square kilometres of territory, so deforestation is driving them back. Cattle ranching on cleared forest has introduced a new prey animal to the jaguar's diet, and made ranchers keen to hunt them down. Killing a jaguar or puma also raises a man's standing in the macho world of the forest and emphasises his testosterone levels. In fact, there's usually nothing heroic in the hunt. It's not as if they stalk one through the bush armed only with a spear or something: most are shot at night when the hunters drift down long sections of river, hugging the bank and shining torches in the hope of spotting an animal drinking. Any number of animals can be dazzled this way, and jaguars are one of them. They are mesmerised sitting targets.

Professional cat hunters use a jaguar caller. It's made from a hollow tube with a taut skin over one end and thongs hanging down inside. Sliding wetted fingers down the thongs vibrates the skin and imitates the rasping grunts of the jaguar. If there is a cat in the area it will answer and approach warily, presumably either to scare off a rival from its territory, or to find a mate. It must be tense work operating the caller, trying to mimic the sound of a jaguar accurately and not succumbing to the temptation to call too often, all the time knowing that a very powerful wild beast is coming nearer and nearer with one of two intentions: to fight you or to mount you. The hunters usually wait in hammocks positioned a long way up trees.

The main prey of the creek-drifting hunter is the paca, a cat-sized rodent with a brown and white coat that has the tenderest, tastiest flesh of any Amazon creature. It has long curved teeth that enable it to penetrate the tough casings of nuts and fruit.

A few years ago, Queen Elizabeth made a visit to Belize and at a banquet she and the other guests were served paca. The Belizeans consider it meat fit for a monarch, far superior to any sirloin of beef, but the worldly British tabloid newspapers thought otherwise. They felt Her Majesty had been insulted, served with some toothy jungle beast. A rodent conjured up only two images: a mouse or a… oh my God!

'QUEEN SERVED RAT!' shrieked one headline.

CHAPTER THREE

The fabled reputation of the Tumucumaque would have it that any river descending from such giddy heights should be a white-water torrent passing through several climatic zones. Henri-Anatole Coudreau, who penetrated these hills in 1888, wrote that the Oyampi Indians 'cross the high passes of the Tumuc Humacs', conjuring up images of trails zigzagging up scree slopes and the crunch of snow beneath bare feet. Eduardo Barros Prado, as late as 1959, described one of the rivers descending off the Tumucumaque as 'being swollen [...] since the thaw had already begun in the mountains'.

So a canoeist paddling apprehensively upstream is grateful to find long stretches of calm instead of the foamy steps of cataracts and the boom of fearsome waterfalls. Obviously the Mapaoni was no stagnant canal coated with green weed: the water surged against us in a smooth, unbroken rush, creating a bow wave and the illusion of brisk progress. We skulked along at the very margins, slapped by wet leaves, urged to stay awhile by the prick and tug of thorns, ducking between the creepers whose root balls trailed in the current picking up debris and nutrients.

At times the current outdid our efforts, pushing us downstream despite the frantic churning of the paddles, and then we grabbed hold of the bushes and hauled the canoe forward, the water still too deep to wade. After several days of this it was almost a relief to reach the string of almost continuous rapids that were to dominate our lives for the next two weeks. The first of these falls was Canapanoye.

Paddling as close as we dared, the canoe bobbing and skittering in the turbulence, we stepped ashore to discover the start of a portage trail made by *garimpeiros*, and I suddenly felt more kindly disposed to their activities and inclined to forgive them an environmental peccadillo or two.

We carried our light canoe the 300 yards of hilly path with barely a pause to rest, stepping over the rotting logs that others had used to roll their heavy boats upon. Two trees had fallen across the trail since it was last used so we chopped detours through the undergrowth to avoid them. Then it was just a question of eight trips each backwards and forwards to move the sacks of provisions and equipment. I strapped up the hernia in a tight girdle of elasticated bandage, nipping the waist into some grotesque hourglass, compressing flab until it bulged out at top and bottom like cream in a pastry.

This tiresome weakness of my viscera was positioned high up near the rib cage, and had appeared many years before as a nut-sized lump. Doctors said it would gradually enlarge until they'd have to operate but was best left alone for the moment. How big it would have to get before they reached for the scalpel they never told me. An orange? A football? Or would my intestines blast out of my belly like that creature in *Aliens*? In consolation, hernias at the top of the abdomen are apparently less likely to rupture or strangulate in some inconvenient place (like the banks of the Mapaoni) than those lower down in the groin.

We made our camp on a flat expanse of rock about halfway along the rapid, just above the main falls. The roar of the cascade, the rocks littered with bleached driftwood and the jungle-clad islets brought back memories of many other campsites in similar locations. The sun was out for a change, so we soaped some clothes and spread them to dry, and stripped naked to do something about the very untropical colour of our bodies.

Heather caught a small piranha for bait, and after that fishing was easy. We sat in the sun casting hooks baited with goujon of piranha and the relatives of the deceased threw themselves upon it. In half an hour we had nine piranhas for supper and a further one to use for bait the next day.

An unfortunate feature of Amazon life is the continual presence of a slab of dead fish under the canoe seat. If there are any doubts about the effect of heat on the rate of decomposition, dead piranhas dispel them. A fish caught in the morning is green and putrescent by nightfall; by the following morning the flesh has turned to some evil jelly that even piranha will push unenthusiastically round the plate.

We might whinge about rapids but they break the monotony and there was a satisfaction in putting each one behind us. Rapids meant rocky margins, pretty scenery, better fishing, and shallow pools with a rocky or sandy bottom to wash in – not those sluggish, spooky places where we'd sink calf-deep in ooze, releasing upwellings of marsh gas, our imaginations seeing dark shapes sidling towards our pale legs, licking their yellow fangs.

Orange and yellow butterflies congregated on the damp rocks or played a follow-my-leader conga up and down the river, seemingly for the pure pleasure of being out of the gloom of the forest and in the sunlight.

Soil is scarce and plants have to squeeze a root down any crevice they can find, only to get buffeted by the current for several months a year. Bromeliads do well in the hotter conditions out on the islets. Attached to the lower rocks is a plant with bright green leaves with the veiny texture of savoy cabbage. This is Podostemaceae, and for much of the year it remains completely submerged, only appearing as the water level falls to bloom with purple-pink flowers on a long stalk. By the time it shrivels and dies, the river level has fallen enough for other plants to emerge and flower, so the rapids are always carpeted in colour.

'Let's try fishing for armoured shad,' Heather suggested. I was sprawled with a novel in a patch of sand, the perfume of Ambre Solaire in my nostrils, enjoying a rare interlude of conventional holiday.

'You know we'll never get one,' I said in an effort to discourage her. This little armour-plated catfish is like a Palaeozoic fossil returned to life, with interlocking bony plates on its flanks and rigid pectoral fins. They live in turbulent water, and would be left unmolested if they weren't so delicious to eat.

'Come on you lazy bugger,' said Heather, flicking water and being tiresome.

'Obviously you're not enjoying your book as much as I am,' I protested, reluctantly putting it aside and getting to my feet before chasing her into the shallows for a spirited water fight.

'With gloves or without?' I panted once we were both soaked.

'Oh, *with* of course. I've got no chance at all without them on.'

We'd brought a pair of work gloves, mainly for armoured shad fishing. On past trips we'd spent hours trying to catch them and attributed our failure to using bare hands.

We waded out into the turbulent margins of the rapid where the water was knee-deep.

'There's one!' A black blur shot ahead of us and dived under a rock.

Putting a glove on my right hand I reached gently into the crevice where the fish had disappeared. There was something insane about this activity, as we'd seen more snakes swimming on the margins of rapids than anywhere else, and while my fingers waved searchingly for the fish, all my reflexes were sending frantic instructions to get that hand the hell out of there. I touched something that moved slightly, but the gloves prevented me from distinguishing what it was. I withdrew my hand and took the glove off.

'I don't think it's possible with this on. You need a lot of sensitivity to feel around.'

Putting my unprotected hand under the rock again I felt the rough sides of the fish. No smooth-skinned trout this: its bony scales rasped like coarse sandpaper. Fluttering fingertips gently along its flanks I moved into position and then seized it firmly. Until that moment it had been motionless, but now it wriggled violently, and the extended bony pectoral fins pinched my fingers against its body. I let go and yanked my hand away.

'Damn! Damn! Damn! Every bloody time!'

Heather laughed and put the glove on. She had a try but the same thing happened to her, and over the next hour fifteen more armoured shad escaped from our clutches. It seemed impossible not to snatch the hand away when the fish began squirming and lashing from side to side like a ball of knobbly muscle.

'I do feel we're getting a bit braver each time,' Heather said, when we gave up and returned to dry land. 'I think it's the sort of thing that when you've succeeded once it's a breakthrough, and you never have any problems after that.'

The next morning dawned cloudy and grey so we abandoned our intention of staying at that campsite and paddled off through the maze of channels above the rapid. Half an hour later we passed a little tributary that was soiling the clean waters of the Mapaoni with a silt-laden slick. A sign nailed to a tree proclaimed this to be part of the mining operations of 'Franck e Cia' whose territory stretched 'from the Jari and Mapaoni rivers to the Tumucumaque Mountains'.

'This must be the gang Abel told us about,' I said, finding myself whispering. 'That's a bit bloody greedy, isn't it, staking a claim to several hundred square miles? We might have to fight Mr Franck if we find the mother lode upstream.'

At least we now knew where to find people in case of emergency, and one glance at the colour of this creek would tell us if they had moved on or not. There was no need to visit them, we decided as we paddled briskly away; relieved because we were already developing the shyness that can afflict the explorer after a period alone or with just one companion.

This had reached ridiculous levels in 1987. After twelve weeks of descending a river, we'd lost our position on the map in a bewildering succession of rapids and had no idea where we were.

One afternoon we'd paused to fish when we heard the sound of an outboard motor approaching, and round the corner, straining against the current, came a large canoe packed with humanity.

'Well at least you can ask them where we are,' Heather said, my Portuguese being better than hers.

We drifted down gently and the other craft, looking like one of those vessels that desperate refugees from Vietnam or Cuba launch themselves to sea in, came closer. There were dozens of people in it, crammed knee to knee, sitting on the gunwales, ten or fifteen standing up. Here was a cross section of Brazil's racial mix from Aryan blond to pure black and pure Indian with every possible shade in between, but all looking poor and rather ragged. They were all silent and staring at us.

I felt an anxiety creeping upon me. There were so many of them! All at once after three months of solitude! How could I speak to so many, and what was I going to say? 'Excuse me. Where are we?' I couldn't ask them that. It would sound really stupid and they'd probably laugh at me.

I was still holding the fishing rod, the bait in the water, so I sat there like Huck Finn with my battered straw hat giving me a gormless air as the boat reached us. Fewer than 6 feet separated the two canoes, and out of the corner of my eye I saw Heather glance at me, waiting for me to speak. I did. Giving a strained attempt at a smile, I said, 'Good afternoon.'

And that was it. I couldn't manage any more. No one in the canoe replied, and gradually they drew away.

'I couldn't do it,' I apologised. 'I'm sorry, but there were too many of them. I was struck mute.'

There was one consolation as we carried on our way, still ignorant of where we were, curiosity unsatisfied about all those people and where they were going. Surely heated debate and conjecture must be raging in their canoe too.

'Those weird gringos! Man, did you see how wild they looked?'

'Like they'd been on the river for months. Did you see the grimace the guy made as he greeted us? Creepy huh?'

'Was that a woman with him? I think it was, but what a state to let yourself get into.'

'Where do you reckon they came from?'

And surely someone will pipe up, 'Why the hell didn't one of us ask them? For Christ's sake, out of sixty-five people not one of us had the wits to speak!'

Although it was still raining once a day, enough to wet the firewood, douse the fire and maintain a maddening drip, drip, drip from above, it lacked the ferocity of the deluges of the first fortnight. This was reflected in the river level that dropped steadily by 4 inches a night, and the first of the sandbanks were beginning to appear. After loitering for the level to fall, we now felt we should hurry up, but we were given few opportunities to paddle; wading up several small rapids, and passing the second large falls of Canapacapán with an easy portage along the rocks.

The next afternoon we came to the pretty falls that Peter and I had named Pineapple Rapid but which the Indians call Canamaracá. Here the river divides in two: one branch dropping 30 feet in a confused 100 yards of spray, while the other spills almost sedately over a large shelf of smooth rock covered in Podostemaceae. The edges of this were drying out, making our route up as slippery as an ice rink. Even rigging a hand line in the bushes didn't help, as our boots were useless on the slick mixture of wet rock and dead leaves. We moved over to wade up the stream itself where the clumps of vegetation gave some grip. We still tripped and fell, fearful now that we'd slide down to the bottom and disappear in the waves below. Heather sprained her thumb as she crashed to the ground, and had trouble gripping anything for the next two weeks.

I badly gashed my own thumb with a saw while cutting a wedge to secure the axe head, which was rather careless for someone who's supposed to be a carpenter. Heather put two stitches in it, and while I hadn't married her for her needlepoint she did a neat job of injecting the local anaesthetic and suturing. It only took an hour per stitch.

Our medical kit probably held more than an average Third World pharmacy: stuff to set a broken bone, sew up a wound, and treat any possibility of illness or infection. Eight different antibiotics should cope with chest, urinary, ear, eye and skin infections. Two of them used together might even control appendicitis for a few vital weeks. Here were drugs to protect us from malaria, and others to cure us when they failed. Injectable painkillers, tablet painkillers, and local anaesthetics should avoid the need to grit our teeth and be stoical in our suffering. Other crises might be met with ampoules of adrenalin, temporary tooth fillings, tablets to control allergies and itches, prevent nausea, help us sleep, kill intestinal parasites and tapeworms, or to stamp out fungal growths. Syringes, scalpels, plaster, sutures, bandages and sterile dressings bulged out of the large bag. Inevitably, many of the creams and tablets should have been kept in cool conditions, ideally in a fridge, but had to bake in the tropical sun along with everything else.

It was very comforting to have this pharmacy with us but we had no illusions. We stood little chance of surviving a major accident, such as a fractured skull, a puncturing wound, a compound fracture, appendicitis or poisoning. If both of us were still able to walk or hop past rapids we might just make it, but with one comatose or incapacitated the other wouldn't be able to manage all those rapids and waterfalls alone. I might just be able to carry Heather, but when we first started going on these expeditions I told her she must have the sense to abandon me and save herself. That had made me feel quite heroic and noble as I said it. What a fine Captain Oates sort of chap I was. Of course, I'd probably react very differently if it ever happened.

'What do you mean, you're off now? You can't leave me here! What about your marriage vows, "till death us do part" and all that?'

Heather had never injected warm human flesh until that day, and though we studied first aid manuals they merely guide you through until the emergency services take over. Several pages prepare you for dealing with electric shocks, which are rather rare on the Mapaoni, except for the eel-inflicted variety.

I'd accompanied a doctor friend one weekend when he was on duty in a casualty department. That experience taught me what silly things people do when they're drunk, and the mess a car crash can make of the fragile human frame, but though I saw broken limbs set and wounds sewn, emergency airways cut in throats, hearts resuscitated, dislocations relocated, the circumstances didn't permit me to get any hands-on experience.

Appendicitis is an obvious worry when medical help is so far away, and in the old days expeditions used to start with a visit to hospital to have that organ removed. Several years ago my GP refused to permit it.

'You can't just rip out a perfectly healthy and inoffensive appendix. That would be quite wrong.'

'Why?' I pressed.

'You must realise that every part of the human body has been designed for a purpose. Occasionally they malfunction and have to be sacrificed, but until they do they are best left alone.'

'What important function does an appendix serve?' I asked. 'Some crucial one like nipples do on a man?'

'The appendix is a blind process terminating the caecum. It's the vermiform appendix of the intestine...' he informed me sombrely, dredging his memory from student days.

'It sounds like an unimportant cul-de-sac to me. Its very name suggests it was stuck on as an afterthought,' I argued, but the doctor was glancing impatiently at his watch. I'd evidently exceeded my seven minutes per patient, so I got up to leave.

'Ninety-five per cent of appendices never cause the slightest problem, and I'm sure yours will be the same, wherever you may take it.'

'But if it's one of those five per cent it will kill me, right?'

'If you don't get to the hospital quickly, yes.'

I began to open the door.

'Of course we could possibly arrange for you to have it done privately. Six hundred pounds should do it I'd have thought.'

There are other medical conditions that require immediate surgery: ruptured spleens, strangulated hernias, burst ulcers or twisted bowels. In fact, a ruptured spleen is not an uncommon complication in malaria. I remember when I was at school one of my friends was in agony from a twisted testicle and needed an operation to sort it out. We thought we had a pretty good idea how a boy of thirteen had managed to upset his testicles and sniggered behind our hands, but it would still be a nasty thing to live with for several weeks.

The feeling of vulnerability would increase with every mile. Once in the mountains we'd be nine weeks' journey from help on the Brazilian side. Maybe Abel's crew would still be around with their radio and supply planes, but we couldn't count on it. Our best protection was caution and prudence, so we carried the canoe around difficult rapids, and stayed alert to the hazards of our daily chores: the open fires, the axe, machete and sharp knives. We took our anti-malarials and tried to limit mosquito bites. We never reached blindly around a tree trunk, picked up logs without kicking them first or put our boots on without shaking them. As we walked along we monitored the ground ahead for snakes, and watched over each other anxiously. I didn't want anything to happen to Heather, especially if it would mean me being left there all alone.

We could have taken a radio, as we had the previous year on the film crew's insistence, but decided against it. This HF transceiver, powered by a car battery and with a 30-foot aerial, had enabled us to contact the Brazilian coastguards on the Amazon River, who would then dial any telephone number that we asked for. With the battery fully-charged, reception was excellent. Our only regret was that we'd chosen the name *Jacaré* to identify ourselves, so whenever we used the apparatus we felt pretty silly broadcasting over the Amazon wastes: 'Calling Santarém. Calling Santarém. This is Alligator. This is Alligator. Over.'

Heather and I had opted to leave the radio behind, as we had on every other expedition. We didn't want to carry a heavy car battery that could spill acid and rot away our canoe, inevitable when all our baggage would be dragged roughly in and out of the canoe five hundred times or more when passing rapids and fallen trees.

There are other gadgets on the market, of course. Satellite phones that would make a wilderness experience seem pretty wilder*less* to me. Other gizmos send a distress call to passing aircraft, so any jet cruising the stratosphere on its way from Rio to Miami would pick up the signal and alert the authorities. I'd always be worried that the thing might get switched on by mistake, and we'd look up from breakfast one morning to find the air filled with searching aircraft, with marine commandos and the British press approaching in speed boats.

Monkeys were the only animals we saw – howlers, squirrel and capuchin – and they regarded us suspiciously from high branches or chattered and fled in alarm. They'd evidently met man before. Several times we heard a jaguar calling but the river was devoid of the tapir, giant otter, capybara and anaconda that I remembered. On the positive side, the number of prospectors' camps was decreasing and looked older, with rotten structures too weak to support our hammocks. Perhaps we'd reached the limit of their operations.

The thin fabric of the canoe couldn't stand much abrasion against the rocks, and after some rough treatment in the rapids small tears had opened in the hull that we patched from the inside with waterproof gaffer tape.

On previous expeditions, when using wooden canoes, we'd carried a supply of fibreglass for repairs, which made patching easy but did have its drawbacks. Two chemicals are needed: lots of polyester resin and a small quantity of catalyst to harden it after the mixture is spread over glass tape. Such chemicals are not welcome on airlines because of their flammability so we'd purchased them in South America.

There was only one company in all of Manaus that used fibreglass, but they were willing to sell us some of their stock. The polyester resin was no problem, we'd brought some 5-litre containers and could screw it safely inside. The catalyst was more difficult because most receptacles would be corroded by the chemical and we couldn't find a glass vessel that was strong enough and had a decent lid. The factory owner recommended using an old powdered milk can, so we poured in half a litre and banged the lid down hard.

'Make sure you keep it upright,' was his only advice.

We transported this chemical cargo back to our cheap, windowless hotel room where a fan stirred the moist humid air. This might have deceived the skin that it was slightly cooler, but under the bed where the catalyst lay it remained over 100°F.

I now know a bit more about this substance than I did then. It is Methyl Ethyl Ketone Peroxide, and in Britain its container is marked with lots of warnings about its oxidising and corrosive properties: 'Keep container in a cool, well-ventilated space. Causes burns. Risk of serious damage to eyes. Contact with combustible materials or other materials generating decomposition may cause fire.'

What a 'material generating decomposition' means I've no idea, but I had experience of its flammability. After assembling a canoe on a previous trip we were left with more catalyst than we needed, and I foolishly tossed a cupful into the embers of a bonfire. The mushrooming fireball removed most of my quiff.

A few hours before we were due to catch the evening riverboat down to Santarém, we dragged the stuff out from under the bed and got ready to pack it up for the journey. The resin was fine, but the lid suddenly flew off the catalyst with a tremendous bang, denting the ceiling, and a fine spray was caught by the fan and blown into Heather's eyes. Fortunately we were on the ground floor and the owner was watering some flower tubs on the patio outside. I rushed out with Heather screaming and covering her face in her hands, wrenched the hose from the startled man and turned it on her, making her lie down under the jet for several minutes. We then went back in to examine the catalyst. A once clear liquid had gone milky white.

It was Sunday so I looked up the factory manager's home number and disturbed his siesta. It couldn't be helped. The boat was going to take us downriver where there would be no more fibreglass suppliers, and in a week's time a bush plane would drop us at an airstrip and depart. That would not be a good time to discover that the catalyst didn't work and that we couldn't put the canoe together, particularly as we had no radio to call the pilot back.

The manager was irritable and I could hear some female sighs, kisses and muffled giggles, and I'm not sure I really had his full attention.

'Try testing it with a little resin,' he said curtly. 'If it still hardens it must be OK.' ('Oh yes, it hardens all right!' cooed a woman's voice, and the manager sniggered.) 'It's probably absorbed some of the coating from the inside of the tin.' He hung up.

Reassured by a test, we hammered the lid shut, tied a piece of string around it, wrapped it in a towel and placed it upright in my backpack.

The riverboat was packed with several hundred hammocks pressed side by side on two decks, and we lay in ours drinking a few beers and chatting over the thump of the diesels. It was lucky we were there and not on the top deck, because the smell of the catalyst alerted us.

Heather reached down and touched my pack. 'Jesus! It's red hot!' she shouted.

A yard away two Brazilians were sitting on their suitcases enjoying a cigarette. Without a word of explanation, like some rabid, crusading health fanatic, she reached out, plucked the butts from their lips and tossed them overboard. 'No smoking,' she told them firmly.

I yanked open the lid of the pack. A cloud of acrid smoke seared my throat; the towel that covered the tin was charred and ragged and looked as though it might be a 'material generating decomposition' to my untutored eye. The lid had come off and the scorched fabric looked about to ignite, so I ran to the rail and heaved the tin and towel into the river.

Most of my clothing was ruined, the pack itself was holed, and we had been on the brink of a spectacular disaster. Seventy-five shotgun cartridges were stored in the bottom of the pack, and 20 litres of equally flammable polyester resin lay alongside in a sack. The wooden boat would have burnt with pyrotechnic accompaniment, and 500 passengers would have had to leap into the dark water hundreds of yards from shore.

It was a sobering thought, but not nearly as depressing as the realisation that I would have to return to Manaus while Heather continued on to Santarém with all the other gear. I spoke to the captain, inventing a story that I'd forgotten some essential documents. I didn't think a confession that I'd almost blown up his boat would improve my case.

'I have to get back to Manaus straight away,' I implored. 'When will this boat make its first stop?'

'Tomorrow morning at six o'clock,' he replied, turning the wheel to avoid a floating log that had been picked out in the searchlight. I looked at my watch. Nine hours' time. On this river a boat's downstream speed is more than double that of one labouring against the current, so by the time they dropped me off I'd have a twenty-four-hour journey back.

There seemed to be flotillas of lighted boats passing us the other way.

'Can't we flag down one of those so I can get on board?' I asked desperately. 'It would be easy to hop across, it would only delay you a moment.'

He shook his head, and despite all my appeals he offered no alternative but to wait until dawn, when I was dropped on a jetty with two other unfortunates. They told me they lived there, but seemed unexcited to be home.

'Where's the town?' I asked. They looked surprised.

'It's not a town, just a few houses over the hill there,' one said, and shouldering their suitcases they disappeared up a track between head-high grass. Heather and 498 other passengers looked down, making me feel like a missionary being dropped off at an outpost of the empire in the Dark Continent.

'Does anyone know when a boat will pass?' Heather called.

'There's supposed to be one sometime tonight or tomorrow morning,' I replied sulkily and sat on my luggage. A bell rang in the ship and many of the passengers disappeared from the rail.

'What's that?' I asked.

'Breakfast, I think. I'd better go.'

'Oh, don't be late for breakfast,' I sneered.

'I'll miss out if I don't get a seat now. You never know, there might be an espresso bar for you up that track. See you in Santarém!'

I waved morosely and when a wag yelled, 'Watch out for headhunters!' I pretended to be amused.

Five minutes later another bell rang in the engine room and a gap opened between the ship and the jetty, but the decks and rails were deserted and there was nobody to wave to.

The village consisted of one street of shacks without a bar or restaurant, and the store only stocked a few rusting tins of sardines. The inhabitants were as listless, depressed and unwelcoming as you'd expect from a lifetime of boredom and malnutrition.

The graveyard was huge, far larger than the place seemed to warrant, and I sat on an elegant marble slab and read a book. This had evidently been a thriving community until the attractions of Manaus had lured all the young and healthy away. I later walked through overgrown clearings, swam in the muddy Amazon, watched the river traffic enviously, lay under trees where I read, dozed, read and dozed again.

Nightfall and mosquitoes came hand in hand, so I returned to the jetty and sprawled out on my folded hammock. If a boat was due no one else was waiting for it. I slept, and was awakened hours later by the thump of engines and a searchlight beam that swept past, paused and came back to fix on me. My watch said 3 a.m. Standing up, I waited for the ship to pull into the jetty, but to my horror it continued its slow cruise upstream. I yelled and waved vigorously, hopping up and down on the creaking boards, and at last the beat of the engines slowed and the large vessel drifted back in the current, brushed the jetty long enough for me to hop on, then moved off again.

'Nearly missed us,' said a crew member as I paid my fare. 'If you'd left it a second later the captain wouldn't have stopped for you. You're supposed to wave a torch to let us know you wish to travel.'

'I'd have swum after you if you hadn't stopped,' I assured him.

He looked at me in amusement. 'That would have been a bit drastic. There's another boat coming the day after tomorrow.'

Twenty-seven hours later I took a taxi straight round to the fibreglass factory.

'Look at this!' I shouted as I entered the manager's office, waving a pair of jeans that had been holed and scorched. 'My backpack and all my clothes are ruined, and I've had to get off a riverboat and come all the way back! It's cost me a fortune and all because you gave me useless advice.'

The manager fingered the holes and shook his head. 'Never seen anything like it,' he said, calling out to his foreman, and soon a small group had gathered, everyone most impressed with the power of Methyl Ethyl Ketone Peroxide.

I'd bought some expensive fruit juice for the sake of its robust glass jar and screw-top lid, and put the new catalyst inside. That evening I caught another riverboat to Santarém where I arrived two days later. Throughout the voyage I clutched the jar like some sacred relic, panicking that it might slip out of my sweaty, nervous hands and smash on the ground. Whatever happened I wasn't throwing this lot overboard or returning to Manaus again. No way. The boat could burn with me and all the women and children in it before I did that.

We continued to catch plenty of fish for our lunches and suppers, but piranha nearly always made up the catch. Only once did we hook an alternative, and that was a sleek 6-pound predator that rushed at the spinner and then performed spectacular head-wagging leaps and rushes in an attempt to escape. A pike-characin I believe it's called, and I've often seen them hurtling after fry in the shallows. This one's stomach contained several almost unmarked little fish. They have a fleshy orange appendage on the tip of their upper jaw which is apparently a lure to attract small fish or insects when poked through the surface film.

After gutting piranhas we grilled them intact – head, scales and all – peeling the skin off when it was charred and cooked. Hoping this predator would have a finer flavour I decided to prepare it for frying. After bashing it over the head I began to remove the scales with the back of a knife, but it kept on flapping its tail and jumping out of my hand. I cut its head off and went back to work, but it still wouldn't stay still, so I slit open the belly and removed all the intestines. Even then it landed in the water and flapped around the shallows, headless, upside down and with the slit of its empty belly hanging open. It was to make one final protest at its untimely death: as I laid it in the sizzling frying pan it sprang right out again.

Some of the piranhas we caught were ugly brutes of 5 pounds or more that flopped and snapped their triangular, razor-sharp teeth until stilled with a machete chop. Losing a finger or toe this way is about as near as the Amazon traveller is likely to get to a piranha attack; the rest of the piranha reputation is very overplayed. There are over twenty species of this fish but only the piranha caju, one of the smallest, with a pink underbelly, is likely to school in enough numbers to reduce a large victim to a skeleton. These favour the backwaters and lakes of muddy rivers, and when concentrated at low water they can certainly be a danger to anything that enters. However, you would have to be rather stupid to swim in such a place. The surface is furrowed by racing dorsal fins and splashing as big fish eat little fish, and even bigger fish eat them. Hungry piranhas might go for you in there, but so would half a dozen other species.

On clear-water rivers the most common species is the black piranha. More solitary, they vary in colour from steel-blue to dark black, and feed mostly on fish fry, fruit, crabs and carrion, but they will tackle larger prey. Sometimes when we hooked catfish they reached the bank with semicircular chunks missing from their flanks and tails because piranhas had been attracted by the commotion and nipped in to take advantage.

So the piranha is a ghoulish little fellow with its grunting and snapping, and one of the few creatures that I can kill with no trace of sorrow. Although there are many tastier fish in these rivers, piranhas make a passable luncheon, and we've been known to strip one to the skeleton in minutes.

It was fortunate that they failed to live up to their lurid reputation, as we had to spend many hours a day wading up the fast current, pulling logs and rocks out of the way, deepening channels, unloading sacks and carefully hauling the canoe up by rope.

Raymond Maufrais had similar experiences when ascending the Mana River on the other side of the hills in the company of a trader taking provisions into the interior:

> All this unloading and loading and unloading! I join the boatmen in humping bags and chests: it all helps to keep me in training for later [...] We jump; clamber across channels on bridges made of dead tree trunks; claw with our feet at the slippery moss-covered rocks; and our shoulders ache beneath the loads. The heat weighs heavily upon us, and as we slip and slide and sweat we call one another every name we can think of.

On the morning of our twentieth day we were carrying some sacks along the fringe of another small rapid when I thought I heard a whistle from the other bank.

'What's that?' I asked, seeing that Heather had paused in mid stride.

'Sounded like someone whistling.'

We peered across the river, but the overhanging trees obscured the view.

'Can't see anyone, but it did sound like a human whistle to me.'

'Me too, but some bird calls can be like that.'

Feeling ill at ease we continued with our portage. Shortly afterwards, two men appeared on the rocks opposite carrying shotguns, one with a dead animal hanging on his back: a howler monkey judging from the rich red of its coat. We waved, and they lifted their hands a short way from their sides in a rather half-hearted greeting. One of them shouted something but the noise of the rapid snatched it away.

'We'll paddle over in a minute!' I called and he cupped a hand to his ear and shook his head. I signalled that we would cross over once we had got the canoe and sacks upstream to quiet water. They nodded.

'Bloody hell!' exclaimed Heather. 'Why didn't you tell me I've got no top on? I've been flashing my tits at them!'

'Sorry, I hadn't noticed. Anyway, I'm stark naked myself.'

'That makes me feel a lot better. My husband isn't even interested in my breasts any more.'

Ten minutes later we paddled across, preparing ourselves for the rusty art of social interaction, but there was nobody there. We called out, paddled a way upstream, drifted down again, but it seemed they had gone.

'You'd think they'd have been curious enough to wait,' I said. 'To get a closer look at your tits at least.'

'I reckon they're still there, just hiding and watching us,' she whispered, and I thought of the shotguns that could be pointing our way.

'Maybe they've got a camp around the corner and we'll see them there. Let's get moving,' I said. Heather looked as pale and tense as I felt.

We carried on upstream scanning the riverbanks, listening for the alien thump of diesel engines. Once we thought the wind brought us a whiff of wood smoke, but an hour later we still hadn't seen anyone, and our way was now blocked by the large fall of Ouyapan where the river fell 15 feet in one abrupt drop.

We'd been going slowly enough against the current for men to follow us on foot, and remembering terrible scenes from the film *Deliverance* (not advisable viewing for those planning canoe trips on wild rivers) I considered loading the shotgun, but that little peashooter wouldn't do much for morale.

We scouted the margins of the falls looking for a way past, and in the shade of the overhanging trees near the left bank I found myself still searching the bushes for spying faces. Mr Franck might be very possessive about his claim and assume we had gold on our minds.

Suddenly there was a clap of sound and out of the corner of my eye I saw the water erupt in a loud splash a few feet from the canoe. My God, they were shooting at us!

Leaping to my feet in the back of the canoe I called out, 'We're friends! Don't shoot! We're not *garimpeiros*!'

Heather turned round in her seat. 'What are you doing?' she asked. Jesus, she was a cool one!

'Can you see where they are?' I asked.

'Who?'

'Whoever just shot at us for Christ's sake! Didn't you see the bullet hit over there?'

'Bullet?' she asked infuriatingly.

'Yes. Bullet!' I carried on shouting friendly phrases into the jungle, emphasising that we were tourists, photographers and biologists.

'That was an iguana,' she giggled.

I stopped shouting and stared at her. 'It wasn't. I heard the crack of a gunshot.'

'You didn't. It was an iguana. It dropped from a branch up there and nearly landed in the canoe, doing one hell of a belly-flop.'

We decided we'd better pull up on an islet and have some lunch so that I could recover my poise. As I waded the shallows casting the spinner I could hear Heather still giggling by the fire. 'Don't shoot!' she mimicked and was off cackling again.

Green iguanas rain from the treetops as you paddle into sight, plummeting 60 or 70 feet into the water to escape. Their flesh is very succulent if you're not squeamish about eating some scaly, warty dragon, so there is good reason for them to be wary of man. They often ricochet off other branches as they fall and the whole strategy looks very painful and unnecessary, as you would never have seen them motionless up there anyway.

Not long ago I heard a BBC programme on the radio where concerned people were talking about the unsuitability of iguanas as pets. Purchased as attractive finger-length little lizards, they then grow to 3 or 4 feet of trouble and became too much for the average three-bed semi. 'What can be done?' asked the presenter, and I was tempted to phone up with a selection of recipes.

There was a beautiful pool below the falls with spits of yellow sand, shiny black rocks and purple flowers. Clumps of foam circled lazily in the eddies, and within two minutes I'd caught a brown high-sided fish, similar in appearance to the piranha but less toothy. I slit open its belly and pulled out the guts, and was about to toss them into the stream when a movement caught my eye. The handful of intestines seemed to be alive and heaving. Hundreds of long white wriggling worms had emerged from the stomach and were making their way purposefully up my wrist. I dropped it with a shudder and quickly washed them off, and soon a shoal of minnows was darting around with lengths of white worm trailing from their mouths. In doing so they temporarily dropped their guard, and a waiting pike-characin hurtled through them, mouth agape, causing several dozen to leap in panic and land flapping on the shore. The shock of the dark shape rushing so suddenly out of the depths caused me to lose my balance and sit down heavily in a rock pool, bruising my bottom. Heather was chuckling again.

Summoning some reserves of dignity I cast the lure nearby, and the rod tip was almost immediately yanked down and line pulled off the reel with a scream. Four, five, six times the sleek body catapulted itself into the air, shaking its head and snapping its jaws to expel the hooks, but they were firmly embedded and soon I dragged it on to the sand and killed the spirited creature with regret.

After an excellent lunch of crispy fried fish fillets we tackled the falls head on, carrying everything straight up the middle where only shallow water covered the rocks and plants. There was a platform on which to unload the sacks at the bottom, but we portaged the canoe first as there was no dry land at the top. On the way up I planted my foot confidently on a patch of Podostemaceae, and suddenly I was falling, disappearing up to my waist, cracking my kneecap against the edge of the hidden blow hole as I went down. I yelled out in pain, but fear still made me hop out of the hole quite nimbly to do my writhing on the surface because such places are popular haunts for electric eels. A deep gash had opened on the knee and the pain was so bad that I was sure I'd smashed it.

Heather bent over to examine the damage. 'Christ, you're bleeding buckets,' she exclaimed.

I was. Alarming red rivulets were running down my shins and staining the rock, but the wound, though ugly, seemed strangely bloodless. The gash on my thumb had reopened.

It took half an hour for the pain to subside enough for me to try standing up and Heather was looking anxious. Would we make it downstream if I had a broken knee, or would she have to leave me behind? Was she worried that the life insurance company might not pay up?

I flexed the joint tentatively. It moved, very painfully, but it moved without the grinding of smashed bone, so I hopped up to the canoe while Heather brought the rest of the sacks up.

We camped at the first suitable spot and for the next four nights the pain of the blackened and swollen knee kept me awake, despite our strongest painkillers. It was difficult to straighten it out and get comfortable in the hammock, so I usually moved out and lay by the fire. In the daytime, once the joint had loosened up and been soaked in the river, it felt less painful.

That knee has given me trouble ever since, particularly when carrying anything heavy, and a recent X-ray showed that it was chipped. A little bit worse and our expedition would have ended right there.

There was only Cachiri rapid ahead of us now, but this is the largest on the Mapaoni, stretching for more than a mile. The river flowed down numerous channels between islands, and it would have paid to explore ahead on foot to find ones where the river dropped once over a high shelf rather than four times in lesser steps that needed four separate portages. But the water was too deep to make such scouting possible, so we had to choose randomly, and we chose badly.

We made one portage of 70 yards, relaunched the canoe, battled with fallen trees and shallow water for 50 yards and took it out again. This next portage was for 200 yards, then 100 yards in the water, then 100 yards on land. By now it was clear that we should have cleared a trail and portaged past the whole lot, and we camped on an islet as it was getting dark, barely having the energy to prepare one of our dried dinners before bed.

According to the packet, the slush of gruel we had just consumed had been Beef Bourguignon: 'succulent morsels of beef marinated in red wine before being freeze-dried'. Oh yeah? Where's the beef? Has this watery gravy ever passed within shouting distance of a wine bottle? We'd brought one hundred dried dinners and our hopes that they'd provide culinary oases in a desert of gastronomic blandness had been cruelly dashed. The Beef Bourguignon was full of rice (as if we needed any more of that); the Vegetarian Hotpot was a stock cube gravy with a few unidentified floating objects or UFOs as we called them; and the Beef in Cream Sauce had a pungent aftertaste of vomit.

We still hadn't finished with Cachiri rapid. The next morning we waded up a channel, crossed the river, waded some more and began to pass the sacks over a fallen tree that lay awkwardly across a small falls.

'Look out!' Heather shouted, snapping me out of some reverie as I manhandled sacks on autopilot. The canoe had tipped and water was pouring inside.

'Hold on! Try to keep it pointing upstream!' I yelled, struggling to keep my footing on the slippery riverbed as the current caught the swinging bow and pushed it sideways.

'I can't!' She was pulled off her feet, head disappearing briefly under water, adding her weight to the waterlogged canoe and making me slip and flounder too. I scrabbled at slippery rocks but couldn't halt our rush downstream or prevent the canoe from swinging. We'd lost it – a capsize was inevitable. Then the bow hit the bank and stopped it turning broadside to the current, giving us another chance, time to hang on to some branches and wedge our feet on the riverbed.

We stared at each other, panting hard. There was nothing to say; we knew how lucky we'd been. When we'd lost control like that in the past, everything had spilled out and drifted off downstream, some of it never to be seen again.

Above the rapid we found a cache of equipment hidden in the bushes. A tarpaulin covered a promisingly large heap, and after beating it to warn any snakes that we were coming in, we peeled back the wrapper with all the excitement of children at Christmas. The covering crumbled in our hands and had obviously sat there for several years, and wooden boxes disintegrated as we pulled at them, revealing a boring horde of salt, axes, picks, shovels and a drum of diesel. Nothing worth having. Some packets might once have held soap and coffee but they were too mouldy to be sure.

'Any gold?' I asked optimistically.

'No,' confirmed Heather as she poked in the last rotten sack. 'Wouldn't it be great to find the stash of some long dead prospector?'

'Mmmm. A decaying hammock still hanging between trees containing the skeleton of the poor wretch, and all around kerosene cans full of nuggets and gold dust...'

'When we get home we could walk into the local branch of the building society, dump a heavy sack on the counter and pay off our mortgage...'

'And of course we'd discover where he'd found it all, so whenever our debauched lifestyle needed new funding or the yacht a refit, we could have a holiday out here and get a few more kilos...'

Dream on.

For the first time in twelve days we'd re-entered calm water and the Mapaoni had narrowed. There were more rocks showing and yellow sandbanks had appeared on the inside of bends, in the lee of large rocks, and anywhere else the current slowed enough to make the river drop its cargo of ground-up Tumucumaque hills. Sometimes the land rose steeply beside the river and huge rounded boulders stood in midstream with a thatch of plants on their summits. Other boulders formed the banks, and the current, failing to do more than smooth and polish these obstructions over millions of years, squeezed between them in deep, dark channels, the light infused with a soft green hue from the overhanging vegetation. We felt sure that we'd see a jaguar raising its dripping muzzle from the stream with its coat glowing and eyes balefully yellow. We had in the past, in just such places. What we did see, and long overdue, was our first group of giant otters; a pair of adults with two almost mature youngsters that chattered at us throatily but kept at a safe distance, diving and then periscoping up with their white fronts showing.

Things were improving. The rapids were behind us, it hadn't rained for forty-eight hours and we seemed to have calculated it just right as far as the river level was concerned. We were also hoping that we'd left all gold prospecting activity behind us, but in the afternoon we rounded a bend to see a gold miner's raft moored in midstream.

We approached reluctantly, but all was quiet. When we drew alongside we saw that its tarpaulin was ragged and sagging with the weight of pooled water, weeds and rust were growing over the machinery, and the long mooring ropes to either bank looked frayed. Nobody had been there for ages. This was a better raft than many, having metal pontoons rather than the usual plank-built floats, so someone had gone to great expense buying and transporting this equipment. It must have been a painful decision to leave it all behind. But that's the way gold rushes often end. After weeks of fruitless prospecting the *garimpeiros* can barely afford their own flight out, let alone pay for all the machinery to be airlifted as well.

Five miles further on we reached the last major tributary of the Mapaoni. It seemed a shame that we were staying on the Mapaoni all the way to the top, as the Caripí looked marginally larger, although both rivers were little more than brooks.

Hoping to find an agreeable campsite and perhaps take a day off after the exertions of the rapids, we paddled a little way up the Caripí. Heather's body suddenly went rigid and alert, and she jerked her nose noiselessly at the bank, like some gun dog pointing at a thicket where a rabbit was hiding. There stood a bird as big as a turkey, black except for a yellow face and a patch of white feathers on its rump. On its head was a forward-curling little crest 'like a windswept toupee' as Gerald Durrell described it. A curassow.

The canoe had drifted forward too far to see the bird any longer, but Heather held on to a bush while I retrieved the shotgun that had been lying neglected down the side of some sacks. It was in a sorry state; covered in rust, water trickling out of the barrel, and I had to bang it hard over my knee to open the breech, but the cartridges were dry in the watertight drum. I loaded, cocked the hammer and we drifted back, expecting the bird to have gone. It hadn't. It wasn't even making the clucking cheeps that curassow do when alarmed, it just stood there 10 feet away, watching us with an inky eye. When I pulled the trigger it was slammed to the ground, feet scrabbling in the leaf-mould and neck arching slowly back before it died.

Until then I had been swept along in the heat of instinct and the chase, but as I scrambled out of the canoe to retrieve it I found my vision clouding with tears. What hypocrisy. One minute complaining that the river seemed empty and despoiled, and then blasting to death one of the first trusting creatures we saw.

Everything about curassows' behaviour seems to render them vulnerable. At night, or when trying to attract a mate, they call with a beautiful vibrating hum, a little like the bass notes of an oboe – *dee dum dum dum*. On hearing that, every hunter in the Amazon picks up a gun and heads their way. Many times when paddling along we heard the frantic peet-peeting of the birds coming from the jungle; they'd seen us, but we only saw them because they gave themselves away. Even when the hunter is approaching with gun in hand and there's still time to escape, they don't fly up and away to safety, but flap into the low branches where they might be safe from their feline predators but not from the shotgun. Poor curassow.

It's the tedium of the diet that drives us to hunt. For a few weeks the firearm remains unused, and edible creatures have no need to fear us. We actually enjoy eating fish three times a day, and can admire the plumage of waterfowl or the shiny coat of deer and paca without thinking of drumsticks or stew. But this period of benign goodwill is short-lived.

Back in England, belly filled with variety and flavour, I remember with shame the monkeys, curassows, ducks, caiman, capybara, deer, pig and paca I have killed. Strange behaviour for a keen naturalist. We'd wanted this trip to be different by bringing more luxuries and dried dinners to keep the diet interesting. One bird in a month was hardly wanton slaughter, but this first blood at the mouth of the Caripí made us attempt to draw up a code of conduct for the rest of the trip.

Curassows are ground-feeding birds that like to peck over the areas uncovered by the retreating floods. We usually saw them in pairs but occasionally on their own or in groups of four or more. We suspected they might mate for life.

While the stew bubbled gently on a low heat, emitting a delicious meaty aroma, we discussed our future shooting policy. Several rum cocktails had left us light-headed, and the sadness of the kill had faded to a sentimental melancholy.

'It's awful to think we may be killing a bird's long-term mate and condemning it to years of loneliness,' said Heather.

'So maybe we shouldn't shoot at any birds in a pair?'

'I guess not,' she agreed. 'Unless we shot them both of course. That way we'd avoid leaving one bereaved.' We chuckled.

'Any bird on its own is fair game,' I contributed. 'It's obviously too ugly or dull to be missed by curassow society…'

'… be almost a kindness to put it out of its misery.'

'Right.'

Lifting the lid off the pot I prodded a huge drumstick. Still not cooked.

'What about a group of four birds? That would probably be two married couples hanging out together.'

We considered the etiquette of such an encounter. 'I suppose we would be shooting one bird's mate, but at least there would be a bereavement support group at hand, wouldn't there?' We giggled drunkenly.

'OK. So here are the rules. We can bag one from a group, one on its own, but not one in a pair?'

'Right.'

'All settled then.'

Surprisingly this sentimental and ridiculous code worked. From then on almost all the curassow seemed to be in pairs and we left them alone.

CHAPTER FOUR

'You know, we've only got about thirty miles to go and then we can leave the Mapaoni for good,' I commented cheerily, preparing a breakfast of absurd complexity. Heather said nothing as she struggled with the hammock knots and hauled down our camp.

'Won't be at all easy though,' I prattled, paring curassow flesh from the bones and chopping it up with garlic and our last mouldy onion. 'We've already covered the bulk of the distance from Molocopote to the Tumucumaque, but the real difficulties are still to come.'

'Great,' she muttered, rolling up a hammock.

The fire had really caught by now and I placed an oiled frying pan on the hot embers and poured in the batter. It bubbled and spluttered in no time and was ready to turn with a debonair flick of the wrist that looped the golden pancake in the air. A choice of tea or coffee warmed in their pots, and I rolled the chopped meat in cylinders of pancake after seasoning with pepper and soy sauce.

'Come and eat while it's still hot,' I ordered, and Heather sat beside me, sleepy and dishevelled. She looked sulky, and I decided to ignore her until the breakfast had worked its magic. The pancake rolls were delicious, and the coffee strong and sweet enough to wash the smoke of a fat cigarette down my interior passages, soothing the defence mechanism's reaction to the strongest tobacco in the world. Tears of discomfort, a wave of dizziness, each inhalation feeling like a light punch in the throat and my blackened, oil-slicked lungs crying out in torment. The first cigarette of the day. Pure bliss.

All too soon there was no excuse for sitting there any longer and it was time to shed our warm nocturnal layers and drag on clammy wet shorts and trainers. Paddling back to the confluence of the Mapaoni and Caripí, we spent an hour fishing the turbulent area where the two streams met. All the signs seemed to indicate piscine plenty: the merging streams laden with food, and the attractive back currents where fish could loiter, waiting for morsels to be dropped into their mouths. We saw fish leaping at butterflies, watched tiddlers scattering for their lives while being harried by predators, glimpsed large scaly backs and flanks break the surface as fish rolled from the sheer exuberance of living in such a spot. A plump otter popped its head up at intervals on its way across the pool and I think I heard it belch.

While Heather enticed the fish with baited hooks, I drew a selection of lures across the pool: red and silver ones that wagged from side to side, golden ones that revolved, copper ones that seemed to struggle in agony to the surface before losing strength and weakly fluttering down again. They all played to the bully in the predator's psyche, showing weakness, exhaustion, sickness and vulnerability. Their vibrations and fluttering movements indicated a quick snack after an easy pursuit.

I wound them in fast or slow. I varied the speed into little sprints and lazy wriggles. I let them stay deep; I kept them on the surface. I cast under bushes, behind rocks, perilously near fallen trees, risking our precious lures among the sunken branches. I cast overhand, underhand, 70 yards from the canoe, and almost underneath it.

I was wily, cunning and skilful and the reel grew hot to the touch, but I caught nothing. Heather got no bites either, only snags on the riverbed. She wound in her line.

'Come on John, let's get moving.'

'Couple more casts.'

Eventually I threw the rod down with disgust and we picked up our paddles and headed up the greatly reduced Mapaoni. Peter and I had arrived here in November 1983 at the end of the dry season, but this year we'd timed it better: in September the stream was 8 feet deeper and 12 feet wider.

We'd camped just up here and rested for three days while Peter suffered an attack of malaria. Tossing and turning in misery, muttering intimate secrets in German, retching painfully, his shivers travelled up the hammock ropes making the branches quiver. While I sat sweaty and naked in the cloying airlessness, he lay in jeans and sweatshirt, wrapped with blankets, teeth clicking like a hypothermia victim, occasionally levering himself out of his hammock to take a few wobbly steps and release the dark yellow urine of fever. Sweat had pasted the hair to his scalp, his eyes were wild and vacant in the yellowy pallor of his skin and he'd aged fifteen years overnight.

Fortunately our malaria attacks had never coincided, and it was my turn to be nurse. This entailed three simple duties: to keep him eating, to dish out the quinine tablets and to check his temperature. If the latter approached 105°F I would sponge him down in cool river water, because 105°F was apparently a dangerous threshold of brain damage and death. Once, failing to cool me with wet cloths, Peter had peeled away my cocoon of blankets, lifted me out of the hammock and deposited me in the shallows while I croaked in rage and lashed out with puny fists, my shivery blue body covered by water of an arctic iciness.

In a British hospital, falciparum or 'cerebral' malaria is treated as an emergency and a patient put on a saline drip with blood pressure checked every hour. There are many possible complications, including liver or kidney failure, anaemia and a rupturing spleen. Death can occur very quickly as the parasites multiply, gobbling up the red blood corpuscles and clogging up the little passages in the brain. The spleen becomes swollen and painful as it tries to remove millions of old or diseased red corpuscles from the circulation.

All we have in the bush to keep ourselves alive is quinine, a thermometer and some damp cloths. However, quinine is miraculous stuff and only two days after beginning a course of treatment the fevers stop and strength begins to return. We could be back to six hours' paddling within four days.

Thumbing through a handbook of tropical diseases produces an agreeable frisson of fascination and revulsion, and could put the faint-hearted off making a trip altogether. But among the gruesome catalogue of worms and parasites, and a memorable picture of an Indian gentleman pushing his scrotum around in a wheelbarrow in an extreme case of elephantiasis, I recently came across an unexpected benefit from the malarial ague.

Malariotherapy was a treatment for tertiary syphilis that earned Wagner von Juaregg the Nobel Prize in 1927. He discovered that syphilis, *treponema pallidum*, was temperature sensitive and that it could be killed if incubated several degrees above the normal body temperature of 98.6°F. So he deliberately infected his patients with vivax malaria, confident that their temperature would reach 104–105°F for several hours. Tens of thousands of syphilitics were thereby saved a sure and agonizing death. Patients weren't cured, but further downward progression of the disease was avoided. This treatment continued until the fifties when it was replaced with antibiotic chemotherapy, but Horton Hospital in England treated over 10,000 patients by malariotherapy between 1922 and 1950.

In the unlikely event that Peter had been harbouring any *treponema pallidum* they were well and truly dead by the time we moved on up the Mapaoni. I'd had four cheerless days to contemplate the depressing view from our camp – eight or nine tree trunks blocked our way in the first 50 yards, a small rapid tinkled between large boulders, and shady margins of sand separated the reduced stream from its banks. And it dropped 6 inches more while I watched.

It was all very different now as Heather and I gave up our fishing and got on our way. The river still filled its channel, and we were in excellent health.

Rainforest rivers have chaotic margins of dead trees, brought down by the current undermining their roots, and these bleached carcasses sometimes float a few yards seawards before tangling up again. Some, with their fin-like buttress roots, look like discarded space rockets. After a few seasons they become waterlogged and sink, and the end of the dry season reveals just how many litter the riverbed.

We had it as easy as any canoeist on a little creek can expect. Only two logs forced us to unload all the sacks that day, and twice more we had to do some slashing with the machete to widen gaps or clear smaller branches out of the way. Peter would have been astonished at our progress: more than 3 miles by late afternoon.

Just as encouraging were the sightings of wildlife. We saw an agouti, the burrow-dwelling rodent about the size of a cat, and then one of the small species of spotted felines, a margay or perhaps a Geoffroy's cat; I have trouble distinguishing them. It sauntered off into the jungle, wary of our approach but not alarmed. Several times it paused to look back over its shoulder, the spotted coat that seemed gaudy in the sunlight blending in perfectly with the dappled shade. It was a difficult shot through the creepers and saplings, but just before it disappeared for good behind some buttress roots, it paused once more. My finger caressed the trigger and the cat fell, kicking weakly... only joking.

With two hours of daylight left, we camped on a rocky outcrop that forced the river to bend round it. After putting up the hammocks I took a mug of coffee and cast a hook baited with a chunk of putrescent piranha into the eddy on the inside of the bend, leaving a bow of slack in the line. Almost immediately the line gave a little flutter and tightened slightly. The current? I kept my hand near the rod butt and soon the slack disappeared, the tip arched, and I felt the weight and power of a large fish that caused the ratchet clutch on the reel to shriek before the line went limp.

Reeling in, I found the hook and wire trace had all gone. Probably the bait had been swallowed deep enough for the nylon line to be in reach of the teeth. Getting another hook I fashioned a longer trace out of our roll of fencing wire and soon had another fish on, but it thrashed on the surface and shook the hook out, giving me time to see that it was a traira.

After losing two fish in a European stream I'd be unlikely to catch anything else for the rest of the day, and in Britain I've crawled on my belly through stinging nettles, dressed in battlefield greens and browns to approach spots where big fish lay. One careless footfall or a hasty movement, and they would melt away and hide for the rest of the day. After all, fishing is a pitting of wits against a creature with a brain the size of a lentil and usually losing.

Such finesse doesn't work in all parts of the world, and Amazon fishermen often beat the surface of the water and splash about to get the fish interested. The commotion of the two escapees had prompted seven or eight traira to emerge from their lairs, and when I hooked one, another immediately seized it by the tail giving me 16 or 17 pounds of fish on the line, while whorls of blood added to the frenzy of the others. Pulling hard, I slid the first fish on to the rocks and only when the second one was half out of the water did it let go its grip and fall back, leaving a tail that was gashed and lacerated.

The purple-brown traira has jaws armed with large teeth and, like many predators, can look straight at you disconcertingly from its forward-positioned eyes. Actually their eyes are their best feature: a limpid, pale pink, like flawless pink-tinged marbles. This one flopped and snapped until I quietened it forever, and slitting the belly open I amused myself by dropping little pieces of gut to the mêlée below, where more than twenty large fish were now rolling and splashing about. The commotion disturbed Heather as she was making the first of our rum cocktails and she came to watch from the bank above. A movement behind me attracted her attention.

'Look out! There's a snake crawling up on to your rock!'

This was not welcome news when the rock in question was only 6 feet square, and I spun around to see that a large brown snake had raised 2 feet of its length out of the water and was watching me beadily, flickering its tongue. If the river hadn't been full of blood-crazed fish in a feeding frenzy I'd have surrendered my island without a struggle by leaping into the water, but the snake seemed the lesser threat. I swished the flexible tip of the fishing rod over its head and it turned and slid back under the surface.

That night's menu consisted of super-fresh fried fish, beans and chapattis, washed down with double rums. Life seemed perfect. Progress had been easier than expected, the rain had held off and the campsite was almost mosquito free. The flickering light of our fire bathed the overhanging branches in red. Bats fluttered past so near that they ruffled our hair, fireflies winked green tracer through the tree trunks, and frogs croaked with drum-like beats.

After every cocktail we fished out the lime seeds from the bottom of our glasses and planted them in the soil beside us. After being pickled in the coarse Brazilian rum it was doubtful they'd germinate, but we hoped to leave groves of fruit trees for the enjoyment of future explorers. Less fruitful is the legacy that Daniel Ludwig has left behind on the Jari River.

On both sides of the lower Jari lies the land of the company Jari Florestal e Agropecuaria, owned until 1982 by this American billionaire who, in the 1960s, was one of the four richest men in the world. Ludwig owned National Bulk Carriers, the largest private merchant fleet in the world, bigger than those of Onassis and Niarchos combined. He also had coalmines in Canada, iron ore mines in Australia, a chain of hotels and much more. He purchased 4 million acres along the Jari in 1967 for $3 million at a time when the Brazilian government was fully committed to a policy of attracting foreign capital. Ludwig was anticipating that the insatiable demand for paper in the developed world would lead to a shortage of wood pulp before the end of the century that couldn't be met by slow tree growth in temperate or cold climates: he was proved right. He thought the tropical heat and exuberance could produce trees at a much faster rate, and he chose the melina from South East Asia that could grow to 20 feet high and 4 inches in diameter in a mere twelve months. It could be ready for felling in five years, compared to a Scandinavian tree that could take eighty years to mature.

The land that he bought on the Jari had all the criteria he was seeking. It was easily accessible to merchant shipping via the Amazon Delta, it had the right rainfall and temperature, and he didn't need to buy up dozens of individual plots, because this huge area was already owned by one consortium of Brazilian and Portuguese businessmen: the Empresa de Comercio e Navigacão Jari Ltda.

Ludwig cleared 250,000 hectares of forest, planting them with melina. There were problems almost immediately. Melina grows well in clay, but not in sandy soils, so he decided to plant eucalyptus and Caribbean pine as well. Twenty miles of railway, 1,600 miles of road and three airfields linked these new plantations. The pulp mill and power plant were assembled on barge-like hulls in Japan and towed across the Indian and Atlantic oceans by tug; a journey that took three months. Ludwig spent $1 billion on the project in fourteen years and it seems that his involvement lacked the caution that he showed in his other business ventures.

Already in his seventies when he started, he devoted all his energies to making a success that he would see in his lifetime. From 1974 onwards he began to dismantle his business empire to provide funds for Jari, selling a construction company, a salt evaporation plant in Mexico, half of his New South Wales coal interests, oil and gas properties in the western USA, half a chain of resort hotels, and one of his supertankers. In 1976 he cancelled an order for three supertankers and built the power and pulp plants instead.

In addition to the pulp operations he planted a large area of floodplain with rice where he was getting the highest yields in the world: 8 tons per hectare compared with an average of 4.5 tons in the USA and 3 tons in South East Asia. He also discovered the third largest kaolin deposit in the world on his land, conveniently right on the riverbank, a deposit he says he knew nothing about when he purchased Jari.

The project attracted considerable criticism from Brazilians who resented the acquisition of such a huge area by a foreign concern. Ludwig was excessively secretive and refused to allow any visitors during the first years of development, forcing one journalist to feign engine problems in his aircraft to gain authorisation to land. It was rumoured that Ludwig was employing slave labour, running a training camp for the Green Berets or illegally exporting precious metals. The name chosen for the administrative centre and main town of Jari, Monte Dourado, added fuel to these suspicions. Why name a town Golden Mountain, people asked, if there weren't huge deposits of the yellow stuff? In fact, the town was named after Rodolfo Dourado who was in charge of the initial work of clearing the jungle.

There were also objections from environmentalists. Jari might become a failure like so many other grandiose projects in the region, ending in the bequest of useless desert to future generations. When diverse tropical rainforest was replaced with three species of foreign tree, disease and blight could run riot down the ordered rows (as had happened when Henry Ford tried to cultivate rubber plantations on the river Tapajós in the 1930s), and the fragile soils might not be able to support single species cultivation for long. It seems they haven't. Tree growth has been disappointing and has suffered from attacks by fungi and insects.

Ludwig's scheme entailed the destruction of primary forest to make way for his plantations. If they had been established on land already degraded by other activities it might have been more acceptable, but the plantations would never have got started on such soils and Ludwig wouldn't have benefited from the extraction of the valuable primary forest hardwoods that offset some of the enormous expenditure in the first years.

What finally scuppered Ludwig was the changing attitude of the Brazilian government. The wholehearted support of the early years was replaced with a maddening political and bureaucratic obstructionism when all the land titles in the state of Pará (which contained about three-quarters of the project) were annulled with a promise that they would be quickly reissued. In fact this didn't happen for years, and without these titles Ludwig was nothing better than a giant squatter, unable to get government grants for the schools, housing and healthcare that he provided for his workforce. After the government refused to help fund this infrastructure, Ludwig put the project up for sale in 1981. By then it was losing about $100 million a year so there were few takers, but he was able to extract a little revenge from the government that had treated him so shabbily. Unless he could get a buyer he would walk away leaving 35,000 employees stranded and with a $180 million obligation to Japan that had been guaranteed by the Brazilian Development Bank. Under government pressure, a consortium of twenty-two companies bought the project, paying $2.7 million each, and the Bank of Brazil assumed the $180 million foreign debt in exchange for 25 per cent of the forestry operation.

All Ludwig could expect to recoup was a small percentage of any profits from 1987 to 2021 and it seems unlikely that these will amount to much. The biggest loser is medical research, as Ludwig announced years ago that he would leave his fortune to the Ludwig Institute for Cancer Research in Zurich. This institute has a staff of more than 500 scientists and technicians working in seven nations, and Ludwig had already endowed it with $700 million by the time he died in August 1992, aged 95.

When Heather and I visited the Jari project in 1990, the slick presentations and glossy brochures couldn't mask the problems. The kaolin mine seemed to be the only truly profitable part of the venture; the plantations suffering from leaf-cutter ants and falling soil fertility. The pulp mill was out of action for the three days we were there due to mechanical breakdown, and the company had just announced a further reduction of a thousand jobs.

There are still 50,000 people directly or indirectly dependent on the Jari project. The technicians and managers live in the company town of Monte Dourado, with its white bungalows and green lawns spread over the hills of the west bank, and the manual workers live in Beiradão across the river. As there is no bridge across the Jari, people are ferried back and forth in aluminium canoes with 15-h.p. engines that keep the river in a permanent froth.

Beiradão is a wooden shanty town built on stilts. In the rains it lies just above the water; at other times it is left high and dry above a festering mudbank covered with all the rubbish and sewage of the town. There used to be a long boardwalk running down the waterfront, lined with stalls, bars, cheap hotels and restaurants, all a great deal more fun than the Midwest suburbia over the river.

Unfortunately Beiradão is no longer what it was. Much of its boardwalk was destroyed by fire in the late eighties, and instead of being confined to the riverbank in one long ribbon of houses, the town has now spread inland with roads and breezeblock constructions. Although I'm sure the inhabitants are delighted with these improvements, it's now indistinguishable from any other town of the interior. Previously it had been worth running the risk of violence to enjoy its bars and clubs. Not any more.

That night we planted a future forest of lime trees as we sat until midnight enjoying our drinks. The limes were beginning to go soft and brown, but we'd never expected them to last so long. Soon we'd have to drink our rum neat, and then our enthusiasm for alcohol would decline – neat Brazilian *cachaça* being as much fun to drink as a mug of paint stripper.

Later we attempted a rather inebriated excursion in the canoe. I think we were looking for nocturnal creatures but seemed to have forgotten that we weren't on a wide, uncluttered river. After shedding blood thrashing about in thorny tangles, I slipped as I got out of the canoe and fell into the water, soaking the clothes I'd intended sleeping in. Our giggles and shouts were typical of those nocturnal cries that shatter the peace of Mediterranean resorts – the English at play.

After trying to dry my trousers by the fire and scorching a hole in a place that was going to make it very hard to wear them with decency in any civilised gathering, we finally tired and crawled into our hammocks.

The river sometimes flowed through areas of swamp where tangles of thorns or clumps of spongy plants took the place of jungle. Many barriers of vegetation completely blocked the stream and we cut tunnels through them with saw and machete, gradually advancing into the heart of the obstacle, standing on severed branches to push them under, yanking the canoe through inch by inch. There was no room for a back swing inside these tangles and creepers danced playfully away from our machetes, causing a deterioration in language, especially when the fishing rod got snagged in the vegetation yet again, bending to snapping point, or the sack of cooking pots fell overboard to begin floating away. Half an hour later we'd emerge on the upstream side of the tangle and swim through the evil flotsam that had been dammed up for months: dead leaves, seed pods, drowned insects, live insects and once the bloated corpse of a capybara that seemed on the point of bursting in a blast of gas and a spray of unspeakable liquids.

Before attempting any machete work it was wise to scrutinise the thicket. That dark patch up there – is that a bird's nest, a pile of debris left by the last flood, or is it a swarm of wasps or hornets that will sting us to death? We'd give a first tentative chop, ears waggling for an angry buzzing, poised to eject into the safety of the river. All quiet. Proceed with caution. The tangles were a biologist's dream, packed with poison-arrow frogs, caterpillars, stick insects, beetles, spiders and ants that dropped upon us as we pulled the canoe through, some stinging and biting, others causing outbursts of mild hysteria.

In the afternoon we reached a fork in the river where the combination of rock, sandy beaches, abundant firewood, dry ground and stout trees the right distance apart made it an idyllic campsite. The only worry was that this tributary didn't exist. Not on our maps.

'Do you think we're right up here?' Heather asked, pointing at a fork on the map three miles from where the trail started. 'I can't believe we've done twenty miles in the last two days, can you?'

'No chance.'

'Where then?'

I shrugged. 'No idea.'

'You don't seem very concerned.'

I was concentrating on lighting the fire and making a reviving cup of tea. My whole body ached and I was going to take my cup and a book and swing in my cradle until supper.

'You have to accept that maps of this region are crap,' I said, 'and there's no point getting worked up about their inaccuracies.'

'Sort of believe them when it suits us and ignore them when it doesn't?' She snorted. 'You're nuts. How are we going to work out where to leave the river without their help? If you intend chopping a trail inland without any confirmation that we're in the right place, you can do it on your own.'

'Of course I'd want to be sure first,' I snapped, irritated by her tone. 'If we start from the wrong place it could be forty miles to the other river, instead of fifteen. I'm not daft.'

'I sometimes wonder. The way you and Peter behaved up here last time, carrying on for weeks after most people would have turned back. It's a good job you couldn't locate the spot to start cutting the trail or otherwise you'd have attempted it – despite being ill, out of food and medicine, with a wooden canoe weighing eighty pounds! Admit it.'

She was off again. I'd heard all this so many times.

'For a while,' I answered wearily. 'And what's wrong with giving something a good try? We'd put in enough bloody effort getting up here.'

'But I think you'd have pushed on until you succeeded or you died, that's what's wrong.' She sat down on a watertight drum. 'I personally don't think this expedition is worth dying for, ruining my health for, or even having a truly horrible time for, come to that. I'll do my best, but I'll refuse to go any further if the risks seem too great.'

'Fair enough,' I replied. Anything to shut her up. We'd had it easy so far, what was she whining about?

She sighed. 'You worry me sometimes.'

'You think I'm prepared to gamble our lives gripped by some obsession to cross the Tumucumaque Hills, even though there's no reward of wealth, discovery, imperial conquest or anything else, is that it?' I scooped some water out of the stream and hung the kettle over the blaze on a pole between forked sticks. 'Do you think I don't see that this is a pretty ridiculous caper? I want to give it another try, but I've no intention of risking our lives any more than we have on past trips.'

'Glad to hear it.' She smiled shakily. 'There's something about leaving the river and heading off inland that scares me silly.'

'Me too,' I said truthfully.

'Does it really?'

'You bet.'

'I'm terrified of getting lost, of walking around in circles and starving to death like Maufrais.'

'We'll be careful.'

'I'll make damn sure you are,' she said, putting her arms around me and resting her face on my chest.

What was I doing involving her in an adventure like this? Was her heart really in it, or was she nobly following her partner, quite literally, to the ends of the earth? What if she refused to go any further and ruined the expedition? I should have come back with Peter, the only travelling companion who never berated me for pushing things too far. With him in fact, I'd struggled to keep up.

'We'll look after each other,' I said gently, feeling cold and distant, play-acting. I'd never forgive her if she let me down.

I drew away, and busied myself rooting out cups and sugar.

'We'll be fine. Now let's have some tea.'

How I missed the rough camaraderie of some trips in the past, uncomplicated by emotional ties.

The worries about the unmarked tributary were groundless; it turned out to be a branch of the main river that had wandered round a large island. As the campsite was unusually perfect we opted to stay there longer, exploring our surroundings on nature rambles where we did inadvisable things like roll over logs and poke sticks down holes. But we only saw one snake: a slender green creature coiled as tight as a clenched fist around a thin sapling. Squatting beside a large hole we debated what lived there. Judging by the freshly turned earth and the absence of any cobwebs across the opening it had a resident. Armadillo, paca, taira (a furry black carnivore of the mink family), ocelot? Lowering our faces we sniffed the warm musky odour in the opening and there was a sudden and extremely unfriendly hiss from a couple of feet away. Bashing heads, we leapt back and ran for our lives.

With the assistance of beetles, termites, fungi, and a mat of delicate root tendrils that seek out their nutrients, the carcasses of fallen trees crumble away much quicker on the forest floor than they do in the river. Quite often all that's left is a hollow trunk that collapses in a soggy heap when climbed upon, and others decay where they stand, propped up by their neighbours, swaying on lianas. Such logs often contain chubby grubs, more than an inch and a half in length and as fat as a gobstopper. These are popular nibbles for the Indians and I tried some once in hungrier days. I couldn't manage to eat them raw; time after time I brought them towards my mouth only for them to wriggle slightly, making me focus on their white bloated bodies and brown faces, and my hand lowered again. They weren't bad fried, but I cooked them so thoroughly that they looked like chunks of charcoal.

In the end we stayed three days at that campsite. Time passed pleasantly to the sway of hammocks, reading, preparing feasts, washing clothes, writing diaries: killing time really. The place to leave the Mapaoni and start cutting the trail over the Tumucumaque couldn't be too far away, and even though Peter and I had spent three weeks up in the headwaters and left with no idea of where we were, nothing was allowed to interfere with our confidence. We attributed that failure to different circumstances: poorer maps, weaker physical condition, exhaustion, malaria and the like.

It seems laughable now but we worried that our trip might be too brief; our objective achieved so easily that we would be home two months earlier than expected. One more week on the Mapaoni, two weeks to get canoe and gear to the other side of the hills, then two weeks downstream to reach civilisation in French Guiana. Five weeks in all. We wanted to spend more time in the jungle than that.

Poor fools. Mooching around, stretching things out, watching the river drop a foot when we should have been hurrying on.

The days at that camp showed the benefits of moving home frequently in the rainforest. Mosquitoes weren't a problem on this river, but other insect pests grew more numerous every day. Stingless red bees circled us with a dreary, persistent humming, and black sweat bees settled all over our faces when we were doing anything energetic. Top prize for the least popular creature went to a little red wasp. Hopefully it might become extinct quite soon, and if it ever gets on the critically endangered list with just one breeding pair left in the wild, I'll break through the cordon of concerned entomologists and blast them with my fly-killer.

This creature has numerous strategies to sting you. It hides its nest in low bushes, positioned with the express intent of waiting for someone with a machete to come and chop it down. It gently tickles the back of your neck so that it can sting a carelessly scratching hand. It adores the festering sores that decorate the bodies of jungle travellers, and makes them leap in the air by starting to probe and eat among the pus. They would alight unseen on my penis, poke their jaws down the urethra and take a good and agonizing chew, safe in the knowledge that I wasn't going to swat them there. The first time this happened my knees clamped together in an agonised reflex, and the trapped wasp then stung my scrotum, giving me new insight into those lyrics about 'Great Balls of Fire'.

On the ground, ants swarmed over the food, crawled up trouser legs, and began to penetrate the mosquito nets and eat holes in things. Other jungle travellers sweep away the leaf litter from an area around their camps and say that this keeps their numbers down. I expect so, but insects rule this environment and man is always going to lose the contest. We just surrendered to their persistence, packed up and moved on.

Back on the river again we entered another swamp that took five days to cross. Places to camp were scarce. The margins, freshly emerged from the floods, were still muddy and almost devoid of firewood, or trees strong enough to hold our hammocks. One night we made do with tying both hammocks in the branches of the same sickly tree, but it meant that one of us lay pressed against the trunk by the other hammock, and any fidgeting disturbed us both. A huge mass of woody liana above us threatened to pull the tree down, and several large branches already littered the ground.

The risk of falling trees is a very real one, as the frequent sustained crashes and earth-trembling thumps testified, so we usually tried to avoid camping under anything that had already lost a branch, looked unwell or carried too heavy a burden of parasitic creepers. That was the theory anyhow. Actually most campsites had a dodgy tree in the vicinity, and we sometimes found freshly fallen trees with foliage intact and seemingly in perfect health. They would have fooled us for sure.

Lying in unwanted intimacy and acute discomfort in the branches of that unhealthy giant, we heard the approaching rumble of thunder. Earlier, I'd been looking at one of its discarded limbs thinking that the scorched bark might have been caused by a traveller's campfire. Now I suspected that the tree's height in an expanse of swamp would make it an irresistible magnet for lightning. As the storm reached us, the wind flexing and swaying the diseased branches, lightning strobed in flashes that the instantaneous thunderclaps told us came from directly overhead. We stared up into the gale-lashed night expecting the *crack* that would be the last thing we'd ever hear, or the blue flash of instant incineration, and I for one re-opened a very poorly maintained and underused communication channel with the Almighty.

The arrival of a deluge of stinging rain forced us to leave our hammocks and crawl under the folds of the tarpaulin on the soggy ground, holding each other tight and burying our heads in the darkness to block out the bedlam. Even then there came a dreaded, if fairly modest *crack,* the swishing of leaves, and a heavy thud nearby.

Morning came eventually with a sunny air of innocence as if to mock us. 'Storm? What storm? You've been imagining things. Look at that sky, does it look unsettled to you? Feel that benign breeze – not enough to stir a leaf.' Only the branch lying across our food sacks, big enough to have smashed our bones, remained as evidence.

The swamp continued with the river, writhing through a flat landscape, disappearing under mats of grass or tangles many yards deep, brushing against the heart-shaped leaves of the anhinga plant that showed an intricate tracery of veins when back-lit. Metallic-green hummingbirds whirred among the spiky red and yellow monkey's brush blossoms in the wall of herbaceous climbers, with a noise like we'd produced as children by putting paper in the spokes of our bicycle wheels.

We labelled each fallen tree according to its character. There were 'breakers' that would crack and sink if bounced up and down upon. There were 'sinkers' that floated low in the water and might sink some more under our weight. There were the 'limbos' that we squeezed under, leaning backwards and brushing our noses on the bark as we passed. Then there were the unprintables that stuck well out of the river and needed every sack removed.

The red pods on the kapok trees fired off their seeds, filling the air with fluff like the aftermath of a giant pillow fight, and one long-dead kapok sprawled its bleached and thorny corpse across the stream, creating a barrier 6 feet high. When trodden on, the bark sloughed off, exposing a slimy layer that stank of rotting meat, and nasty squelchy matter squeezed up between our bare toes. We hurried to get away, tossing sacks out, heaving the canoe over, tossing sacks back, but it was enough time for dozens of fire ants to swarm onto our naked bodies.

Tiny creatures with none of the size and awesome mandibles of their cousins, they are aptly named. Their stings feel like flames licking over the body. Why South American torturers ever went in for all that fancy electrical equipment when they have so many free and effective agents around them in nature I don't know. A week in the forest with no mosquito net would do. Cover the victim in sugary syrup, tie him to a tree and those droning, tickling, red bees will make him crack. For the real hard cases, bring out the fire ants. They seem to favour those tender, moist areas – the armpits, groin or neck – producing a burning and stinging that had us whimpering in the shallows trying to soothe ourselves with soap, water, cream and fistfuls of antihistamine tablets.

We paddled in torment between the many fallen trees and tangles, wanting to camp but finding no dry land. The river twisted, looped and doubled back, the needle of our compass swinging in almost every direction except the north-west we wanted, while rain lashed us into a dumb, frozen misery. Even when we found a little patch of rocky terra firma it was still raining too heavily to do much except smooth more cream over the raised weals, don dry clothing and get in the hammocks. It was eight in the evening before the rain stopped, but by then the effort involved in poking through the dripping night searching for firewood and trying to get it lit seemed too much. We stayed hungry until morning.

'Next time you see me get starry-eyed and nostalgic about life in the rainforest,' I said to Heather at breakfast, 'just remind me of yesterday, will you? That'll bring me down to earth again. Do me good to be reminded of the discomfort, biting insects, torrential rain, hard labour, misery, going to bed with no supper, and all the other charms of these adventures.'

Every day we expected to find the fork in the river that would show that we were nearly done with the Mapaoni, but our progress was probably not more than 2 miles a day and much less as the crow flew.

Several capybara families squatted like giant brown guinea pigs, paralysed save for flaring nostrils, trying to make sense of our unknown odour. The males with bulbous scent glands on their noses usually opted for caution, letting out a bark and leading a rush for the security of the river. With ears, eyes and nostrils set high on their heads to clear the water, capybara are truly amphibious and can stay submerged for many minutes when alarmed.

Monkeys trotted to the tips of branches to see us better, chattering throatily but no longer scattering in panic as they had downstream. Their memory didn't seem to include man in their demonology, evidently forgetting the Swiss and English assassins who might have murdered their grandparents back in '83. Running short of supplies, with fish getting scarcer, Peter and I had been hunting monkeys by the time we got up here, luring them towards us by clowning, scratching, whistling, shaking saplings gently, manipulating their inquisitive intelligence. After sighting a furry brown chest, muttering a request for forgiveness and squeezing the trigger, the dead monkey was hopefully already tumbling headlong to the ground amid the outraged shrieks of his family and friends before the echoes of the gunshot faded away. Much worse was a wounding, the victim clutching a useless arm, the troop screeching the equivalent of 'Run, man! Run!' and covering the retreat by breaking off branches and lobbing them down. This was usually the time when the cardboard shotgun cartridge had become too damp and swollen in the barrel to eject, and precious moments were wasted prising it out with a knife before we could reload and fire again.

On one occasion a victim crashed to earth but was still alive, crawling its way through the leaf litter, whimpering and glancing at me over its shoulder with a wide-eyed look of pain and terror. I had no more cartridges and it watched me search hastily for a stout stick to kill it with, but everything crumbled in termitey dust. I seized it by the tail, intending to brain it against a tree, but it arched back, snapping at my hand. How could I silence the cries that shrieked through the bloody bubbles when there wasn't a strong piece of wood anywhere to be found? I ran to and fro seizing and rejecting rotten club after rotten club. In the end I held the gun by the barrel and brought the stock smashing down on its head. Rather too hard. The skull split open and the gunstock shattered too, but the monkey was dead at last. I sat and cried for ten minutes.

Such is monkey hunting. Such is all hunting, in my opinion. There is no joy in it, only an occasional thrill when the quarry is being stalked, but that turns to sadness and guilt when the bloody pile of fur or feathers is retrieved. Fortunately Heather and I still had sacks and sacks of food. Maybe by journey's end we'd be forced to hunt for our survival, but the monkeys were safe for now and even the curassow had the good sense to walk the neighbourhood in pairs.

Finally, one late afternoon we reached a fork; the tiny river dividing into two feebler streams, one slightly clearer and decidedly colder than the other. Our arms and shoulders ached from repeatedly unloading and replacing sacks, and the canoe looked as if we'd tried to camouflage it, so covered was it with twigs and leaves dislodged as we squeezed through tangles.

Which way?

It didn't look promising. The land stretched swampy and almost flat as far as we could see. Only 2 miles up the left-hand fork should be the start of our trail route that followed the ridges of the Tumucumaque, and that seemed to rule this tributary out. It was all too flat. This confluence must be unmarked on our map; we'd have to press on up the right-hand fork until we reached the next branch. It was disappointing, but we weren't in any doubt about our decision. We'd have to carry on.

Suddenly there was a loud droning and buzzing that approached so fast that my head jerked up, expecting to see an aeroplane flying down the valley. Instead a black cloud of smoke seemed to be billowing towards us on windless air. Heather was overboard already, but by the time I realised that I was looking at a huge swarm of wasps I'd left it a little late for a graceful slide into the water. I let out a squeal, dropped my paddle and leapt, getting my feet caught up in the canoe seat and taking it with me.

Trying our best to make our heads look like clumps of aquatic weed, we watched the swarm pass a few feet above, then turn around and fly back the other way. The queen, or whoever was in charge, didn't seem to know where to go but led them round and round until our teeth chattered with cold. They seemed to prefer the right-hand fork, so we dragged the canoe up the left, staying in the water until the air seemed clear enough to get aboard. It was nearly dark by the time we found dry land, and erecting the tent we lay down on our blankets and went almost straight to sleep, too exhausted to bother with food.

After eleven comatose hours we breakfasted on oatcakes, packed and headed back to the other stream. Within ten minutes I'd been stung five times by some bees whose nest was hanging in the middle of a tangle, giving us no option but to drag everything through a section of muddy swamp. Five minutes later Heather was stung seven times and me four by some large wasps that looked very much like those of the previous evening. I swam cautiously forward to spy out their position. There they were. A swarm the size of a beach ball, a solid mass of hundreds.

This section of the river flowed between vertical muddy banks that made it impossible to portage past. We'd have to sneak through as quietly as we could.

Heather's cheek looked like it held a wad of chewing tobacco, and I'd grown several angry red swellings on my arms and shoulders that were to smart for many hours. A few dozen stings from these fellows would kill you for sure. Placing battered straw hats on our heads, we slipped into the water armed with secateurs. This may seem a strange choice of equipment to take to the jungle where gardening and flower arranging are rare pursuits, but we'd brought them for precisely this sort of operation.

Holding on to the canoe, we swam forward slowly and reached the tangle only 10 feet below the swarm. There were two fat branches and several creepers barring our way. Very slowly I picked up the saw and smoothly sawed through the branches. Gently, gently. That only caused tiny tremors and no more than a dozen wasps left the nest on patrol. Now the creepers. Chopping with a machete would have been suicidal but the secateurs snipped them gently out of the way.

We eased the canoe through, pleased to have got past unscathed. Just a few more yards upstream and we could get aboard and paddle off...

'Look out!' called Heather. Something had gone wrong. 'Ouch! Ouch!' The air was full of brown specks and an irate buzzing.

'That creeper's hooked up!'

We ducked and cringed as the wasps looked for someone to blame. A cut length of creeper had become hooked around the sack of pots and pans, tightened and swayed the swarm. We waited for them to settle, submerging regularly and making only calm movements. The urge to run like the wind was overwhelming.

That afternoon we finally reached an area of terra firma jungle containing the full variety of Amazonian vegetation rather than just those species that can survive with their roots submerged for half the year. It looked magnificent after five days in the swamp and we luxuriated in the solid ground underfoot and the abundant firewood. Feeling desperately tired with raw foot-rot between every toe, lower back pain and tendonitis in our wrists from heaving the heavy sacks, we flopped into our beloved hammocks.

Being short of books already, I reluctantly picked up Raymond Maufrais' journal. I'd read it many times before and his experiences so accurately mirrored our own that it failed to distract. Sure enough, on the upper Ouaqui, Raymond:

... got to the marshes again. I move across a network of lianas and grasses and shrubs that need cutting through — and yet at the same time I have to punt through a jungle of submerged trunks. I keep rousing wasps' nests, and they cause me a lot of trouble. It seems as if I'll never get clear of this ghastly vegetation.

That sounded vaguely familiar. While keen to be finished with these unnavigable waterways, he shared our fear of leaving the river and heading off inland:

Oh God — Nature is so hostile, and my advance so slow. I feel alone, terribly lost, and so far from the world I am used to. I lose hope of seeing the end of it all — of one day getting there. Sometimes when I'm on the river I look hungrily at the forest — the infinite blue-green mass, and the hard green light that envelops it all. I wonder if I shall be brave enough to plunge into it. There's salvation in this river after all. Sooner or later, if I paddle far enough, I shall come to a village, to the sea, to Life. In the forest there's nothing, nothing, nothing [...] No hope at all once you lose your way. Once you're in the forest, once you're its prisoner, you can't allow yourself anything. You can't give up, you can't get tired, you can't lose heart. You've got to get on or die.

Oh what cheerful escapist entertainment. I laid the book down, anxieties reawakened. Fifteen miles of hilly jungle to cross with no trail to follow and no one to lead the way. Even with the lightest possible canoe it was still a formidable challenge. How would

Heather cope? She'd been splendid so far, but the punishment was so relentless, unvarying, monotonous. In other parts of the world exertion of this magnitude would be rewarded with fabulous views, glaciers breaking off into emerald tarns, hanging cornices of snow and ice, fabled cities in the clouds, oases of earthly delights. Here, one tangled creek replaced another in a forest that never changed, with the same discomforts of heat and biting insects, dreary food and unceasing chores. How would *I* cope, come to that? In the past it had been made worthwhile by the sightings of rare animals, by the novelty of undiluted adventure and risk, but on rivers much less restricted than this.

For the first time I could stand back and take a detached look at our journey. It was masochistic, joyless, unrewarding and boring. Yes, boring. The wildlife was scarce, the river too shallow to amuse ourselves with piscine battles and too tangled to make satisfying progress. And the worst was still to come.

How could I possibly complain if Heather just sat down one day and refused to go further? Most people would have done so already.

A jaguar called for most of the night from only a few hundred yards away, giving three or four rasping grunts at five-minute intervals.

'It is then that a man and his rifle develop a kinship so close that they fuse to become as one single entity,' Eduardo Barros Prado assures us in *The Lure of the Amazon* (1959). 'The rifle is more than a thing of wood and metal, it is a unique friend, shield and protector calling for affection and respect [...] Of all the living animals, the jaguar is the most deadly. He has plenty of intelligence, is utterly pitiless and his ferocious cunning is combined with complete fearlessness. A man has as much chance against a jaguar as a mouse has against a cat.'

This is typical hunter's talk, the necessity to portray the victim as pitiless in order to justify his own brutality. One feels that even if a jaguar succeeded in killing and eating Señor Barros Prado, the testosterone in his body would kill it, or one of his giant testicles would lodge in its throat and choke it.

We took it in turns to get up and tend the fire, particularly when a second jaguar began to answer from far away. For a while it seemed possible that they might rendezvous somewhere over by Heather's hammock and we searched the surrounding forest for firewood stocks. However, they then seemed to lie down and stay put, calling from the same spots for the rest of the night. We managed to doze off for such long periods that the fire had subsided to dying embers each time we awoke.

The river dropped 4 inches overnight and in most places was now less than knee-deep. We had to unload over plenty of logs, but a rapid delayed us most; a tortuous 200-yard portage that included walking over a large flat expanse of rock, sloshing through a stream, crossing an island and then hopping from one mossy boulder to another, clambering over five tree trunks on the way.

We met a gang of giant otters and inadvertently managed to separate a juvenile from the family group. The others had sneaked past but this one hesitated, lacking the courage to proceed. We saw it make three attempts to pass us along the far bank only 5 yards away, but each time its nerve failed and it retreated back upstream. It made some beseeching calls, but if they were answered it was at a pitch undetectable to our ears. We withdrew into the jungle for fifteen minutes to help it along.

The late afternoon was spoilt by 100 yards where we had eleven large trees blocking our way one after the other. Sacks out, canoe over, sacks back. A short wade and then sacks out again. We camped immediately afterwards while we still had some good humour left.

A lizard had unwisely chosen to travel with us in the canoe, and would appear in periods of inactivity to bask on the load. Enough insects fell into the bilges to satisfy any reptile, but it was also a dangerous habitat where heavy sacks were tossed back with a crash, and clumsy humans walked across them to get in or out. And so it was that Larry met his end – we found him crushed when we unloaded that afternoon. I'm sure he wouldn't have objected to me sticking his mortal remains on a hook as fishing bait, but within five seconds of casting into the pool the line was broken by a long black fish with a pointed snout and scaly body. At about 15 pounds in weight it seemed a big fish for such a diminished stream, and a species that I'd never seen before.

I scoured the bank for something else to use as bait and found a bright yellow and black poison-arrow frog. There are many different colorations of these small frogs and they are used by the Amazon Indians in their brews for arrow and dart tips. It's true that they give off a very toxic secretion from their skin, but the most common ingredient of arrow poison is curare made from the root of a large forest creeper, the strychnos vine. This is chopped into shavings, soaked and strained, leaving a reddish brown liquid that is boiled all day, and the glutinous sap of a palm added to make the mixture gummy. During the preparation frogs, tarantulas, stinging ants and even red chilli peppers are added, but most of these contribute nothing to the toxicity. This poison is extremely stable and the treated arrows will maintain their strength for years if kept dry.

The poison works by paralysing the nerve centres, causing muscles to relax and the lungs to cease operating. Curare is used in modern surgery as a muscle relaxant, and it has the virtue to the Indian of never letting his dead monkey victims remain hanging in the treetops with a post-mortem grip. The poison has no effect on the meat. If one's companion is shot with a poisoned arrow, he or she can be kept alive by mouth-to-mouth resuscitation to keep the paralysed lungs working until the poison wears off. You never know when such information might come in handy. One day in the shopping arcade someone may run amok with a blowpipe and poisoned darts, and you could earn yourself a headline in the local paper with your presence of mind.

Anyway, the poison-arrow frogs are varied and beautiful, and I felt regret as I whacked this one with a paddle and squashed it flat. Putting a plastic bag over my hand, I gingerly baited it on to my hook. Now an experiment. Will the fish instinctively know that these frogs are poisonous? Are they resistant to the poison? Are they too greedy and stupid to care?

I cast in, and again there was a swirl, a glimpse of what I swear was the same damn fish, a brief struggle and the ping of breaking fishing line.

John Steinbeck summed up the feelings of the unsuccessful angler in *Travels With Charley*: 'A remarkable amount of my fishing is like that, but I like it just the same. My wants are simple. I have no desire to latch on to a monster symbol of fate – prove my manhood in titanic piscine war. But sometimes I do like a couple of cooperative fish of frying size.'

Lacking those, it was going to be pasta with oil and garlic again.

CHAPTER FIVE

Hearts hammering from excess caffeine we stood beside our laden canoe, trying to muster the tiniest enthusiasm for the day ahead. We'd strung breakfast out for as long as possible with three brews of coffee and a rigmarole of pancake production, but now the sacks were all aboard and we'd run out of excuses. Our wet clothing snuggled its clammy way into our cracks and crevices, and sand in our canvas trainers inflamed raw patches of foot-rot. A bend blocked any view of the river upstream but how far would we get before an obstacle forced us to unload everything again?

Only 100 yards it seemed. A tree had recently fallen from a long way back so that its bushy crown had landed in the stream, and so far it seemed unaware of its misfortune. The leaves remained glossy and green and it still produced flowers that were visited by insects and hummingbirds.

I stood on some of the outermost branches, sinking waist deep as they bent under my weight, and attacked the mass with saw and machete, trying to clear a route through to the main trunk. Suddenly the air was filled with angry buzzing and in the second or two before my reflexes cranked into action I was stung on hands, arms, face and neck with sharp jabs of pain. Not again! Still clutching the machete I toppled backwards into the water, yelling a warning: 'Wasps!'

By now no word in the English language was guaranteed to galvanise Heather into action so effectively. She performed a majestic and technically difficult backward roll, exiting from the canoe with fluid grace, and was beside me in the water before I'd even surfaced myself.

'Ouch!' Another one had got me on the hand in an act of totally unprovoked aggression, and spying their nest wedged in a fork, I scrabbled for the shotgun.

'Right. They've asked for it!'

'John, wait! Wait! Don't shoot at them, you'll only wind them up.'

'I'm sorry, but they've got it coming. I'm going to blast the little bastards.'

'Zap 'em with the nerve gas then, but don't fire at them,' she appealed, referring to the can of insect killer that we used against intruders in the tent. Probably made from one of Saddam Hussein's recipes, this Brazilian concoction was so choking and toxic that after every squirt we had to rip open the tent flap and wheeze in the cool night air, eyes ruby red, lungs aflame.

'Good thinking,' I agreed with glee. 'Make them die in pain!' A calamity was about to fall upon this community, so terrible that it would be talked about from generation to generation of wasp, and youngsters would shiver at the telling of it.

By the time we'd found the spray the wasps had calmed down and gone indoors.

'Give them hell!' called Heather, taking the canoe to a safe distance as I swam forward, can aloft, and hauled myself up to position the nozzle for maximum devastation. The gentle shaking of the tree caused an angry buzzing and rustling from inside the nest and a dozen of their crack airborne defence appeared in the doorway.

Psssssssssst. A two-second burst knocked them off their feet and swirled up the opening, drifting fog-like through the chambers and alleyways within. They fought bravely to the end, even getting in two more stings to my head between my duck dives, but soon they began to cartwheel out of the sky and the water downstream was full of splashing and commotion as fish gobbled up the victims, spreading poison up the food chain.

Ten minutes later all was quiet and there were no survivors. Out of curiosity I took down the nest and opened it with a machete, discovering an airy paper construction of chewed wood pulp, with corridors choked with dead wasps and chambers housing white grubs. I felt almost ashamed of myself as I tossed it into the river and got back to work.

In 1983, somewhere not far from here on the upper Mapaoni, Peter had had a worse encounter. He'd been vigorously slashing at a tangle when a large dark mass that we'd assumed to be a bird's nest, suddenly separated and drifted outwards in a cloud.

'Look out, Pete!' I yelled, but he'd already seen the size of the hornets heading his way and sprinted for deeper water, letting out a scream and clutching his head before he dived under the surface. We stayed in the water for fifteen minutes, only popping up for air while the hornets droned menacingly overhead, massive and terrifying.

'Ten of those stings, man, and you'd be dead,' said Peter with conviction, fingering a large swelling that made him look as if he was about to sprout a horn. 'Shit, that hurts!'

The hornets had now settled, and feeling I had to do the decent thing and retrieve the machete from where Peter had dropped it, I crept forward, eyeing that seething mass and debating whether we could do without the machete after all. The insects were still angry and many cruised around looking for trouble. I inched through the shallows keeping as submerged as possible until I could grab the machete and retreat at last.

We decided it would be best to portage the canoe through the jungle, but felt that an act of revenge was called for. Sneaking to within 15 feet we fired the shotgun at the swarm, then turned and sprinted for our lives. But we collided with each other and fell in a heap in the shallows as the first of the hornets reached us. One landed on my arm – I remember seeing it alight a split second before I submerged, but it must have been washed off just in time. The water was only 18 inches deep, and we crawled our way along the bottom heading for a pool downstream, clawing our way over the shingle, concerned above all that our bare arses should not stick above the surface. Reaching deeper water we surfaced at last. All clear. We looked at each other, gasping and pop-eyed from fright, and burst out laughing. That would teach us.

At midday we arrived at another fork in the river but our excitement was short-lived. Something still wasn't as it should be. Neither branch headed off in quite the right direction, and over the last few days we'd noticed that the Mapaoni had been leading us too much north-east for our liking; the map showed the final miles before the fork as flowing north or north-west.

We camped at the confluence on a levee with a sandy foreshore, the land rising sharply on the other bank from a chaos of boulders bewigged with ferns, moss and bromeliads. The sun filtered through the trees and the gravel of the riverbed glowed yellow in the clear shallows. Six giant otters came upstream, their submerged bodies creating a bow wave on the surface. Traira dominate in headwater streams of this sort, and it's estimated that they make up to 90 per cent of the fish in weight at the end of the dry season. The streams are packed with a variety of fish a few months earlier as other species migrate from downstream to spawn, but the voracious traira eat most of these. Otters keep traira numbers under control, helping to maintain a higher fish diversity.

After a dull lunch of plain white rice I waded up the left-hand tributary and peeked around the corner. Not a pretty sight. At least twelve fallen trees in the first 100 yards. It wasn't a place to take a canoe unless we were certain it was the right way, so we decided to explore ahead on foot. Hanging the compass round my neck, carrying machetes and as naked as the day we were born we set off up the creek, ducking under logs, clambering over others (careful with the splinters), wading through shallows and stepping over the chaos of driftwood. Then it became deep and swampy, forcing us to swim for several hundred yards through dark, stagnant water where the bottom was lined with muddy ooze and the surface scattered with debris. Then more shallows, with logs or thorny tangles, banging our shins on submerged wood, shivering in the shadowy underworld. Out there the weather had settled down to the dry season norm of sizzling heat and blue skies, but not much of that reached us.

Two miles was enough to confirm that the tributary was flowing predominantly from the north, and not north-west as it should. Our excursion ended when we came to a log that blocked one of the deep sections, its top 3 feet above the water and the bottom edge 2 feet below the surface, all topped with a toupee of thorny vegetation. Treading water and holding on to the side of it I swung the machete, clearing a space to clamber up, but a slight movement under my left hand made me look down, and there was a snake's tail wriggling under my palm.

I followed its length for 4 feet upwards and saw the head raised and angry just beside where I had been chopping. I'm no herpetologist but this looked venomous, with a triangular head and darker diamond patches along a coarse-scaled brown body, and the tail that had been under my hand vibrated angrily. I lowered the machete towards it and it bashed its nose in a strike, causing the metal to ping. I'd been lucky, but I wasn't so much afraid as angry at the way it was interrupting our progress. I thought of trying to chop its head off, but was worried by the consequences of missing.

'Shoo!' I said, smacking the machete behind it. 'Piss off!'

It held its ground.

'Leave it alone John,' Heather appealed. 'You'll only make it angrier.'

I continued striking the log until I got a response. It had been a lousy day and I wasn't going to be dictated to by some reptile. I was only asking it to wriggle away a few feet and let us pass.

Finally it moved. Not along the log as I'd anticipated, but down the side of it, plopping into the water 2 feet from where I was treading water.

'Now you've done it!' yelled Heather, swimming off downstream. I immediately stopped waving my legs, and promptly sank, expecting to feel the fangs fasten on to my leg, or in my nakedness, worse. Lifting an arm to grab the trunk, I hung there motionless for a couple of hundred years before I plucked up courage to move. Time to head back to camp.

Splashing despondently through the shallows and swimming the icy pools, I could feel the chances of finding the trail slipping away and another heroic failure on its way. This tributary wasn't the one.

Putting on two layers of clothing we huddled round the fire, our blue fingertips and chattering teeth making us fear a malaria attack was on the way. A flock of thirty grey-winged trumpeters unwisely chose this moment to come trotting down the hillside opposite and congregate on the bank. Not being great fliers they viewed the stream with a certain amount of dismay, but flapped across it one by one, landing a few yards from where we sat. I reached for the shotgun, sighted on the nearest and the shot lifted it off its feet to land in a jumble of feathers. The others didn't know what had happened and strolled away calmly, scratching and pecking like chickens in a farmyard.

As their name implies, they can be noisy birds, setting up a great commotion when pursued and trumpeting at night in a chorus of throaty honks that starts fast, but becomes slower and deeper in a descending scale, with each bird's call overlapping the other. Handsome birds too I discovered as I ran my hands over the feathers – predominantly black with just a tinge of grey and brown on the back, greenish legs, and a patch of beautiful rainbow feathers on the throat. By the time I'd plucked everything off we were left with only a pheasant-sized roast, but enough to help cheer us up after a grim day.

Our well-thumbed maps were soon spread around our feet. We had an aeronautical chart with a scale of 1:1,000,000 that was useless, a photocopy of a Brazilian map of the Mapaoni with a scale of 1:250,000, and a map of southern French Guiana that we'd purchased from the Institut Geographique National in Paris. The latter had a scale of 1:200,000 and was by far the most trustworthy of the three, and fortunately it also covered about 10 miles of territory on the Brazilian side of the border. It even showed the route of the Indian trail.

The French and Brazilian maps didn't agree on much; in fact it was hard to believe they depicted the same region. But both maps showed a fork in the river about 2 miles from where the trail would start, though their interpretations of the course of the Mapaoni after the fork were very different. The Brazilian map showed no further tributaries, but the French one marked another branch 5 miles upstream with the two streams swinging away in the same directions as these two did by our camp. Also, the river between the two forks was shown to travel north-east or east.

It seemed possible that we'd gone too far, and that the tributary we'd rejected three days before was the one we wanted.

'It makes sense,' argued Heather. 'Crevaux described the trail as marshy even in the dry season and impassable in the floods, so it can't be used all year round. So wouldn't the Indians aim to connect sections of rivers that are navigable during the driest months?' She waved a hand at the view in front of us. 'Not tiny little creeks like these.'

Jules Crevaux had been a doctor in the French Navy and initially gone to French Guiana to work with yellow fever victims. In 1877 he had crossed the Tumucumaque to the Mapaoni in the company of Wayana Indians and became the first European to descend the Jari.

Heather was making sense, but there'd been no high ground back at the previous fork. The trail wouldn't start in a swamp.

'We'd better explore the right-hand tributary before we make up our minds,' I said, 'but I can't face any more of that today.'

'We'll check it tomorrow. If it corresponds with the French map I suppose it means we'll have to go back.'

I sighed at the memory of the choked creek behind us, and at the irony of going too far.

A couple of hours wading up the other stream the next morning confirmed that it headed eastwards, so we reluctantly turned the canoe round, pulling it on to the bank to get its 18-foot length facing the other way in the tiny river. Swift progress cheered us up; by lunchtime we'd covered the same distance that had taken a day and a half on the way up, and we could have got further but Heather had bad back pain and I felt shivery with a sore throat. The river was about 6 inches lower than it had been, but that didn't make a lot of difference.

It sounds foolish to lie suspended 3 feet off the ground when big cats are around, and in the old days I used to keep a fire going all night, even though the most carefully laid blaze needed tending at regular intervals. Now we threw a few extra branches on the cooking fire before retiring, but by midnight it was reduced to a heap of cold ash. I certainly wouldn't let that happen if there were tigers, lions or leopards about, but there's something curiously unthreatening about the jaguar.

'Man, to the majority of jaguars, must be an unknown quantity to be treated with curiosity, caution or indifference, but only exceptionally as prey, and the scent of man holds no significance for them,' writes Richard Perry in *The World of the Jaguar*. Most Indian tribes don't seem unduly concerned about them and there have been no maneaters, or even many recorded incidents of jaguars killing people, that I've found. This unblemished record is probably explained by the abundance of space that has let them retreat from man's intrusion. On other continents big cats have been forced to live in close proximity to humans with fatal results.

When I've seen them on the riverbank, magnificent and powerful yet strangely benign, I've been encouraged to do silly things like follow them on foot into the forest trying to grab another photo as they swish their tails in irritation. If you keep your distance they watch you calmly, bemused by your novelty, giving plenty of time for men to react as Raymond did with Gallic enthusiasm for '*la chasse*' and in keeping with his age:

On the bank a jaguar — a splendid, very large one — watched me go by. I fired, and he ran off with a tremendous bound. What an animal!

If approached, however, they will generally retreat, and such timidity from a creature powerful enough to drag a steer for half a mile further encourages one's delusions that they're really just big pussycats. Heather didn't quite share my conviction that jaguars or pumas wouldn't do us any harm, and liked to sleep beside towering inferno pyres that bathed a huge area with an orange glow, especially on the Mapaoni where the jaguars were so vocal. These too were normally cold ashes by midnight.

'Don't worry about it,' I told her. 'If a cat comes into camp we can scare it off.' I told her how one had started licking the cooking pots once, until Peter and I had driven it off with some banshee howling.

In 1987 she saw a jaguar on the third day of her first trip to the jungle. Rounding a tight bend, paddling in silence and hugging the margin, our senses barely registered a spit of sand and a heap of reclining orange that leapt to its feet with an ear-flattened panicky snarl, and whirled for the cover of the forest, dugs swinging beneath the belly. All in two seconds and 8 feet away, and so fleeting that we needed to get out and see the pugmarks to convince ourselves it had been real.

'John! Wake up!'

'Mmm, ugh... what?'

'Wake up! What's that animal?' Heather's anxious whisper and the shaking of my hammock finally brought me back from a lovely dream. It was too dark to see a thing, but footsteps crunched nearer, heavy yet stealthy, already less than 30 yards away. Not heavy enough to be a tapir, too heavy to be a paca, an armadillo, an ocelot...

I reached down for the torch under my hammock as the creature halted 15 yards away, sniffing the air loudly.

'It might be a jaguar,' I said, trying to quieten the quickening of my breath. 'Let's have a look.'

The beam was answered by a flash of eyes, startlingly near, glowing like the headlights of an approaching car: I expect our jaws dropped and we gasped profanity and awe. It was hard to unlock our gaze and shift the torch to one side for a flank of spotted gold to confirm our fears. The jaguar watched us with calm intensity.

'We'll give a good yell,' I whispered, 'and that should see it off. After three... One. Two. Three!' Leaping up in our hammocks we let out an ear-piercing scream that woke some roosting parrots and made them squawk in alarm. I was watching the jaguar for a reaction. It bared its teeth and snarled noisily, doing a good impression of the Metro Goldwyn Mayer lion.

'Try again! One. Two. Three. Aiiiieeeeeee!'

Same response. This was having the wrong effect. The relaxed nighttime wanderer had crouched and flattened its ears, scared and threatened by scents and noises it couldn't identify. I was going to have to get up, resurrect the fire and find the shotgun.

Handing the torch to Heather with instructions to warn me if the jaguar did anything – anything at all – I slid reluctantly to the ground. Where was the other damn torch? I crept over to the fire and fanned optimistically at the dead coals, my scalp prickling at the thought of the jaguar's killing bite to the brain.

I'd have to get some rubber and kindling, but first I found the shotgun and checked it was loaded. A single-barrel 20-gauge shotgun is not the sort of firepower one wants when facing a charging jaguar. Old bull-balled Eduardo Barros Prado wouldn't be caressing this peashooter and drivelling about fusion into one single entity, he'd be screaming for his Magnum or radioing for an air strike.

Unable to find the other torch, I groped blindly for some rubber and dry kindling that I tried to light with a shaky hand. Idiotically, at the same time I was having an internal debate about the rights and wrongs of pulling the trigger on such a beautiful and endangered creature. I'd have to be very convinced it meant me harm before I could bring myself to shoot it, I decided. A canine pressed to each temple and hot breath on my bald patch might just be enough.

I heard some movement.

'What's it doing?' I squeaked, waving the gun around wildly, principles forgotten. It needn't die in vain – I could always make a nice car seat cover out of its pelt.

'It's taken a few paces over to the left, but it hasn't come any nearer,' Heather reassured me. 'In fact, it's just sat down.'

I raised my head and saw the jaguar sitting back on its haunches like some huge domestic cat, patiently waiting for its owner to operate the tin opener. Now we'd stopped shrieking and screaming and upsetting the neighbourhood it had recovered its poise.

A crackling blaze eventually drove away the darkness and most of our fear. The jaguar too. Next time we looked up the cat had gone; just a final flash of eyes as it glanced over its shoulder.

Heather was staring at me accusingly. 'Just one little yell and they run, eh?'

I shuffled sheepishly. 'I promise you it worked last time – the thing shot off like the proverbial scalded...'

After travelling downstream for more than two days we feared we might blunder around a bend and unexpectedly ram another big wasp swarm, one bit of the river looking pretty much like any other. We needn't have worried because one of the perimeter guards dropped out of the sun and stung Heather on the wrist, giving us abundant warning and outraging her sense of fair play. 'But I wasn't even doing anything!' she protested.

It would need more than a can of fly killer to annihilate that lot: a flamethrower perhaps, but we'd not packed one of those. It was now out of the question to sneak by as before because the river had dropped, exposing a thick trunk underneath the nest that would have to be cut, and there were no volunteers for the task.

I climbed up the steep bank and the first 10 yards of soft, fleshy fronds dropped satisfyingly under the machete, but the chaos of liana that followed was completely impassable without some vigorous chopping that I feared might disturb the sleeping foe. Emerging sweaty from that, I expected a respite, but an enormous tree had recently fallen, dragging five others with it. Trunks too high to even look over, branches 6 feet in diameter, and a mess of splintered wood and creepers as thick as my thigh blocked the next 50 yards.

I sat down despondently on a section of broken branch that was covered with wispy lichen and some bush-sized epiphytes. It was all too much. There was never a quick and easy way. Getting around a wasps' nest should have meant a 10-yard portage through the woods. Not here. Oh no. Everything developed into a bloody epic. If I hadn't learnt my lesson I'd have fired the shotgun at them out of pique.

We began chopping a trail but the vegetation was so thick, and the detour to avoid the fallen tree so long, that it took two hours. Then we had to get the sacks and canoe up the sheer 8-foot bank and carry everything to the other side. Good humour was an early casualty.

Arriving back at the fork in the river we examined the other stream with interest. It seemed, if anything, smaller than the one we'd been on, and the water was noticeably murkier and warmer. Perhaps we really were only a couple of miles from the head of the trail now and could have finished with the Mapaoni for good by the next evening. That mood of optimism whipped us along for the rest of the afternoon and we made good progress. The creek meandered along a wide, swampy valley, doubling on itself in infuriating loops, making a mockery of the two straight miles represented on our maps. In consolation, we managed to squeeze under a few more logs than usual, and float over others, the prickles of a plant with mimosa-like leaves grabbing at our skin and leaving trickles of blood.

What worried us, as it had Peter and me in the past, was the absence of any hills worthy of the name. The ground rose slightly at the margins of this wide valley, in one or two places soaring to an imposing height of, well, 50 feet or more, but that was it. These were supposed to be the Tumucumaque Hills for heaven's sake, and here we were, still in a swamp, without seeing a rapid for days and with nothing remotely spectacular in the way of high ground. Either we weren't in the right place or these ancient hills really had seen better days. We began to sympathise with the geologist Hurault: after spending a while up here it would be easy to lose patience with the exaggerations of the explorer Henri-Anatole Coudreau.

Hurault singles out Coudreau for spreading many of the myths and legends of these hills after the latter had explored some sections of the Tumucumaque between 1887 and 1891. Arriving in French Guiana to work in the colonial service, Coudreau later crossed the far eastern portion of the Tumucumaque from the Oyapok to the Araguari, explored tributaries of the Oyapok and briefly entered the headwaters of the Cuc, a tributary of the Jari. He died from malaria on the Trombetas in 1899.

Raymond Maufrais had met Hurault when on his way to the Tumucumaque:

> And there too was J. Hurault, whom I'd met in Paris at the Service Geographique. He was just the same. He wore battle-dress and had several Bonis [Bush Negroes] with him. They made themselves at home in my shelter without asking my permission to sit down.

Hurault was one of the jungle experts who had tried to persuade Raymond to change his plans:

> I'm bound to say that Hurault and I had more than one sharp disagreement about my projects.
> 'Come on Maufrais, why don't you come back with us to Cayenne, and then on to Paris? You've done quite enough here already. With the rainy season coming on, it's too late for you to start anyway. If you go on alone you've an even chance of not coming back.'

Raymond wasn't going to start listening to sound advice this late in the day:

> They all said the same. But my father is a man of the Beauce: obstinacy itself, that's to say. I've decided to make this journey, and I'm not going to shorten it by so much as a yard. In my own eyes, and when I have to face my own conscience, I should see it as a renunciation of myself. The work would not have been done. I'll win through. Yes Messieurs les Pessimistes, I'll win through!

The next day was less kind to us. Not content with scattering the stream with the usual number of fallen trees, the malevolent forces had placed them in clusters of three or four in quick succession, without even the 18 feet to fit the canoe between them. It was easier in these places to cut a trail along the bank to bypass the lot. We did this with careless vigour, slashing at a common plant that had four tall floppy leaves emerging from tubular roots that lay half-submerged in the mud like radiator hoses. They were nice and cucumber-soft to slice through, exposing a core that I thought might be edible.

Only recently, reading Nicholas Guppy's *A Young Man's Journey*, have I discovered that the Dieffenbachia has a blistering sap and would be an unwise addition to a salad. It was 'the dumb cane' of the West Indies, 'where the juice was used by the Spaniards for torturing slaves; a few drops in the mouth caused the tongue to swell and made speech impossible for several days.' Alternatively the slave would be beaten with sections of the root, raising painful weals on his back.

Further reading introduces other hazardous plants. The *Ryania speciosa*, or *mata-calada* in Portuguese (the silent killer) has almost legendary poisoning properties according to John Hemming and James Ratter's report on the Royal Geographical Society's Maracá expedition. This common small tree produces ryanodine, a poison so strong that even a tiny amount ingested causes immediate death; even inhaling the smoke from burning sections of the tree can kill, and caiman are hunted by rubbing a meat bait with its leaves. Apparently a number of participants at a forest barbeque had dropped dead because the meat had been skewered on ryania wood, which made us realise how many times we played Russian roulette with our stick bread. After kneading the dough we wound it in a spiral around any suitable stick and toasted it slowly over the fire until it browned.

Lunchtime came and went without us finding anywhere in the swamp to rest and eat, so we chewed tablespoonfuls of sugar for a little surge of energy to deal with a fallen kapok tree that had sprawled across the river in a way calculated to cause maximum distress. With three enormous branches and a colossal trunk, this was the equivalent of four fallen trees in one. Sacks came out, sacks went back; came out again, went back again; sacks slid off precarious perches into deep water; sacks were passed over wide gaps or handed up heights that the human frame was not equipped to cope with; the canoe drifted off downstream when we weren't looking; biting black ants stung our bare feet and the sun baked us mercilessly.

After that we camped as soon as we could in what I described in my diary as 'a shitty place with a swampy margin'. It had no virtues as a campsite, having a steep bank that made washing or collecting water difficult, a soggy foreground full of thorns, and the jungle, when we cut a path into it, turned out to be tangled and rocky with hardly any flat ground. Its only advantage was that it came before a group of five fallen trees that we couldn't face dealing with that day.

Our hammocks hung on the steep slope of a little hillock of dry land, almost touching the ground on the uphill side and with a 6-foot drop on the other. The fire threatened to roll away or pitch supper into the dirt, and bumblebee-sized mutuca flies lanced us with painful jabs. We escaped to the river, washing the debris out of our hair and soothing the bites, scratches, stings and aches of a tough day.

The evening sun picked out all the myriad shades of green, illuminated the white tendrils of liana that hung from the few tall riverside trees and softened the canopy of the forest that rippled across the surrounding hillocks. The cool clear water, clean enough to drink without worry, gurgled around us over a firm bed of sand where fool's gold winked and mica flashed. Some creepers had lowered down tassels of root fibres from the branches above that jiggled on the surface of the water, capturing flotsam.

Another plant had exhibited as near to a thought process as a plant is ever likely to have. Probably beginning life as a seed deposited in a bird dropping on a high branch, it had drooped earthwards seeking soil to establish its roots, but its questing tip had found the river instead. Unable to perform a right angle turn and support itself for 6 feet sideways to reach the bank, it seemed to remember that on its way down it had passed the branch of a bush. Performing a U-turn, it had snaked and twisted back up itself for 15 feet until it moved over to the bush and continued on its way.

A toucan headed for its roost with the characteristic five flaps and glide, five flaps and glide – the weight of the beak causing a dip and loss of altitude every time it stopped flapping. The insect life of the forest was in that relatively quiet lull between the day and night shifts, and our worries and frustrations were swept away by the refreshing waters and the beauty of our surroundings. It's easy to approach the forest in a mood of combat; life too dominated by the difficulty of progress and the discomfort. Camping early enough to have a few hours relaxation in daylight when the worst heat of the day had passed, gave the opportunity to appreciate just how lucky we were to see this beauty so far from the depredations of man.

But the pleasure of our bathe, and the happy realisation that we might be less than a mile from our goal and nearly finished with canoeing on the Brazilian side of the watershed, was shattered by the raucous call of a caracara – the Neighbourhood Watch of the Amazon – the first to spot intruders and screech out a 'Ca-Ca-Ca-CAAAA! Ca-Ca-Ca-CAAAA!' It's an unbearable racket. Halfway between a vulture and a hawk, this black and cream bird sat in a nearby tree and went on and on, jangling our nerves and driving us out of the water.

We were suddenly impatient to finish with the Mapaoni and walk off into the hills on the second stage of our journey. Raymond had felt the same:

I long to get out of the boat and strike out on foot. I've had enough of this river! Before, there were the rapids; and now all these fallen trees. I don't know what I want; yes I do — just to get there very soon. But alas, the days are short and full of harassment; I move very slowly.

The following day we left the hammocks in place and carried on upstream with an empty canoe. That way we'd be able to heave it over logs quickly and wouldn't have to swim through the occasional deep sections where the dark stagnant water was not inviting. Electric eels and anacondas might favour such spots, and toothy fish appraise our flailing pale legs. As it turned out, there were no sections more than knee-deep, but we led the canoe for a nice walk through tangles, over fallen trees, and zigzagging around driftwood in the shallows. We were looking for areas of high ground where the land rose steeply from the shore, because to our way of thinking a trail should start at such a place.

The only descriptions we had from the early explorers were not very illuminating. Edgar Maufrais, searching for his son, travelled up the Jari and Mapaoni in 1952 in the company of Oyampi and Wayana Indians. He described the trail head as a cul-de-sac, with several abandoned canoes. Crevaux, in 1878, merely stated that the Mapaoni was 10 metres wide (considerably more than it was here) with some granite rocks and numerous fallen trees. Its water had a temperature of 23.2 degrees. Not much useful information there.

We found only one section of terra firma forest, but the hills were on the south bank, not on the north. We climbed them anyway and it opened up a vista of hilly country that we'd seen no inkling of from the river. Our view was interrupted by trees, but in the area behind our camp there seemed to be a succession of ridges. Nothing spectacular, but enough to head home with a little hope in our hearts.

There's a little bird in Amazonia whose song can stop you dead in your tracks. It sounds just like a man whistling through rounded lips. It could be a house painter up a ladder.

In the jungle when you haven't seen sight or trace of man for weeks it's truly alarming. There's someone there, hiding and watching, letting you know by whistling his tune that he can see you even if you can't see him. It is Hannibal Lector, or a mad axeman, or even worse, a chirpy Cockney house painter.

In fact it's a nondescript little brown bird called the musician wren, but when one started to sing on our way back to camp I could see the colour drain out of Heather's face, and felt the same shock myself. Our heads swivelled in unison to a section of bank, certain we were going to see a human being. The call has that element of intentional attention seeking. It's a melodious 'Pssssst!' or 'Coooeee!'

Nothing is scarier than the idea of a prowling man, and in that we share the fear of nearly every creature in the forest. Our scent caused panicked stampedes, leaps, dives, snorts, barks or yelps of alarm. We scared the hell out of them. I guess it was only fair that we should share the same feeling, even if it was just the product of our imagination.

Back at camp I wandered inland to see if the ground climbed up as much as it had seemed from the previous viewpoint. After crossing 100 yards of floodplain I started to climb gently, and kept on going up for a considerable distance. Even better, the ridge swung north and continued heading in the right direction. I left further exploration to the next day but on the way down I discovered a little stream that entered the Mapaoni 100 yards upstream of our camp, and one of the maps showed such a creek near the trail head.

A network of Indian trails exists all over Amazonia, some only a few miles long, others much longer. Several cross international boundaries with a nomad's freedom and disregard for bureaucrats and boundary commissions because they were using these routes before the frontiers were created, before Europeans even arrived in South America.

They use these trails to travel to the next river, to visit other villages, to go on long hunting and foraging trips, to raid or trade. To a westerner the Indian's sense of location seems extraordinary. Childlike and helpless without our compasses and satellite imagery, we marvel at their ability to travel through the forest without getting lost. William Curtis Farabee, travelling on the Corentyne River in Guyana in 1917, noted that while it was an unknown river to them, his Indian companions knew where they were. 'None of them had ever been in the region before, but when we were descending the river Corentyne they told us many times quite accurately what places were directly west of us on the Rupinimi and Essequibo and how many days' journey it would be if there were a trail.'

Obviously the trail that we were searching for had never been much of a path by our standards, accustomed as we are to scarred hillsides from the tramp of many boots. Marked with a few broken saplings, this would have been used by thirty people a year perhaps, barely disturbing the leaf-mould with their bare feet. And since the village of Molocopote had been abandoned in 1980 and the last Wayana moved to French Guiana, no one would have crossed the Tumucumaque. In the old days there would have been a few canoes parked at each end of the trail. Leaving yours there, you picked the most serviceable one on the other side. In the unlikely event of there being no canoe to take, you felled a tree and hollowed out a dugout, or peeled off the bark and made a canoe from that.

How clumsy and hopeless we must seem to forest people. Relying on guides and porters, we stick to the rivers if we can, only making brief forays into the jungle. Rivers can pose their own difficulties as we knew all too well, but an overland journey involves carrying a huge pile of gear that we regard as essential. We haul our canoes along because we haven't the skill to make one on the other side, and we weigh ourselves down with food and equipment because we can't feed ourselves from the forest or improvise shelters. Anyway, these considerations were a little premature. First we had to discover if we'd stumbled upon the right spot to head inland and blaze our own path.

After a huge breakfast of porridge we took compass, maps, machetes and binoculars and headed up the hill. Reaching what seemed to be the highest point we headed down the other side, due north, expecting to come to a valley between one hill and the next. It turned into a horrible tangle of bamboo, so tightly packed that the machete couldn't clear a way through but thick enough to take our weight. We hoisted ourselves up and poked our heads into the sunlight, getting a good view of a steep hillside stripped of the usual forest cover, where perhaps a landslide had let in enough light and heat for the bamboo to take control. But over to the left, the hilltop we'd just come from continued in a ridge that curved round to the north and descended in a more wooded slope.

We returned up the hill and explored it. Things were starting to look promising again. For a start it was a sensible route for a trail, taking the easiest route along ridges to avoid the tangles and swamps. Could this be it? It seemed ironic that a camp made hastily, in exhaustion and to postpone climbing over some fallen trees, might have put us in almost precisely the right place.

While Heather went through all our gear, checking the food bags for damp and doing an inventory of our supplies, I started to cut the trail. This had to be good enough to follow easily without fear of getting lost, and wide enough to stop vegetation catching on our loads. Soon my shirt and trousers were heavy with sweat but I cut a mile or so up the hill and along the ridge; the day's work coming to an end when I stuck the machete smack into an unseen nest of large wasps that was attached to a sapling at knee height. Fortunately they reacted very slowly, and I had time to yank the blade out and run like a sprinter on steroids before they could reach me. After that adrenalin boost I left the trail cutting for the day and explored ahead to see the lie of the land.

The ridge went on for half a mile westwards before turning north, dropping down very steeply to a clear stream flowing through marsh. On the other side the ground rose up again so I ascended the next hill. All seemed as it should be from the map.

I was very conscious of being totally alone, a vulnerable little speck of humanity in the vast forest; more than 2 miles from camp, and out of earshot even if Heather tried to lead me back by firing our ammunition into the air. I could die a horrible death of hunger and exhaustion if I got lost, stumbling through the unfriendly terrain with dwindling strength until I fell down for the last time. And poor Heather waiting day after day, not knowing where to start looking, or how long to leave it before she could assume I was dead and think of saving herself. In two weeks, animals would have scattered my bones and I'd leave only a greasy stain on the ground.

Such morbid thoughts were upsetting my concentration as I peered through the trees at what lay ahead. There should be further hills in front, including Temomairem, 453 metres high with a distinctive bare and grassy summit or flank according to Crevaux and Edgar Maufrais. It was really the only distinctive feature on the trail, and a confirmation that we were on course. I peered through the trees, alternately rising on tiptoe or crouching to peep through little gaps. There! That was a large bare hillside wasn't it? Perhaps... it was hard to be sure. I tried to climb a small tree to get a better vantage but with no success, all the time the dread of getting lost plucking at my sleeve. Best to leave this until morning. It was a fair walk back to camp and Heather would be worried.

I descended the hill, crossed the stream and climbed again, dispelling any doubts with the compass. I walked on and on, far further than I remembered ever coming that day, seeing nothing that I remembered passing on the way out. It might not be the same ridge at all, and I broke into a panicky trot, dodging through the saplings, fending off the branches with my raised arms. Already the sun was low. Why had it been necessary to go so bloody far? I could have left it until the morning. At the very least I should have marked my way.

But then I noticed a highway opening before me, an avenue of cut saplings whose severed bodies lay wilting on the ground, contrasting with the brown of old dead leaves, and I flopped down to catch my breath and quieten those terrors that had been flapping through my guts.

I strolled down my trail with a contented stride, machete idle at my side. For the last two hours I'd been weaving and ducking, occasionally crawling under the thickest obstacles, clambering over logs, being hauled back by lianas that hooked around my neck or legs, snagged by spiders' silk as strong as sewing cotton. Now I could walk upright, unimpeded and unchecked. Ten minutes later I saw the blue of the tarpaulin through the trees and smelt the smoke from our fire. Heather's hammock shook as she sat up and pulled aside the mosquito net to peer out, smiling at my sweaty, exhausted appearance.

'You're bloody late. I was worried.'

'Sorry, I should have rung.'

We laughed, me with a trace of hysteria, and I gave her a kiss.

'Let's have some coffee and you can tell me all about it,' she said.

Home sweet home.

The previous year I'd been up the little river Ximim Ximim with Peter and a small film crew. One day we stopped for a midday rest, and I decided to pass the time while lunch was cooking by wandering off to take some photos. A group of howler monkeys was active nearby and I decided to stalk them as they moved slowly inland to escape my unwanted attentions.

Forty minutes later, satisfied that I wasn't going to get any better pictures, I gave up and decided to head for home. Then I suddenly realised that I didn't have a clue where 'home' was. I'd been so absorbed in harassing the monkeys that I hadn't been paying attention to where they were leading me.

I knew that I must still be within earshot of my companions, but I was reluctant to call out to them. Pride and embarrassment stopped me. I was expedition leader, for heaven's sake, chosen to take the group into the jungle and bring them safely back. I hadn't even followed my own emphatic advice never to leave camp without a compass. How could I now go around shrieking like a novice?

Looking around at the featureless jungle that surrounded me, I convinced myself that I knew the way back and trotted off in that direction. Five minutes later I wasn't so sure, and decided I'd have to seek some assistance.

Opening my mouth I let out a good yell. Not the word 'help' of course, more a vague sort of scream that could be explained away later as an attempt to shoo away a marauding jaguar or something.

No reply.

I had been a bit timid, I thought, so next time I drew in a good lungful and really let rip.

Still no reply. Nothing at all.

I learnt later that Peter couldn't hear me because he was listening to his Walkman and had headphones clamped to his ears. The film crew had heard my calls but hadn't appreciated that I was hoping for a reply. Maybe they thought I'd gone into the jungle to practise my yodelling or something.

I walked a bit further and tried again. Well actually, to be more truthful, I flailed through the undergrowth with a strange bleating coming from my throat, and tried again.

Still nothing.

Instead of sitting down and controlling my panic, I trotted hither and thither for ten minutes yelling at the top of my voice.

Back at camp, Peter finally removed his headphones and heard my faint cries.

'Is that John?'

'Yes. He's been doing that for a while now.'

When their distant cries reached me they came from the last quarter I would have expected. I was heading the other way. In five minutes I'd have been out of earshot forever.

And what did I do when I got back to camp and found them calmly eating lunch? Did I fall on their necks and smother them with kisses of gratitude?

The hell I did.

'That was a safety drill,' I snapped hoarsely, strutting around like a drill sergeant. 'Why didn't you answer my calls? This isn't some bloody game you know, you're going to have to shape up. Imagine if I'd really been lost out there!'

CHAPTER SIX

Blunt again. Taking the file out of my back pocket I squatted down, held the machete between my knees and rasped at the cheap Chinese steel. Heather thought I was over-zealous in my continuous filing and honing, but the blade would only hold its edge for several hundred cuts. The best machetes for sale in Santarém had been made in Sheffield, and with one of those we might have cut from river to river without once using a file, but that English craftsmanship had come too dear. Anyway, I had the voice of my carpentry instructor still barking in my ears from many years before. 'A blunt tool in your hand is as worthless as a limp tool between your legs,' had been the teaching of that particular philosopher.

Heather urged me to drink some water; my shirt was saturated and my trousers sagged with sweat. 'Take it a bit easier,' she encouraged. 'There's no point giving yourself a heart attack.'

Nothing is guaranteed to spur a healthy and fairly fit man of young middle age into more frenzied bursts of physical activity than such appeals. Nobody told you to take it easy ten years before, but now you're expected to slow down, get early nights, buy some slippers and give up on gentle exercise like cutting a trail for 15 miles across jungle hills in stifling heat. I was on my feet in a flash, chopping to left and right, and the newly sharpened blade was deadly and keen.

Heather sighed in exasperation and followed behind, clearing the stuff that I'd missed, checking the compass bearing and telling me where to head. In a day pack she carried water bottles, some lunch, binoculars and a compact camera.

In thick forest our trail was as obvious to the eye as a motorway through a bluebell wood, and agoraphobic animals probably stood in awe at the edge of it summoning up courage to sprint across. No chance of us losing our way here. But sometimes the vegetation thinned into uncharacteristic sparseness where our minimal chopping made the trail much less visible, so we scattered torn up pieces of paper as markers. Not happy with hacking several thousand plants to death, we were strewing rubbish around too.

The trail made little kinks and turns. Round the wasps' nest that I'd kebabed the day before and which was now avoided reverently like the habitat of some endangered species. Round fallen trees that we didn't want to clamber over, skirting extra-thick tangles, and even sparing particularly vigorous saplings that might soon be noble mahoganies.

We left the ridge and zigzagged steeply down, the dead leaves still wet and slippery, arriving in a squelchy valley bottom where we paused for a picnic of plain cold rice and water. Prisoners on the Burma Railway were probably given better lunches. The crowns of the palms above clattered in a breeze we could not feel, and discarded brown fronds carpeted the ground. It was twilight-dark, muddy and depressing and the claustrophobia of the deep jungle was already affecting our spirits. Once lunch was over there seemed little pleasure in sitting on a decomposing log in a bog any longer, so we chopped on up the next hill, called Mapaony-Epoyane on our map. It was from the top of this that I'd tried to see the land ahead the day before, and finding a tree that had conveniently fallen and rested against a neighbour at a gentle angle, I climbed up and hacked away some obscuring leaves and branches.

'Here, come on up!' I called, and Heather soon stood beside me on a branch. 'See, through there, that browny-coloured patch ahead? I reckon that must be Temomairem.'

The view was still blocked by a screen of higher trees and it was necessary to focus through them on sunlit expanses that lay behind. Sometimes I achieved it and sometimes not. The binoculars made it even more confusing. Maybe I was imagining it all. Heather probably thought so, but she did her best.

'It's like a patch of autumn woodland,' I explained. 'But the browns must be patches of sunburnt grass and rock, and that's how Crevaux described the slopes of Temomairem.'

'Oh yes, yes! I can see something!' she exclaimed with conviction; and then she must have blinked and changed her focus. 'Or at least I did for a second there.'

We took a compass bearing on it, almost due north, and descended to the ground. We then extended the trail for another 200 yards before heading back to camp. The rough machete handles had rubbed blisters on our hands, my right elbow ached from the swinging and jarring, and there wasn't a dry patch left on our clothes, but we felt that weary satisfaction of a job well done. Confident too, that with 2 miles cut we were well and truly on our way.

Two more days slashing took us over a further three hills, and according to our map Temomairem would be the next. Sitting in another swampy valley we made plans to start moving gear up in the morning. Temomairem was supposed to be a third of the way along the trail, so here would be a natural location for our next camp.

'We'll have to put the hammocks on the hillside where it's drier and the trees are stronger,' I mused aloud. Heather nodded absently; she was deep in mathematical calculations and not taking in the dismal surroundings that held none of the prerequisites for a decent camp.

'This is the pits!' I continued. 'Nowhere to wash, no sunlight to dry our clothes, crap firewood full of termites...'

But Heather was having a parallel conversation.

'It'll take at least five trips to get the gear moved up here. Do you think we can get all of it squeezed into five packloads each?' she asked.

'... mud and ooze underfoot! Tie hammocks to these trees here and they'd just bend over and plonk your arse on the ground.'

'If the trail really is fifteen miles long that means that by the time we've gone backwards and forwards carrying the loads we'll have walked a hell of a way.' She paused to work it out. 'One hundred and fifty miles at least, not to mention the miles covered when chopping the trail or exploring ahead.' She was gabbling excitedly, and I left my appraisal of the inadequacies of the valley to watch the play of emotion running across her grubby features: optimism, confidence, happiness... and a trace of anxiety. We were about to leave the Mapaoni lifeline behind and immerse ourselves in the Tumucumaque. I was too tired to do much except smile wearily and watch her with love and pride.

'And hell knows how many feet of climbing! Twenty-five thousand feet? Thirty thousand? The equivalent of Everest!' She shook her head in disbelief. 'This really is a dumb venture.'

I couldn't deny that. 'Splendidly pointless, almost magnificent in its stupidity,' I said in a Prince Charles tone. I felt so numb and exhausted I could have sat there forever, but Heather seemed to be bursting with new energy.

'Thank God we found where to start cutting the trail so easily. Three weeks should see us over these hills and into sunny Surinam!'

The next morning we surveyed the pile of food and equipment at our feet, and tried to separate it mentally into ten packloads. The fishing rod could be taped to a paddle, the shotgun dismantled to fit inside a pack, and parts of the canoe strapped to our backs. Canoe poles and watertight containers would have to be carried by hand.

We decided to move food first: packet after packet of rice, beans, flour, oats, spaghetti, sugar, salt and 7 litres of cooking oil. There seemed so much left.

'Let's jettison seven or eight kilos of rice,' Heather suggested.

'Don't be daft.'

'Why not? We've got tons of it left.'

'Because you never abandon food supplies until journey's end, that's why. It's obvious why not.'

'Look how little we've used up so far. It's crazy to carry it all over the hills only to dump it later. And four kilos of salt! What do you intend to do with all that?'

'We're not getting rid of any food. Who knows how long we'll be? What if we get ill or injured and have to camp for a while? There'll be no fish to catch where we're going, hunting will be difficult and we'll burn up tons of calories. Throwing out food is like tempting the fates. We're taking it and that's that.'

'Well you can bloody well carry it then,' she said, tossing a few packets down in anger.

'Oh grow up. A few kilos more or less isn't going to kill us.'

'Grow up yourself! You're always fussing and fretting. We've found the route of the trail, we've cut a third of the way, you should be feeling more relaxed about things.'

We could only agree on leaving behind a couple of spare notebooks, the axe, two bars of laundry soap, books we had both read, and two waterproof sacks that were too holed to be much use. A reduction of 6 kilos at the most.

I helped Heather on with her pack and she winced at the weight, her legs buckling. I tried to swing mine on but couldn't lift it high enough, so I put it on while sitting down and then hauled myself painfully to my feet on a creeper. It was absurdly heavy. Before taking a single step we were sweating heavily and the straps cut off circulation, reducing our arms to tingling paralysis. Heather seemed to have sunk a few inches into the leaf-mould.

'I don't know if I'll make it,' she gasped. 'I've never carried anything as heavy as this.' Two years before we'd walked the Pyrenees from the Atlantic to the Mediterranean and thought our packs heavy then, but they were mere day sacks compared to these.

'You'll make it. Little by little, with lots of rests,' I encouraged, wanting to throw off the absurd weight and flop to the ground. Tightening the waist belts we tottered up the hill away from camp, stopping every few steps, thighs aching, choking for air; and at the top of each hill we sprawled like two soldiers on a forced retreat, sweat spreading across our shirts like Rorschach tests. Mutuca flies stabbed us viciously and we were too laden to do anything about it.

Three and a half hours after leaving the Mapaoni we'd climbed the last hill and were descending into our new valley home, hanging on to saplings to avoid running out of control. The wide area of swamp at the bottom hadn't seemed too bad before, but the weight of the packs pushed us down through the layer of dead fronds to the slime below. If we could hop quickly along all was well. Hop? We sank over our boots and things wriggled in our socks.

Choosing a spot of high dry ground, we unloaded the parcels of food into a waterproof sack. Heather was quiet and grim, her face grey with fatigue, and I felt no better. That was just a fifth of our gear moved a quarter of the way across the hills. Should we call it off now? I lay back on the dead leaves with a sigh, and as I did so a searing pain in the gap between shirt and trousers made me scream and leap to my feet like a springbok.

'Get a stick and poke around where I was lying!' I shouted between rather unimaginative repetitions of the same four-letter word. 'Careful! It might be a snake!' The pain was so excruciating that I was alternately hopping up and down, then dropping on my knees to cringe and hug myself, rubbing the growing aches that radiated from a spot above my left kidney.

'Can't see anything,' she said, turning leaves over carefully. 'Sure it wasn't a thorn?'

'Of course it wasn't a fucking thorn! Would a thorn do this to me?'

She lifted my sweaty shirt-tail. 'No fang marks. There's a big red swelling though.'

'You don't say! Keep looking for what it was.'

'There's a bloody big ant here,' she called later. 'More than an inch and a half long and jet black.'

'That's the bastard!' I leapt on it, stamping and grinding the heel of my boot, but on the soft soil it emerged intact and scuttled off.

'Oh no you don't!' I cried, whacking it with a piece of wood. 'Come back here you shit!' I finally succeeded in mashing it against a root.

I could see that Heather thought that I was making an inordinate amount of fuss about an ant bite.

'These solitary black ants have stings ten times worse than those wasps we met the other day – a bit like a hornet sting,' I explained later. 'In fact, they even look like big hornets without wings, don't they? Great pointed lances sticking from their abdomens and great jaws at the other end. Their stings can kill children, for Christ's sake.'

'I see them all the time, but I never realised they were so dangerous,' she said more sympathetically. The pain was fading but an ache had radiated out from the sting and I felt slightly feverish.

Later, after nibbling a soggy cold chapatti, we walked slowly back to the Mapaoni, our steps feeling almost bouncy now that the weight had been lifted off us. Taking some aspirin I climbed in my hammock, tucked the mosquito net in and was soon asleep, dreaming slightly deliriously of far-off places – polluted urban sprawls of traffic and bustle, seediness and squalor, crammed with a wealth of earthly delights. That probably sums up my restless nature, because when I'm at home in the city my dreams find their way up Amazon creeks.

I dreamt of being in a Rio taxi, hurtling through the tunnels at the mercy of a mad driver who refused to slow down, which is a familiar reality to anyone who's taken a taxi in that city.

'I'm not supposed to die this way!' I pleaded. 'I've come to Brazil to risk death on your rivers, not your roads!' The driver turned round, laughing insanely through decayed teeth, and increased his speed.

A few years ago, when I used to hitch-hike everywhere, I travelled several thousand miles of Brazil by this most sociable and entertaining of methods. It was reasonably easy for someone so obviously blond and foreign to get a lift, but some drivers viewed hitch-hikers with suspicion, calling me a *marginado* or good-for-nothing. Nothing new or exclusively Brazilian in that.

However, once I'd secured a ride I came to dread the smooth open tarmac highway. I preferred the unpaved roads because the corrugated rutted dirt acted as a traffic pacifier, and any truck or car that went too fast would break its springs and wreck its tyres. Journeys might be agonizingly slow – 10 mph or less as the trucks rocked and swayed, slid and stuck – but the only danger came when one vehicle wanted to overtake another. For long, tense seconds we drove blind on the wrong side of the road, unable even to see the end of the bonnet through the dust, exposed to a head-on smash.

On tarmac, however, there were no restraints to the natural exuberance of the Brazilian temperament. The road was smooth, samba was on the tape deck and the foot was on the floor. Only twice in all my hitch-hiking in forty countries have I ever insisted on getting out of vehicles in the middle of nowhere because I was sure I would die otherwise, and both occasions were in Brazil. Drunken driving, inappropriate speed for wet or mountain roads, lunatic overtaking – in fact, just about anything that you're not supposed to do, they did. The statistics confirm the ensuing bloodbath: the state of São Paulo alone having 9,000 traffic deaths a year, more than all the United Kingdom.

Outside Bahia I put down my pack, stuck out my thumb and set off on the 1,200 miles to São Paulo. I expected it to take several days, but almost immediately a VW Combi pulled up and the driver told me they were going all the way.

Only when I climbed in the back and met the eight people on board did I realise that it was going to cost me dear.

'Have you found Jesus?' asked one.

'Do you love the Lord?' asked another.

'Why didn't I take the bus?' I asked myself.

Here was a bunch of rabid evangelists heading back to São Paulo after some gathering, and they had me at their mercy for the next forty hours.

The Combi rocked along to religious pop songs of such nauseating sweetness that they made a typical Cliff Richard hit sound like an incitement to riot, and everyone joined in, singing, clapping and beating tambourines. I was squeezed in beside a beautiful girl whose shapely brown legs had a light dusting of blonde hairs. Her face gleamed with a rather unreal innocence and ecstasy, and I admired the jiggle of her breasts as she bashed her tambourine, my head filled with undevout thoughts.

There were two old men, a pretty woman who was the girl's mother, two children under thirteen, and two men in their twenties.

We drove through scenery of grassland dotted with outcrops of black rock, and whenever we passed one of these near the road, the driver stopped and the team got out with brush and white paint to desecrate the landscape. 'Read the Bible!' they daubed. 'Find Jesus before it's too late.' 'Sinners repent!'

We rolled along all day, and I was forced to explain my lack of faith and to listen to numerous readings from the Bible, but when things got too tiresome I pretended to doze. In the intervals I felt I was building up a nice little relationship with the luscious

Miranda, and had hopes for some devilish seduction when we reached São Paulo.

After dark, while we discussed the thorny subject of Darwinism (which was evidently an unknown branch of scientific theory to these Protestant fundamentalists), I was aware that the driver was tiring, and his driving was deteriorating even from his pretty abysmal norm. He hated to miss out on the great debate that was taking place in the back, and spent most of the time with his body turned towards us and his eyes off the road.

I hadn't had much time to prepare my case but I thought I gave a spirited potted version of *The Origin of Species by Means of Natural Selection* of 1859. My Portuguese wasn't up to translating crucial words like 'hominid' or 'oligocine', but it wouldn't have helped my argument even if it had. The idea of sharing a common ancestry with the apes had everyone scratching at their armpits, hopping up and down and making monkey noises. All very droll. The driver was laughing so much that we left the tarmac, bounced across the rough verge and clipped a fence before ricocheting back. The laughter barely faltered.

When he'd already been at the wheel for fourteen hours I asked him if anyone else was going to take over.

'No one else knows how to drive,' he answered. Forget the 'else' I thought.

'I'll drive for a while if you like,' I offered rashly. There could be all sorts of problems at police road blocks with my lack of insurance papers, and my driving licence was many thousand miles away in Britain, but I knew that otherwise they intended travelling through the night with one driver all the way. I might sneak into heaven if we all died in a crash, there was enough religious fervour here for me to hide in the crowd at the Pearly Gates, but I preferred to risk a lone application much later.

A few minutes later he pulled to the side and I took over. I immediately discovered that he'd had a few mechanical handicaps to deal with. The steering wheel turned loosely in either direction for at least 4 inches before there was any turning of the wheels. The brakes were ineffective and the headlights glowed feebly over the road a few feet ahead.

I settled down to it and the passengers seemed happy with my progress, returning to their singing, clapping and prayer.

Three hours later, when the road was climbing up into a hilly region in twists and turns and the traffic piled up behind some slow-moving lorries, I felt I knew all the quirks of the Combi. Seeing a gap in the approaching traffic I pulled out to overtake. At first things went well, until I was about halfway past the long rig and trailer, then power seemed to fade. My foot was on the floor, the engine revs were climbing, but speed was decreasing. Clutch slip. Seeing the glow of headlights coming around the bend ahead, I dropped back to tuck in behind the truck again, but the gap had closed. A small lorry had moved up tight behind it and there was no room.

As the lights of approaching vehicles bore down on us, panicked cries rose in the back of the Combi.

'Pull in for God's sake!'

'What's this crazy gringo doing? He's trying to kill us all!'

'He's driving on the left!'

A blast of klaxons and squeal of brakes came from the huge lorry that was barrelling down the incline towards us, and there was still nowhere for me to go on the right-hand side of the road. At the last minute I glimpsed an access to a shack and petrol pump on the left, and veered off, bouncing violently over a shallow ditch, and skidding in the loose gravel.

We came to a halt, and the inheld breath from nine pairs of lungs escaped in a long communal sigh. At least that had stopped the bloody singing for a while. Then an excited babble filled the van. My co-driver reached over and switched off the engine.

'I think that's enough of the English way of driving,' he said. 'Dear God, I've never been so scared in all my life!'

Hauling myself up the vicious inclines, then slithering down the other side with the pack swinging me off balance, threatening to toboggan down the slope in a clank of canoe parts, I grabbed anything to steady myself, including palm trees that embedded black spines into my hands and saplings protected by over-zealous ants. Twice in two days fronds swept my face and neatly flicked out a contact lens, sending it flying to join a million glistening raindrops on the dead leaves. Over the years I've spent many hours searching for lost lenses, patting my bathroom floor with gossamer touch, once cordoning off the aisle of Ely Cathedral while I approached the altar like some penitent on hands and knees, but I knew I was beaten here. I just kept on walking.

Many times I questioned the sanity of this enterprise, ridiculed myself for concocting such a ludicrous plan, laughed mirthlessly at the supreme folly of it all, but I never seriously thought of giving up. Anything seemed preferable to an ignominious retreat to the Jari with nothing accomplished. If Heather was feeling differently she showed no sign. On the contrary, she pushed herself to the point of collapse, face set in a grimace of pain and obstinacy.

Finally only one last load remained and it was time to leave the Mapaoni for good and establish our new camp in the forest. I waded into the stream and stuck the axe as deeply as I could into a fallen tree as a temporary sign of our passing. It was unlikely to perplex anyone. Since the Caripí we'd seen no sign of man, and Peter and I had been the last intruders many years before.

Once that little ceremony was complete we turned our back on the river with mixed feelings. The river was a lifeline, and that night we'd be sleeping 4 miles away from it with pieces of our folding canoe scattered around us, and even less chance of making it to safety in the event of an accident. Attempting to push these apprehensions aside, we stumbled along our trail where the stubs of cut saplings stood up like sharpened spikes, fraying and tearing our trouser legs, threatening to trip us and send us crashing to the floor, with the weight of our loads ensuring that we'd be well and truly impaled.

Raymond Maufrais left the river Ouaqui and headed into the forest, physically weakened by dysentery and sores on his legs, carrying no food supplies at all. He was following a faint track through dense undergrowth, but with too much stuff to carry in one load. He first moved up one pack, and then went back to fetch the other:

> This is how I measure distances. Every hundred yards — every hundred and forty paces, that's to say — I take a leaf and put it in my pocket. When I stop I count the leaves and have a rough idea of the distance I've covered — 2,000 yards the first day, 1,000 the second, 1,000 the third, rested the fourth, and 2,000, I suppose, the fifth. A tortoise could do as much! I want to get on but I can't. At every stride there's a new trap, a new obstacle. I stagger along like a drunken man, sweating and cursing, pursued and harassed by flies.

While I fixed the hammocks on the slope above the swamp, Heather prepared lunch. The last weeks had finally whipped us into the sort of shape we should have been in before leaving home. Fat had been replaced by muscle and we both had lean flat stomachs. Pulse-rates might soar to a gallop while climbing with our noses almost touching the ground, but within minutes of resting they had slowed to a laid-back beat. So, fortified by gluey pancakes made of flour, swamp water and chocolate powder, we felt ready to grab machetes and continue cutting up the next hillside, first winding a bandage round my right elbow to alleviate the pain of the jarring machete blows. Tennis elbow, I diagnosed.

(That would be the day, Heather must have thought, when we'd go on the sort of holiday where I could develop tennis elbow through games of mixed doubles.)

There was only time to cut halfway up the slope that afternoon, but early next morning we set off carrying a camera, tripod, books, food and even suntan cream for our visit to the exposed flanks of Temomairem. If we'd had deck chairs we'd have taken them too.

Eleven hours later we were back: sapped, hungry and demoralised. We'd been up the mountain, back down again, three-quarters of the way around the side of it, and never left the forest for a minute. No bare rocky patches. Just another jungle-clad hillside like all the rest.

At daybreak we headed off again, hoping the one sector of hillside we hadn't explored would reveal all. But the last vestiges of hope faded when we found some nicks on tree trunks that we'd chopped to mark our way the day before. We'd circumnavigated the hill.

Flinging the machetes to the ground we sat down on a mossy log. For a long time we didn't speak, and I smoked some of my dwindling tobacco. The jungle was in an uproar. Scarlet macaws screeched contentedly and discarded half-eaten fruit with a plop. We tried to ignore the omnipresent screaming piha's irritating wolf whistle, and something else that was making a sound like a squeaking swing. Then a flock of mealy Amazon parrots outdid one another with the full repertoire ranging from a melodious chuckling and gargling to piercing screeches. The ear registered these familiar sounds without interest, and there was a similar lack of visual stimuli. In this limited world of greens and browns only the rare patches of colour attracted our attention: golden or reddish tree bark, variegated plants like ones that we had in our living room at home, or the new leaves that began their lives in beautiful mauves and crimsons.

We waited for the lumbering mutuca flies to settle on us and then swatted them easily, collecting a satisfying number of corpses at our feet.

'What the hell do we do now?' I asked finally, feeling more ennui than anxiety. 'We could be chopping across the wrong section of hills for all we know. If we left the river too soon we might have twenty or thirty miles to cut instead of fifteen.'

'I don't get it. Those first two mountains seemed right, didn't they?' Heather argued, checking a patch of leaves for hazards before stretching out and closing her eyes. 'Just what the map showed. We crossed streams in the right places, and we've been keeping to a compass bearing,' she paused, searching for any other grounds for optimism. 'And we saw that mountain through the trees, remember?'

A woodpecker drummed a tattoo in a fast flurry of blows, five or so a second, its head probably moving back and forward in a blur.

'Every damn hill around here looks exactly the same, that's the problem,' I sighed. 'They're all steep, they're separated by little streams or swampy ground, and they have flattish summits. Some are a little larger than others, but not enough to be distinctive.'

We stared at the heavily stained map, but it taught us nothing new. 'We should have checked this bloody hill before we left the Mapaoni, and not moved our gear until we'd found Temomairem,' Heather muttered.

'Right,' I agreed. 'But it makes no difference because we're not going back.'

She raised her head and gave me a cold look. I expected her to protest and resurrect the accusations of obsession, but she just sighed and lowered her head back on the ground.

'We might have to go back if we're still wandering around blindly in a week or two,' she said wearily, probably too tired to argue further. Maybe she could see that going back was no longer an easy option. It would take a week to get the gear back to the

Mapaoni, and the river would be almost unnavigable now. We'd seen it drop 18 inches in the last ten days. It felt as if our retreat was cut off.

We cut miles of exploratory trails in the next few days trying to find where we were, searching for a glimpse of Temomairem through an obscuring screen of foliage.

On the third day I pulled myself up on a dangling liana, locking my feet as if climbing a rope, head swimming with vertigo (which for me starts at about 10 feet off the ground), until I reached a sunlit branch, anxiously listening for tearing noises as the liana ripped away and dropped me 70 feet. Heather's upturned face was a pale dot, and that quick downward glance made me press my face into the mossy bark and fight for control.

The view was almost worth it: a succession of hills stretched for miles into the distance and over to my right an almost continuous ridge headed north-west, broken by three or four valleys. Perhaps we should have been over there, and had started our trail in the wrong place? At that moment I didn't give a damn. An ant had crawled up my nose and had to stay there because my hands were engaged in hanging on for dear life. I just wanted to get my feet back on the ground and have a smoke.

I scattered the last dusty powder and twiggy stems of tobacco along the cigarette paper, hands still fluttery with fear. This was my last smoke and it was going to be a poor affair. In a moment of stupidity I'd opted to bring less tobacco than I'd need to last the trip, in order to kick the habit. Holding it horizontally so that the dry weed wouldn't fall out of the end, I eagerly inhaled the acrid smoke. The paper flared and the embers burnt back to me in four good puffs. One final suck and that was it. I flicked the tiny butt on to the ground.

'That was the last smoke of my life,' I announced. Heather looked sceptical and unenthusiastic. She'd heard that many times before and seen my sweet nature evaporate through nicotine withdrawal. 'It's never too late to stop smoking', we're told;

the body can repair the damage caused by decades of tobacco abuse and the chances of contracting heart and lung disease diminish almost as soon as the last butt is stubbed out. All good news in the long term, but other health hazards seemed to take priority for the moment. Promises of increased life expectancy for giving up tobacco didn't have the same allure out in Amazonia, legendary land of parasitical horrors and potential disaster. Somehow I doubted that while watching my leg balloon up from snakebite – perhaps so much that the skin would split from knee to ankle – blood trickling from gums, nose and ears, my insides haemorrhaging, I'd still be thinking, 'It could just as easily have been a heart attack if I'd continued with that filthy habit.'

I began to sleep badly for the first time in my life, with nightmares and sweaty panic. Dreams of being lost, of carmine fingers jammed in severed arteries, of compound fractures and huge hornets pursuing us with no river to hide in. Heather had similar dreams, but then she's prey to night terrors at home too, emitting ear-splitting screams that probably make our neighbours think that I'm beating her again.

The last weeks on the Mapaoni had been pretty grim, but our lives on the river now seemed rich and varied. It was impossible to keep in good cheer when cutting miles of trail that were usually abandoned, wearing clothes that never dried, camping on the fringe of swamps, living in a perpetual half-light. We either snapped at each other or only talked about the practicalities of our reduced lives: what we would eat, where something was stored, what was to be cut or carried.

Heather's most innocent failings would make me boil with irritation. Her cooking had too much sugar or not enough salt, her pasta was overcooked and soggy, her progress on the trail too slow, she wasn't observant enough, and she either failed to amuse and distract, or intruded on my moments of privacy. My foibles were equally infuriating to her, especially my growing caution and concerns about our safety.

'Honestly John, you're becoming a right mother hen, clucking and fussing all the time!'

'In the old days you used to call me a reckless loony,' I reminded her, 'disappearing into the jungle without a thought for my safety. Now you say I'm a pernickety, super-cautious old woman,' I sneered. 'Well I can't be both. The reason I've always come back from my trips is because I'm careful and don't have your sloppy, lazy nature.'

'I'm not lazy!' she objected.

'All right,' I conceded, 'but you're often sloppy and inattentive. You'd probably die if I wasn't here to look after you.'

'Pah!' she scoffed. 'I'll probably die of boredom more like, waiting for you to decide on the safest option! Anyway, we've still got plenty of opportunity to kill ourselves.'

Couldn't she appreciate that I was being extra cautious for her benefit? I'd made plenty of journeys with men before without feeling any obligation to be protective and get them home safely. Our destinies had been linked; we'd looked after each other, depended on each other's strengths, muddled through together. Heather and I did much the same of course, but expedition life for me was now complicated with emotional ties and a burden of responsibility. Prior to our departure, Heather's three sisters and countless of her friends had asked me to look after her and make sure that I brought her back safely. Being cautious and avoiding unnecessary risk was my way of doing my job. Small thanks I got for it.

'This is your third trip out here,' I argued, eager for a row, 'and you still just drift along leaving it all to me. You haven't learnt how to tie a knot, read a compass or do anything useful. It's all left to old muggins here to make the difficult decisions an–'

'That's a bit rich when you don't let anyone else have a say!'

'Oh come on. You make me out to be some sort of dictator! Am I really that scary?'

She laughed mirthlessly. 'You – scary! That's a good one. You're just a bossy bastard who loves getting his own way, especially out here in the Amazon – the great John Harrison's area of expertise! I gave up trying to have an input ages ago.'

'I don't know why you bother coming if it's all so awful.'

'Because in moments of stupidity and weakness I think it might be fun to spend a few months in an interesting place with my husband.'

'Fun? Interesting?' I snorted. 'How likely is that?'

'As you love telling me: I learn absolutely nothing.'

I caught her eye and looked quickly away. We'd come within a whisker of smiling at each other.

'Right. But you could take some of the burden off me by trying to do things properly.' I looked around and seized on her hammock to criticise. I walked over and examined the way she'd tied it to the tree trunk. 'Just look at these knots! The granny knot's a pretty shitty knot to start with, liable to slip, and what have you used here? *Three* granny knots piled one on top of the other! By morning we'll have to break our nails and teeth undoing it.'

'It's the only knot I know,' she said.

'Well maybe it's time you stirred yourself up to learn another! Look at mine. It does the job perfectly, it doesn't suddenly slip and send me crashing to the ground, ripping my mosquito net, and in the morning I just pull lightly at this loop here and it undoes with no struggle at all.'

Heather clapped her hands in mock admiration. 'You really are a master of your environment!' she cooed. 'Are you part Indian?'

'Oh bollocks,' I said, suddenly struck by my priggishness. 'You're just hopeless.'

This time we did smile wryly at each other.

'Let's try to remain friends,' she said.

'If you insist. I suppose we're not doing too badly. I think we have more rows on our way to Tesco's. How we cope with all that serious stress back home, I don't know.'

'All those life and death decisions we have to make every day. Where to park? Baguette or wholemeal? Film or meal out?'

We poured ourselves a strong mug of rotgut and tried to make it bearable with a spoonful of sugar and a dash of water. Leaning against the rough bark of a tree, I put my arm round her shoulders and she snuggled against me.

'I'm not really turning into a fussy old fool, am I?' I asked.

'Yes you are. Really. You dither and fret and worry, with anxious creases mushrooming all over your face.'

'Great.'

'It really drives me nuts, and sort of worries me a little at the same time.'

'Why's that?'

'Because your indecision gets the better of you more than I've ever seen before.'

'There are weighty decisions to be made,' I said sombrely.

'Alone, of course.'

'With absolutely no input or help from any quarter. It's lonely at the top.' I paused. 'What's for supper?' It was her turn to cook.

'You're not asking me to make a decision on my own are you?'

'Of course not. I just want you to suggest rice so I can steamroll over you and get the spaghetti that I really want.'

We laughed and she took a playful swipe at my head.

In the early 1980s, when I made several trips to Amazonia in the space of two or three years, I had difficulty recruiting companions. Friends knew me too well to contemplate spending months alone in the bush with me; others organised their lives so badly that they couldn't take six months off work just like that. I was forced to place advertisements in newspapers and magazines.

Mine wasn't quite as laconic and off-putting as the one that appeared in *The Times* of 1907: 'Men wanted for hazardous journey. Low wages, bitter cold, long hours of complete darkness. Safe return doubtful, honour and recognition in the event of success.'

Or as sporty as the one that Peter Fleming answered from the same newspaper in 1931: 'Exploring and sporting expedition, under experienced guidance, leaving England June to explore rivers central Brazil, if possible ascertain fate Colonel Faucett. Abundance game, big and small; exceptional fishing; room two more guns; highest references expected and given.'

I aimed at a wording that would deter the faint-hearted and leave no doubts as to the probable level of discomfort: 'Companion wanted for tough and hazardous canoe trip to Amazon. Five months. Genuinely adventurous, yet risky. No sponsorship or back-up. Risk of malaria. £2,000 needed.'

It's an indication how out of touch I am with the holiday ideals of my fellow man that I was amazed to get only two replies. One of them asked for more details before informing me that I was 'a nutter'; the other arranged to meet me in a pub, but brought along a friend who also wanted to go. This caused immediate problems as I'd planned a two-man trip in one canoe, but as no one else was interested I had to agree to take them both.

We travelled by riverboat, truck and bus to the town of Sinop in the northern Mato Grosso, meeting an Italian backpacker on the way who asked if he could join us. We agreed and set to work making two canoes at one of the town's sawmills.

The two Englishmen complained incessantly about the heat, the food, the dirt and the people. They missed their workouts at the gym, improvising bench presses with sacks of beans on the hotel floor. We argued publicly over items of expenditure so miniscule that beggars organised whip-rounds in our support. I just held on to the hope that Ben and Mike might adapt to expedition life once we got on the river; the period of acclimatisation, buying supplies, canoe-making and gruelling overland travel is always a tedious introduction to a river adventure.

One morning I knocked on their hotel door and only Ben appeared with the news that Mike was feeling ill. Peeking my head into the room I saw the invalid wrapped in a blanket, looking rather sorry for himself but giving me a tiny, brave smile.

'I'd better stay with him for a couple of hours to see if he's all right,' Ben whispered. 'Probably join you later.'

Andrea and I worked until dusk with no sign of the others, and no one answered our knock when we got back to their hotel room.

'Maybe he's sicker than we thought and they've taken him to the hospital?' Andrea suggested, and we went to inquire at reception.

The manager seemed surprised. 'They left this morning about ten o'clock. Paid their bill and went to the bus station I think. They left this note for you.'

'Dear John and Andrea,' it read. 'We've had enough. Gone to Rio. Good luck.'

'Bloody hell, they've buggered off,' I muttered in stunned disbelief.

'Oh good,' said Andrea. 'I always thought they were a couple of wankers, but what could I say when you'd chosen them? We'll have a much better trip now.'

And so we did.

Two years later I went back to the Amazon with a new companion: Mark, an Australian who threatened to fill most of the canoe with his 6-foot-8 frame. Once a week before departure we met in a pub to discuss our preparations and even then we sometimes struggled to keep the conversation going. This lack of common interests didn't bode well for those months when we'd be each other's sole source of entertainment. Dating couples would have called it quits after such evenings, but there were no other candidates and at least he was refreshingly enthusiastic and eager, in a way that made me feel rather jaded and world-weary.

For four weeks we travelled up the Jari, past the 60-foot falls of Santo Antonio and countless more rapids. The going was slow and hard but Mark kept cheerful and we actually enjoyed each other's company. I think he'd been hoping for a more 'sporting' expedition, and when he moaned about the impossibility of stalking animals in thick forest, I suspected he was more used to driving around the open scrub of Australia dazzling kangaroos with a spotlight. He'd expected 'the going to be hard, but the living to be easy' with pig roasts and jungle fowl luncheons, but we only shot one small monkey in four weeks.

Things started to go wrong in week five. I had my first bout of malaria, then getting up in the dark to cope with a large catfish that we'd hooked on a static line, Mark tripped over a pot of beans simmering on the fire and badly scalded his foot.

We stayed ten days at what became known as Burnt Foot Camp to give the badly blistered skin time to heal. Strong antibiotics kept infection at bay, but the real damage was psychological. After the shock of the injury, and in the boredom of our enforced idleness, he lost the will to carry on.

We both realised that our expedition had its problems. We'd used up half the food supplies and all the fibreglass for repairing the canoe, our fishing tackle was running short of essential items, and now Mark's accident had exhausted the supply of sterile dressings and much of our medical kit. With several months' journey through uninhabited country ahead, Mark argued that we couldn't carry on. Even if it meant going back past all those rapids to get to town, we had no choice but to get more supplies. Although I rather agreed with him, I opposed the idea because I didn't trust him to return to the jungle afterwards. I preferred to press on and cope as best we could, rather than give him the opportunity to pull out.

I did my best to be solicitous and supportive to the invalid but I grew to resent the gulf between his macho posturing and the feeble way he was prepared to give up after only five weeks. One day I blurted out what I really thought, which led to four days without exchanging a word: cooking our own meals, boiling individual hot drinks, going about our business without so much as a grunt – a triumph of pig-headedness in a jungle clearing of no more than 9 square yards.

Finally we sat down and talked it over. Mark vowed that he was keen to continue up the Jari once we were properly equipped, and I relented and agreed that we'd have to go back downstream and buy supplies. So after hiding some equipment in the bushes for our return, we paddled down to the little settlement of Carecaru where we arranged to leave the canoe with a homesteader. While we were inquiring about the chances of finding a gold prospectors' canoe going downstream, a plane arrived at the airstrip bringing a team of geologists, and we successfully begged a flight down to Monte Dourado.

Mark had his foot treated at the hospital in Belém, but two days later he too suffered an attack of falciparum malaria. Frankly, I doubt if he'd ever intended going back up the Jari, but this illness provided him with just the excuse he needed. So that was it. He now planned to go up to the States and continue his trip round the world. The Amazon had been interesting but it was time to move on. As for me, I had gear at Burnt Foot Camp, the canoe at Carecaru, and no hope of continuing the journey on my own.

We parted none too amicably and I headed upriver for Manaus and my flight home, on the way meeting a young, bespectacled Swiss backpacker named Peter Strub.

'I'd like to go up the Jari with you,' he said one day as we sat on the roof to escape the fetid bowels of the riverboat.

I looked at him with suspicion. 'What makes you think you'd like it?'

'I've really no idea,' he answered honestly. 'I've never paddled a canoe before, but I'm an outdoors type, done lots of climbing and stuff. I like animals and wildlife. I can swim. I'm a very good cook.' He laughed and lifted his arms in a shrug. 'What more can I say?'

I didn't know how to reply. My instincts told me he'd be all right, but the experience with Mark had left me cynical of youthful enthusiasm. Anaemic and jaded after another attack of malaria I'd begun to reconcile myself to going home, cheered somewhat by the thought of luxury and self-indulgence. The idea of donning the hair shirt of spartan, celibate, ascetic jungle life again seemed a poor alternative.

Peter was insistent. 'Look,' he argued. 'You chose Mark despite your doubts, right?' I nodded. 'Would he have come out to Amazonia if he hadn't met you? No. So he wasn't really interested in this part of the world.'

I remained silent, staring over the huge brown river, the wind of our passage drying the sweat on my brow for what seemed like the first time in Brazil. Peter persisted with his job application.

'Well, I'm interested enough to be here already, and I intended doing some sort of river trip. So I think you should take me.'

By the time the boat reached Manaus I'd recovered enough energy and enthusiasm to be persuaded. After buying provisions, treating my malaria and enjoying a little rest, we flew to Santarém, took a riverboat to Monte Dourado, and then an eleven day journey by *garimpeiro* canoe reunited us with our own. We healed its cuts and scrapes with our new supplies of fibreglass and then paddled off upstream for the next four months.

You know the rest.

I'm sure Raymond Maufrais would have relished even the dullest of companions:

This is a bad day today. I try in vain to excuse myself on the grounds that I'm tired, or that my feet hurt, or that I simply have to take a day off in order to start in better trim tomorrow. It's not fatigue though, or my feet, or my need of rest, that makes me linger on, dreaming and writing in my hammock. It's just plain homesickness, and it's come to stay. Ah, it's not easy to dominate that feeling when you're alone... My solitude weighs on me — especially in the evening when I think of the joys of the scout campfire, when we sang the whole night through. Bobby is a good companion and an affectionate one; but his eyes, though expressive, haven't much to say to me.

In desperation Heather and I retraced our steps back along the first part of the trail to convince ourselves we really had seen a bare-flanked mountain through the trees. There it was again, and it seemed relatively near.

'Let's pack the tent and some food and keep chopping till we hit the damn thing,' I suggested. 'That way we'll find out what it is, and won't waste so much time returning to camp every night.'

Carrying food for a week, the shotgun, tent, and some emergency medical supplies we set off the next day. By late afternoon we'd crossed a large stream, that at 10 feet wide and 2 feet deep wasn't much smaller than the Mapaoni that we'd left behind. Its presence added to our confusion but we seized the opportunity to float in its coolness and send grimy soapsuds downstream.

The lightweight dome tent was cramped and airless, and would have been small for just one of us. I could feel Heather's naked thigh against my own in unwelcome intimacy and shifted away, peeling apart our clammy skin with a sound like Velcro. How could my body produce so much sweat? I recoiled from an odour that wasn't like normal BO, more a sickly-sweet effluent, as impurities and toxins, fats and proteins, sebum and subcutaneous junk were flushed out of the pores to fester on the surface.

Heather suddenly woke with a yelp of pain and scrabbled around for the torch. A large ant had clamped her earlobe with forcep jaws. It was a soldier leaf-cutter, and the tent was swarming with its fellows.

'Why's there always some insect screwing things up?' Heather hissed, as we shook all our bedding outside, then swatted a hundred ants that remained in the tent. They'd chewed a small hole through the groundsheet to get in, and we doused the area in Saddam Hussein's special recipe to deter them from returning.

Settling down again, I told Heather of the only practical use for a soldier leaf-cutter ant. 'If you've cut yourself badly but don't have any sutures you can catch a few of those ants, push the edges of the gash together and get them to lock on with one jaw on either side of the wound. It hurts and it bleeds, but then you have the pleasure of pinching their heads off afterwards.'

'I'd enjoy that.'

As they take leaves underground to prepare a compost that nurtures an edible fungal growth, the leaf-cutter's passion for nylon makes no sense. On past trips we've had clothing and packs ruined by their nibbling, and we were lucky we'd caught them in time to save the tent.

One of the climbs the following day went up and up, developing into the longest ascent so far. At the top we sat down for a rest, and I automatically searched in a shirt pocket for my tobacco pouch until I remembered that that little avenue of pleasure was now closed off. Feeling fidgety, I told Heather to stay put while I explored ahead along the ridge. That way I could foray around without marking my route, and she could guide me back to the trail when she heard me calling.

I followed a long ridge, ducking and weaving around the obstacles, forcing my way through at a brisk pace, conscious that when I wandered off like this I was rarely gone more than fifteen minutes. But the ground still sloped gently up and I had to see the summit. Then ahead of me came sunlight through the trees, windows of blue sky, and with growing excitement I passed through a zone of thinning shrubs, patches of rock and clumps of bamboo until suddenly I was out in the open, eyes squinting from the glare. On three sides sheer cliffs dropped 200 feet or more. I was standing on a rock pulpit with miles and miles of forest undulating below me.

Conscious that I'd already been gone nearly an hour I snatched a quick look around, noticing a little marker left by human hand on one of the rocks, then ran all the way back as fast as the creepers and uncut jungle would allow me. When I felt I'd covered about the right distance, I stopped and yelled Heather's name.

No reply.

'HEATHER!'

Silence. Just the beating of my heart and the mocking jungle noises.

'Poor little white boy,' cooed some doves. 'Lost and alone!'

'Lost! Lost! Lost!' shrieked a macaw.

What had I done wrong? Had I strayed on to another ridge? Should I push ahead or retrace my steps? Had I gone too far, or not far enough?

Better to go forward first, I thought, trying to control a panicky trot, conscious that later I might need all my energy, aware that I was already parched with thirst and my stomach was empty. I wanted to yell Heather's name every few paces like some lovesick fool, but I made myself wait until I'd walked for five minutes.

Then I stopped, muttered a prayer, drew in a huge lungful and screamed. 'HEATHERRRRRRRR!'

'Over here,' replied a conversational voice, and looking to the right I saw her calmly sitting on the ground 15 feet away.

I gave her a huge hug that left a sweaty imprint on her dry clothing, gibbered incomprehensibly a little, drained a water bottle, and then told her the good news.

Marking our way with a few chops of the machete we returned to the glorious summit of brown grass, small shrubs and black rock, and stripped off our sodden clothes to reveal grimy bodies of an under-the-flagstones pallor. Eyes used to focusing 15 feet ahead in the dark forest had trouble coping with sunlit infinity.

I called Heather over to a little patch on one of the flat expanses of rock. About a foot square, it stood 3 inches proud of the surrounding granite.

'It's been made with cement. Cement and chippings collected from around here. Who the hell would come poncing around here with a bag of Blue Circle?'

Set in the middle was a small, round, button-like object. 'It's some kind of marker, but it doesn't say anything that I can make sense of.'

We stared at it in frustration. It had Paris stamped on one side, a French name above that, and the number sixteen stamped twice on either side of a depression in the centre. Someone had been up here and taken the trouble to insert this into a rock, but who? How long ago? Was this Temomairem?

'Probably arrived by helicopter,' I guessed. 'Nobody's going to carry cement around if they're on foot. There's enough space for one to land here.'

Heather got bored with my prattle about the logistics of carrying building materials around the Guiana Shield and moved to the edge of the cliff to enjoy the magnificent view. Apart from an impressive molar-shaped mountain slightly north-west of us, we were standing on the highest point in the vicinity. Range after range of forested hills surrounded us in every direction, rolling away to the horizon. Several of the slopes had natural clearings where no soil covered the black rock, but there were no spirals of smoke from distant Indian villages or other signs of man.

I studied the map closely, trying to spot landmarks that might tell us where we were. That tall peak ahead, that should be marked, and the one we were standing on might show the cliffs. Over there, 4 miles to the west, was a totally bare sugarloaf of a peak...

Suddenly I had it, and let out a whoop of excitement that had Heather running over.

'I know where we are! Hee hee! I know where we are!' and laughing manically, I caught her up in my arms and danced a naked jig. She laughed with me but her eyes narrowed with concern. Had I finally flipped?

'Look at the map here,' I panted when I'd calmed down. 'This isn't Temomairem – we're one range of hills away from it. That's Temomairem over there.' I pointed due east to an unremarkable hill that had patches of rock showing like black tarmac through brown grass.

'And that big mountain ahead is Paloulouiméenpeú, the highest around here at 707. We're here,' I tapped the map, 'on this unnamed peak marked as 527 metres high. See the shading of the cliffs around the summit? And this clinches it. That sugarloaf far over there is Maloulekountop.'

Our faces ached from unaccustomed smiling.

'So we must have passed the true start of the trail,' Heather said. 'Gone a mile or so too far along the Mapaoni and got on the wrong succession of hills and ridges.'

'Right. And that big stream we crossed yesterday was the Mapaoni again. See how it loops around here? And those higher hills over to the east must be the Massif de Mitaraca.'

'And that's what we kept on seeing far away through the trees,' she nodded at the imposing bulk of Paloulouiméenpeú. 'Its height and bare brown slopes make it visible for miles.'

We stopped babbling and stared about us. My eyes swung north trying to imagine the route we would be following. I was still excited, but other feelings were present too. Relief, certainly. But the view showed us all too clearly where we were.

In about as near to the middle of nowhere as it's possible to be.

CHAPTER SEVEN

After two weeks in the Tumucumaque we'd progressed about 5 miles, at an average speed of 700 yards a day. In Raymond's words, 'a tortoise could do as much', but what the hell? We'd evidently left the Mapaoni in the wrong spot, but were less than a mile off course, and that seemed an acceptable margin of error hereabouts.

'We'll have to make a detour back up here and take some pics. This place is fantastic,' said Heather, staring out over the cliff edge, naked as an Amazon warrior. A hundred and fifty feet below us the forest canopy rose and fell as it followed the contours of the land 100 feet lower still. A few emergent trees thrust themselves clear, and one species was flowering in pale mauve. Birds, agoutis, bats or the wind had dispersed its seeds most effectively; they were spaced at regular intervals throughout the valley below us.

Our sweat-drenched, filthy clothing was being aired on the rocks and within fifteen minutes had stiffened in a rigor mortis of encrusted dirt. The folds and crevices of my body seemed to dry out for the first time since we left the Mapaoni, and a gust of wind even managed to stir the lank hair on my head.

A couple of evenings before, I'd gone down to the little stream near our camp taking a saucepan to scoop up water and give myself a sluicing. The tiny brook somehow managed to have a bed of firm white sand but flowed through a swamp with margins of treacly peat, meaning that most of the benefits of the wash were annulled in the short walk back. As I undressed, sinking slowly into the mire, a sudden rank odour of wild beast made me whirl around in fear. It was one of those gamey whiffs that waft out from zoo cages where carnivores lie asleep in concrete corners and gnawed bones litter the floor. Was I was being stalked? I scanned the undergrowth for a crouching beast. Nothing there that I could see, but the odour still hung in the air, animal and pungent. Only later when I lifted my arm to soap the armpit did I realise the wild animal pong was coming from me.

Heather had a head of Medusa curls that could well have contained a snake or two; my beard was growing into a gingery fungal growth; our bodies were a dirty white, and our clothes had dried with white salt rings that marked the high tide of past sweats, and assorted stains of food, sap and general filth. I'd started the trip with an impractical pair of white tennis socks that were now brown and exiled by Heather to spend their nights a long way from the tent. I forced my feet into them, the sun having baked them to the consistency of old leather.

'We'd better get a move on.'

We didn't want to leave the sunlight and return to the claustrophobia of the forest, but the sun was beginning its descent. I looked across the valley at Paloulouiméenpeú, rearing up almost devoid of forest cover except for a thin band of trees halfway up. It would be quite an easy scramble once you'd cut across the expanse of jungle floor to its base.

'Maybe we should make a detour and climb that,' I suggested.

Heather stopped pulling on her boots. 'John Harrison,' she said sternly. 'Don't you think we've got enough on our plate without making 'detours' as you call them to climb extra hills?'

'Might never have been climbed before, that's all.'

'We'd probably find that it's covered in little concrete monuments, because if a helicopter managed to land here it could certainly land over there. The French will have beaten you to it.'

Before we returned to the jungle we stood over the little sign on the rock at our feet.

'16. CLAYOLET. PARIS. 16.'

What did it mean?

The next morning we crawled stiff and cramped from the tent, breakfasted on porridge and coffee, and began cutting north-eastwards; first crossing the valley floor with a large area of swamp to our left, then starting to climb. Soon we were hauling ourselves up on saplings among rocky outcrops, until our way was finally blocked by a wall of rock 20 feet high.

As there were few handholds and the vegetation looked impenetrable at the top, we followed the base of the cliff around the mountainside, walking in the shade of the overhang where the rain never fell. It would have been a fine place to camp but for the absence of water. There were shallow caves where we expected to see blackened walls from camp fires, skeletons, a jaguar playing with her cubs, or at the very least some graffiti: *'Jules Crevaux. May 1871'* or *'Raymond Maufrais était ici 1950'*. After circling half the summit we found a cleft in the outcrop that we could scramble up.

Two days before we'd have been ecstatic about the view, but the previous day on '527' had spoilt us. Here the panorama was largely obscured by trees; only on the north-western tip could we step out into the sunlight and it showed us little that we hadn't seen much better already. Below was the brown patch of open ground where the trail would cross, but we were sure that any Europeans who had passed this way would have been drawn up here looking for signs of other travellers, or to leave a mark of their own, so we scouted around in the undergrowth. Crevaux's empty champagne bottle would make a fine souvenir.

'I would have loved to have lingered a little on this crest of the Tumuc Humac,' he wrote, 'but the Indians pointed out that we lacked that indispensable element: water. I didn't want to leave this important spot that separates the Maroni Basin from that of the Amazon without leaving some sign of my passing. I carried in my baggage a last bottle of champagne that I'd wrapped protectively and kept for the baptism of the mountain, to which, in memory of my native land, I gave the name Lorquin. The empty bottle will serve as a testament to the first passing of a Frenchman through this unknown region.'

Also, somewhere on Temomairem there might be a marker stone erected when the border was demarcated. That's what the map seemed to indicate, and that would be the best possible proof that we had truly found our way.

We almost missed the only sign of man that was there: a piece of artificially grey stone peeking out from a mat of soil, roots and grass, not black enough to be the natural igneous rock. I chopped and pared the undergrowth away and there was a little cement slab about one foot square.

'*MISSION. 21. 11. 37. P5. BIS FRANÇAISE*' was what it appeared to say. Fractured by the power of the roots that had engulfed it, some letters were indistinct. November 1937. Less than two years before the outbreak of the Second World War some French soldiers on an exercise had crouched here, sacrificed some water, and mixed a mortar, just for the purpose of writing in it. These French Kilroys were obviously in a different league. The roots would certainly cover it all up again before anyone else came this way.

It had been a long day without food and water and we returned to our tent parched and giddy. The stream was several hundred yards away downhill, and clambering back up with two full water containers finished us off. We lay in the dirt staring up at the graceful fronds of a nearby assai palm, replacing lost fluids with water laced with sugar and salt until strength returned and we felt energetic enough to build a fire before nightfall.

Unlike most other species of palms, the assai always looks glossy and green because it sheds dead fronds immediately. The clusters of fruit hanging date-like from the crown were still green, but when they turn purple and grow to the size of a small grape they can be grated and boiled up into a delicious drink that is rich in iron and reportedly an aphrodisiac. Maybe we should go in search of some and reawaken our dormant sexual drive? Tomorrow maybe. More importantly, what's for supper?

We spoilt a plate of rice with one of our dried dinners, and were asleep by 7 p.m.

The following day we returned to the base of the cliffs, but this time continued round them rather than climb up the cleft to the summit. Soon we saw the open expanse ahead, but the transition zone between the jungle and the grass and rock was a foul tangle of bamboo, thorns and twisted shrub that needed an hour and a half of frenzied machete work. Then we stepped out into the sunlight.

The high grass was burnt brown and grew in clumps between expanses of black rock. Three hundred yards of open space stretched ahead, looking like the Great Plains to our close-focused eyes, dropping away gently to our right, and further up the hill to our left the jungle started again. The rocky summit where we'd been the day before was behind us. The bare rock patches sounded hollow under our feet and had sloughed off in thin sheets, like the layers of an onion, from baking in the pitiless sun and then cooling at night. Wearing only our boots we explored, searching for any sign of man, but only found three stones piled together to form a miniature cairn, and a large sun-whitened turd that could have been deposited by man or dog, but was probably a jaguar's. No rubbish, no graffiti and no marker stone.

We squatted down beside the apology of a cairn, the stored heat in the rocks scorching our bare buttocks, and I prodded the turd with a stick, breaking it down to a powder, exposing what looked like fish bones and clumps of fur.

'There's no actual proof that this is Temomairem,' I muttered, after Heather told me to leave the thing alone.

'Of course it's Temomairem you old curmudgeon,' she countered with a laugh. 'You saw for yourself from 527. Everything tallied with the map.'

She was probably right, but there'd been no actual proof. 'It would just be nice if we could find something to confirm that.'

'What have you got in mind? A map with a 'You Are Here' arrow?' she snorted.

'It's possible of course that the trail never came out here at all,' I reasoned, after we'd explored the clearing and its fringes once more. 'This open space might be psychologically important to us Europeans but the Indians would stay in the forest lower down the flank of the hill. That fringe of bamboo and thorn would deter them.'

Raymond Maufrais' father, Edgar, passed this way in 1952 guided by Indians, and he mentions only one moment where the jungle thinned enough to afford him a view of the Tumucumaque:

We reached the crest of a small rocky mountain which was free of trees and undergrowth and from where we had a fine view of the Tumuc Humac chain ahead of us. We were interested to find a cement slab there with an inscription. I copied it down and I photographed it, but, like everything else, copy and film are lying on the bed of the Maroni [due to a later capsize] and I have to trust to memory. I believe that the reference was to Heckenroch the geographer, and that the stone marked the Koulimapopane, or meeting of three trails.

This doesn't sound like Temomairem at all, and the hill of Koulimapopane was still ahead of us, also called the Point de Trijonction where Brazil, Surinam and French Guiana meet. Crevaux's hill that he had toasted with bubbly could also have been Koulimapopane. So it seemed possible that this bare flank of hill was a diversion that the Indians didn't usually bother with. And why should anyone demarcating the border go to the trouble of commemorating this hill that was still several miles from the frontier? It seemed more likely that there'd be a marker and an abundance of grafitti on Koulimapopane.

As the day was still young we hacked our way through another belt of bamboo into the jungle on the other side of the clearing and calculated the likely new compass bearing. The land dropped precipitously so we cut a zigzag route that we knew was going to be murder to descend when we had heavy loads on our backs. Then the going got easier for a mile until the land dropped once again into a valley with enough level ground, stout trees and water to fulfil our criteria for a campsite. This could be Camp Two.

We set off at first light to collect our first load from Camp One. This bit was fine; an unladen stroll in the jungle of early morning, gazing around us in curiosity, light on our feet, feeling cool and content. My right elbow was inflamed from the thousands of cuts that had opened each mile of trail and I couldn't straighten the arm; I walked along with the forearm parallel to the ground as if about to shake hands.

A few hours later we were back, stumbling and tripping, lungs rasping, clothing pasted to our bodies, staring fixedly at the ground ahead, with loads on our backs that snagged in the undergrowth and toppled us off balance. Raymond described the feeling:

Walking in the forest means bending your back beneath the knapsack, tottering, slithering, falling full length, or grabbing hold of a tree and finding it's full of sharp spines! You take hold of another, and it's rotten and leaves you covered with red ants; you skirt one liana and fall into another; you put your foot on a trunk and it gives way and lands you in water up to your knees.

There were some particularly awful stretches: the river crossing where we had to remove boots and trousers, carry the packs in our arms diagonally across the stream, squeezing under one fallen tree, and clambering over another; the climb up to Temomairem and the climb down again, and the thorny stretch on either side of the open clearing where we hadn't been able to hack a good path and where creepers and thorns would ensnare one of us until the other returned to offer assistance.

It was a relief to find the last camp undisturbed after our seven-day absence. Human interference was unlikely, but a herd of wild pigs could have sniffed out the sacks of food and caused mayhem, or leaf-cutter ants carted the plastic wrapping away.

One of the few advantages of these backpacking days of moving gear, if we managed to complete the trip back and forth by two o'clock, was to snatch a few hours off, swinging in our hammocks, reading or sleeping. Decadent stuff. Military commanders would have had us polishing our boots, powdering our crotches or whitewashing the surrounding tree trunks to fill the time.

For reading material we would have liked undemanding thrillers, sagas, horror stories, science fiction; anything that wouldn't tax our underused brains, but such books could be read too quickly and we were restricted in what we could carry. So intellectually weightier tomes had been chosen instead. The interesting *A History of the World* by M. Roberts covered everything from the origins of life to the modern day, but had to be absorbed in small, digestible pieces. My progress through it has been so slow that it's actually been on three Amazon expeditions with me and I've only just reached the Middle Ages. *Tales from the Arabian Nights* was another good read, but slightly repetitive after a while. The least read was an anthology of poetry that we'd chosen so that we could memorise our favourites.

Mark, my Australian companion in 1983, had selected Debrett's *Etiquette and Modern Manners*. This was a bizarre book to read in a jungle setting, or anywhere else. Unwashed, uncombed and uncouth we learnt the appropriate way of tackling an artichoke, how to address minor members of the aristocracy, the duties of a bridesmaid, or what dress to wear at the Henley Regatta.

Heather's civilising influence kept some of my baser instincts under control, but men on their own in the forest quickly lose that thin veneer of manners and civility, reverting to scratching, belching, spitting, flatulent, nose-picking slobs, and Debrett gave us plenty of chuckles. It was like reading an anthropological account of the rituals of some strange and distant tribe, and they don't come much stranger than the English middle classes getting hung up about which fork to use at dinner. It ended its days as surprisingly rough toilet paper, and I've been tempted to write to the publishers and complain.

Of course there was always Raymond's journal if we really wanted to be transported far away. By now he was fighting a constant battle to feed himself:

The forest is still oddly empty. Bobby, his stomach hollow, his ribs sticking out, shows his tongue and whines. Poor dog, what an appetite he must have. But he's more than once lost me a good target. He knows how to smell out the prey, but he can't bring it into position. He just drives it away with his barking. I fired at a bird, and providentially I killed it. I had to fight Bobby for it — he ran to pick it up, got there first, and had already begun to eat it. I just plucked it more or less, took out its insides, and ate it raw, bones and all, leaving only its beak and claws. It wasn't much, but disgusting as it was, I felt myself getting stronger. Fresh meat revived me. I long to drink blood. It's a desire that haunts me and never leaves me. I feel my own strength draining away and long to feed on that of others.

I laid the book down on my knee, and gazed thoughtfully out through the blue net curtains of my mosquito net and there, on cue, saw a curassow come pecking and scratching its way down the hillside. What would have been Raymond's salvation for a couple of days at least (*'I put my rifle to my shoulder and, with my heart beating wildly, I pulled the trigger. Got him! Hurray! I made haste to light a fire and roast one of its legs. I ate it ravenously, and then another leg, and then a wing, and then the other wing... I couldn't stop eating.'*) just woke conflicting emotions in me. I wasn't desperately hungry, but boy, a stew would be nice. The bird was alone and therefore vulnerable in the Harrison Code of Hunting Etiquette, but I let it head off to roost unharmed.

Two mornings later on our way back to the previous camp to pick up a load, stepping lightly and quietly in the dawn freshness, I reached the top of one of the hills and a sound made me pause. Heather caught up and I silenced her with a raised hand. There it was again: a movement in the vegetation and a low squealing and grunting.

'Peccaries,' I decided, and as the sounds had come from our right and not along our path, we continued walking cautiously across the flat summit.

The white-lipped peccary (*queixada*) of the pig family can stand 3 feet tall at the shoulder and weigh over a hundred pounds. They get their name from the white on the under-jaw and lower cheek, and we'd heard enough of the *queixada* to treat them with respect. A new arrival to Amazonia, as the French photographer Yves Manciet had been in 1966, could view their threat differently. He was out shooting with a Brazilian hunter one day when he noticed that the latter was looking anxious:

'Something in the jungle was not normal: the silence, an oppressive silence.

'Perhaps we'd better go back,' he said.

The words were hardly out of his mouth when we heard a muffled sound, like a distant thunder approaching.

'Quick – up a tree – it's *queixadas*!'

His face had gone white, and after a quick glance around him he ran for a tree that was easy to climb.

Until that moment I had only seen one *queixada*, in Belém Zoo: it was an animal as big as a large pig that liked having his back scratched. He would come up to the fence for this, and when anyone obliged he would close his little eyes and grunt with pleasure. I had no intention of fleeing before a thing like that. I slipped a bullet into the chamber of my .22 and waited – but not for long, for soon the gaps in the trees about 50 yards away darkened with a moving stream of brown.

I realised what an idiot I had been and leapt towards the first tree I could find.'

As Heather and I crossed the flat top of the hill, the jungle suddenly burst into a startling eruption of stampeding feet, smashing vegetation, squeals, clicks and snorts of alarm. Shaking vegetation showed that some animals were passing only a few yards away, but neither of us actually saw a pig. Eventually the commotion ceased, leaving an acrid musky smell hanging in the air, like a men's changing room magnified a thousandfold.

'I guess they smelt us,' I commented lamely with a shaky smile.

'There must have been over a hundred of them!' said Heather in awe. 'Did you hear those tusks clicking!'

Peccaries have a reputation for being the most aggressive creature in Amazonia: the males having 5-inch tusks that they rattle by vibrating the lower jaw with extraordinary speed. The herds can be very large. On the river Napo in Ecuador the explorer F. W. Up de Graff watched a herd that he estimated to be two thousand in number, swimming across the river in a black mass at a point where it was 300 yards wide. When the leaders were climbing the far bank, those in the rear were still streaming into the water on the other side.

Reassured that this herd had run away from our trail, we carried on our way. On the way back, three hours later, we were descending into a valley when the jungle once again exploded with splashing and stampeding pigs as they left the river or raced across it. It was even more frightening this time as they'd been silent until we were right upon them, and the whole herd had been concentrated just in front of us. We saw why. A large area had been rooted over and churned up and the mud was dented where they'd lain to pass the heat of the day. The smell was nauseating. Peccaries possess a large oily gland on their backs a few inches in front of their tails and when the pig is angry, frightened or sexually aroused, the erect hair on the back exposes the gland.

After fording the river we loitered in the valley bottom for more than an hour, giving them time to move off, trying to work out a strategy for handling a pig attack. The herd had raced back up the hill where we'd disturbed them first, and there is probably a limit to the amount of times that peccaries will consent to being pushed around in this way.

'We could shrug the packs off, find a large tree to lean against, and use the packs to protect our fronts,' I suggested. Heather looked dubious, and who could blame her.

'Personally, I'd prefer to get up a tree than play matador with a succession of charging peccaries. It wouldn't take long for one to shove the pack aside and knock our legs from under us, and then it would be like feeding time around the slop bucket.'

Amazon trees tend to have smooth trunks and no convenient low branches to pull oneself up on. The creepers on the other hand would be strong enough to hold our weight. We practised shinning up a few, but Heather's arms tired easily and it was unlikely that she'd be able to hang on long enough.

'Mind you, with a hundred stampeding pigs below me, I'm sure I'd find amazing reserves of strength!'

Each choosing a hefty piece of wood to use as a club, we continued reluctantly up the trail to face an inevitable porcine confrontation, yelling fiercely to let them know we were coming. The jungle was impregnated with a musk that was probably the basic ingredient of those aftershaves that are supposed to drive women wild, but Heather seemed immune. I was getting the impression that even a couple of buckets of the stuff poured over me wouldn't make me sexually attractive to her these days.

We reached the top of the hill and were beginning to relax when it happened again. Pigs to the left of us and pigs to the right, the tusk clicking sounding like a demented flamenco troupe in full swing. There was the usual rushing to and fro and the trampling of vegetation, but the squealing and snorting had subtly changed, or so it seemed to our nervous ears. Before, it had been a panicked alarm call but now it seemed more defiant; a call intended to intimidate us rather than warn each other.

In other circumstances we would have gone straight back to camp and left them alone, or made a long detour through the bush to keep well clear, but there was no tent or hammocks at the camp behind us, and we couldn't run the risk of leaving our trail and possibly never finding it again. We had to carry on.

The peccaries hadn't raced off this time. They were still on the hilltop, milling about in confusion, so the males hadn't led them all away. We walked slowly forward, peering anxiously into the undergrowth and whispering instructions to each other. I suddenly saw them and pointed to four dark shapes that stood facing us about 30 feet away. They were large and angry males that rattled tusks and squealed threateningly, and it was clear from their posture that they weren't going to be pushed around any more.

They were standing 3 yards to the right of the trail. If we approached nearer we'd provoke a charge, so we moved parallel to the trail through the bushes, keeping it within sight but increasing the gap between us and the pigs that we could see. What the rest of the herd were doing we couldn't tell, we'd just concentrate on these four for the moment.

All was going well when a sudden rush of movement on our other flank threw us into a total funk. We'd been whispering encouragement and pinpointing certain trees to run for in times of crisis, but the drumming of feet from this unexpected quarter made us dash for cover. Trying to shrug off huge packs while we ran, at the same time keeping an eye on each other, and still waving our ineffectual clubs menacingly, we must have looked a comical pair. Fortunately we were near the protection of a giant tree that had plank buttress roots curving out in front of it, and in our scramble to get there we saw a small pig run out of the bushes, squeal with alarm when it saw us and veer away. It hadn't been a charge after all, but the safety of the buttress roots seemed too good to leave. We squeezed in with our backs to the tree, the high roots protecting our flanks, and there was only a 3-foot wide opening that we could block with our packs. We could fend off a serious attack with our clubs from there.

A single male peccary came slowly towards us, the bristles along its back erect, its posture stiff-legged and its white tusks chattering. Its small eyes stared at us and when it halted less than 10 feet away we held our breath and stared back. It snorted angrily, as if to admonish us for not having the guts to come out and fight, then turned away to join its fellows.

We squatted in our shelter for another hour.

'We took a hell of a gamble back there,' I said.

'Mmmm,' Heather muttered. 'Scary stuff. But how I wish we'd had the gun and could have shot one of them!'

Our appetite was increasing as the fear passed away. On another expedition we'd killed a smaller species, a collared peccary, and roasted it over a fire on an improvised spit. For three days we gorged, waddling with distended guts from our hammocks to hack off some more, tossing the gnawed bones over our shoulder into the bush. The meat was lean, with none of the fat of domestic pork, and it had been a magnificent orgy of gluttony that made us feel quite ill.

And what of the photographer Yves Manciet who we left up a tree?

'I was astride a branch when they arrived, and only then did I realise I had chosen my tree badly, for this one had thorns as thick as my thumb all the way up its trunk, and I was covered with blood.

As I was bleeding profusely, the creatures had picked up my scent and were forming a circle round the tree, peering upwards and clicking their jaws together.

Two hours later they were still there. Then I noticed that they were nosing about for truffles. With their enormous tusks they were rapidly digging up the earth round the foot of the tree – and all of a sudden I realised the danger. In the Amazon the trees have horizontal roots, for the layer of soil where they find their nourishment is hardly ever more than eighteen inches deep.'

Manciet then began shooting, and had to kill thirty-four before the remainder of the herd finally moved away.

I once opened a copy of *The Times* and came across the eye-catching headline 'ROTTWEILER SAVAGED BY PECCARY'. Some vandals had released four peccaries from a wildlife park, and while three were quickly recaptured, the fourth 'seven-stone hog from South America' caused some excitement at Herne Bay in Kent. Ian Hossick, 47, a publican, was walking his dogs when they pursued the peccary, and a fight started. 'It was like a maniac with a cutlass on the loose,' Hossick said. 'I hit it several times with a piece of wood but it simply shook itself and got up.' His 11-stone mastiff needed 120 stitches and his 10-stone Rottweiler, 50.

We had just dumped our loads at camp when that same curassow came pecking its way down to the stream, lifting its feet fastidiously, heading to its favourite roost. We'd seen it the last four evenings and left it alone, but now I took the shotgun and headed towards it, making it peet nervously. By keeping out of sight behind tree trunks I was able to get 15 feet away and crouched on the ground. The bird cocked its head and watched me, and as I was silent and still, it calmed down and its anxious peeting diminished.

I wanted the meat, and now that we were away from rivers and the possibility of fish there was some justification in thinking that our bodies needed more protein than they were getting. Our food sacks were emptying fast and my belt buckle had advanced four holes, but could I pretend we were hungry? Bored with our stodgy diet, certainly, but it wasn't really necessary to shoot this amiable bird:

> I'm visibly thinner, I can feel my heart beating wildly, I'm always out of breath, I totter to and fro, I find even the rifle immensely heavy, and when I try to take aim I shake from head to foot.

That was Raymond's hunger, and Peter and I had experienced something similar in 1983.

The curassow strolled behind a large tree and out of sight, and I let fate decide for me. If it emerged in view nearer to me than before I would shoot; if it was further away I wouldn't. I waited and willed it to fly away, but it made a bad choice. Round the side of the tree it came, and I cocked the gun and shot it dead. At least at that range it was instantaneous, and I took it back to camp and busied myself making supper, feeling suddenly tearful, vision wobbling as I wrenched the feathers from the warm body, and inserted my hand to extract the guts. I shall leave the gun behind next time, I thought, if I get so upset every time I use it.

Later, when I'd started cooking, I pulled a pot of bubbling oil and sizzling garlic off the fire to stop it burning, and a slight movement caught my eye in the patch of leaves just before the hot base of the pan landed upon it.

'Oh, Lord,' I muttered, and lifted the pot quickly away to expose the thrashing agonies of a brown frog, whose perfect mimicry of a fallen leaf had been its downfall, and which I had to finish off with the heel of my boot.

Tears welled up again, and I turned my face away so Heather wouldn't see, torturing myself with memories of other times when my hunting had left wounded monkeys that I held under water to drown... or when I'd fired at what I thought was a grey dove to find I'd killed a gorgeous fluffy owlet... the time I'd shot at a giant otter thinking the surfacing head was a capybara (and fortunately missed)... of the paca whose jaw I shot away...

Enough, enough. As the curassow pieces grilled over the hot embers I made an effort to think of less traumatic incidents. One time I'd shot a curassow at dusk, but by the time the bird was plucked and gutted it had started to rain too hard to mess about with sodden firewood for most of the night while it cooked. Heather noticed me stowing it in the folds of the mosquito net underneath my hammock.

'Are you sure that's wise, putting it so near you?'

'I'm worried the ants and bugs will get all over it. The net will keep 'em out until morning.'

'What about the cats who might be attracted by the smell of fresh meat?'

'That's a thought. I doubt if a cat would come that near, but maybe I'll stick it in the canoe instead.'

The canoe was moored about 12 feet away from our hammocks with the stern pointing out into the river. We had a plywood canoe on that trip and it had small decks that covered the first 2 feet of bow and stern. I walked down the canoe and wedged the plucked bird into the stern under the decking.

In the morning I went to retrieve it but it had gone. On examination I saw large pug prints leading to and from the canoe. While we slept a jaguar or puma had climbed into the canoe, walked to the far end, hooked out the bird and carried it away.

'Aren't you pleased you didn't have it under your hammock now?' asked Heather.

Dead right. It also made us wonder just what visitations we had to our camps while we slept peacefully with the fire out. This cat must have thought it was his lucky day. No feathers, no guts: just an oven-ready bird for the taking.

I smiled faintly at the memory, pushing my sadness back.

After collecting the final items from the previous camp we made a detour to get some photos from the top of 527 Mountain. It was going to be a long and tiring day so we left at dawn and carried rice and curassow pieces for lunch. Reaching the spot where the trails forked, we dumped our packs and continued with camera equipment, food and water. We had two cameras: the SLR with its zoom lenses, and a compact waterproof that was more robust.

'How are they for batteries?' Heather asked.

'Oh fine,' I replied as I selected three films of different speeds to take along. I'd used both cameras the day before and they'd been OK.

We climbed the large hill, and followed its ridge upwards. As the vegetation thinned we called out in case a jaguar had chosen that sunlit place to catch the breeze. By coming from our direction we'd be cornering it on the cliff top, forcing it to rush at us or squeeze past, and we'd had enough animal encounters for that week.

All was quiet.

The summit seemed just as magical as the last time, and our clothing came off again just as fast. We picnicked on the rocks beside that enigmatic marker, and Heather prodded the central disc with a knife. Suddenly it came loose and she prised it out and peered at it.

'Of course! How thick!'

'What? Have you worked out what it is?'

'It's the metal base of a shotgun cartridge isn't it? Look, here's the central percussion cap and those numbers – it's a sixteen-gauge.'

Those Frenchmen had gone to their usual lengths to mark their passing. We were content to scratch our initials and the date on the rock, but it was unlikely to last more than a few years.

A manufacturer had donated some clothing to test out in the jungle and wanted some pictures of us wearing it in exotic settings for publicity purposes. Unfortunately we had now been wearing the trousers day and night for weeks, and the colour was undetectable under the encrusted dirt. Also, the bottom 12 inches of our trouser legs were shredded from tangling on the cut stems of saplings. Manufacturers like pictures of their garments in wild settings with dramatic backdrops, but somehow clean, still creased from the wrapper, with the colour still visible and not obscured by filth.

Maybe this company would be more discerning. We dressed reluctantly, mounted the SLR on the small tripod, set the timer and moved into position to have the best views behind us. After two pictures the camera stopped working. All the sophisticated metering faded on the LED display and the shutter froze open.

'What's wrong with it?' Heather demanded.

'I don't know,' I said. I hadn't owned the complicated piece of Japanese wizardry for the necessary five years to get the basic idea of how it worked.

'Check the battery,' she suggested.

I pressed the appropriate button, and it showed that the battery was completely exhausted. So was Heather's patience.

'Oh for God's sake! Didn't I ask you if they were all right? We've got five replacement batteries for this camera in our packs down there, so why are you so mean with them? I asked you to check it, didn't I? Didn't I?' she shouted.

I nodded, and hung my head like a whipped cur.

'We'll just have to use the other camera, but the 35mm lens makes everything seem so far away. Honestly! Our one opportunity to get some superb pictures, and you're too bloody careless to check if the camera's in working order!'

I put the waterproof compact on the tripod, set the timer and went over to stand as near to Heather as I dared.

The shutter clicked and the film automatically wound on, but very arthritically. I hoped Heather hadn't heard the slow grind, but she was on to it.

Pressing the shutter again she listened to it advancing the film at a snail's pace, and glared at me venomously.

'Oh great! Fantastic! Not one camera out of action, but two! Another one needing new batteries! Are you planning on taking all those batteries home or what? Bloody hell!'

'It's still working,' I protested. 'Maybe we can get all the photos we need before it won't wind on any more.'

Some hope. It managed two more shots before the wheezing mechanism came to a halt.

What a mess. It was too far to contemplate going for replacements and we wouldn't be passing this way again. All this marvellous scenery laid out around us: the peak of Paloulouiméenpeú across the valley; the extent of the Tumucumaque spread in all its ancient glory; bare rock and jungle in every direction.

I took the batteries out of the cameras and laid them on the hot rock in the sun, hoping that they would gain some charge from being heated. I kept clear of Heather's wrath and sat and watched a troupe of spider monkeys that had climbed into the bare branches of a tree on the next hill to our left, graceful silhouettes as they installed themselves comfortably to rest. There seemed nothing for them to eat over there, but like us they'd come for the view and to get the warm sun on their fur. Through our little binoculars I saw that two of the females had babies on their backs. They saw us too, and their mournful high call floated across in greeting.

Without much optimism I reloaded the batteries and tried the shutters. Machinery whirred, lights flashed!

'There,' I crowed triumphantly. 'There was no need for you to get so hysterical, or be quite so abusive either. Everything's working fine.'

'Lucky for you,' she said, 'and I don't see why you should take any credit for it!' We laughed in relief and spent an hour taking three rolls of the scene from every angle, and time-exposure shots of ourselves in our unappetising state.

All too soon we had to move on.

'Wouldn't it be great to spend the night up here?' I said. 'Imagine the stars!' But it wasn't possible. We had exhausted our water bottles already and had nothing to sleep on.

Reluctantly we turned our back on the view, but as soon as we entered the trees we realised how late it was. The jungle was already gloomy, and we had miles to go. Walking briskly down to collect our packs, we marched as fast as the loads would allow towards Temomairem.

By the time we got to the cliff it was almost too dark to see, but out on the bare flank we could make our way easily enough. On the edge of the forest we stopped.

'We can either sleep here,' Heather said, 'or carry on with our one torch. Any preferences?'

'Not much of a choice.'

We decided to carry on, as we had nothing to lie on or protect us from the chill, and began a silly stumble through the pitch-black forest, me first taking a few steps with the torch, and then shining it back on the ground for Heather.

There was a steep zigzag descent soon after we started and it was here that I lost my footing. I had moved down and was turning to shine the torch when the weight of my pack upset my balance, my feet slid from underneath me and I went barrelling down the hillside.

Faster and faster I went in a clank of cooking pots, with the weight of the pack speeding me along. I knew from walking above this valley many times that the drop was about a hundred feet, with a nasty area of rock and boulders near the bottom. It was crucial that I stop myself before then.

I still had the torch in my right hand while I scrabbled with the left to slow my rush. I was almost sitting upright as the rucksack didn't let my body lean further back, keeping the beam pointing more or less ahead to see what I might run into.

Run into something I did. In a split second I realised that my feet had taken different routes past a 6-inch diameter sapling, one on either side, and that my crotch was about to get splattered into the bark of its trunk.

My hands flew to my groin and were skinned for their act of sacrifice as I slammed into the tree. Better them than my testicles, but a great deal of the impact reached them and I let out a yell of pain. My hands were trapped between my legs until I could dig my heels in the dirt and ease myself a few inches uphill.

I could hear Heather's worried calls from a long way above me as I lay there too winded and nauseous to reply. I flexed my hands and fingers to check that no bones were broken.

The torch! Oh God, where was the torch? All was dark, and there was no sign of it glowing further down the slope.

'Don't leave the trail!' I called. If Heather wandered down to help me we might not find it again. 'I've lost the bloody torch!'

I hauled myself to my feet and pulled myself up the slope until I reached her.

'You all right?' she asked anxiously.

'Nearly got my balls embedded in the bark of a tree!' I replied, shrugging off the pack, wincing from my sore fingers. 'Greater love hath no hands than to lay down their lives for their friends,' I muttered, but she probably thought I was ranting.

'I'll have to see if I can find the torch. You sure there's not another in one of these packs?'

'No, the other one's at camp.'

'I'll use this cigarette lighter then.'

I let myself slowly down the hill, following the groove in the debris that I'd made earlier. I found the torch near the bottom, but my relief was short-lived – the glass was broken and it didn't work.

I'm not sure now why we didn't just build a fire there and then and curl up on the ground to sleep. Homing instinct I suppose: the strong urge to finish a long day in some sort of comfort. We were hungry too and had no food with us.

In the side pocket of a pack we found a candle, and set off with that held aloft like characters from a Victorian melodrama.

It was very hard to follow the trail and we lost it frequently, casting around for a cut sapling or a scrap of paper. The candle burnt down and we used the lighter from then on, but if I held the flame on for more than thirty seconds it would start burning my thumb, forcing us to pause and let it cool.

We took one of these opportunities to shed our packs and have a break.

'The messes we get ourselves into!' chuckled Heather. 'Blundering around the Tumucumaque in the dark, with just a cigarette lighter!'

'And a lighter that hasn't enough gas to get us back to camp anyhow,' I added.

'Hasn't it?'

'Look.' I showed her the outline of the liquid butane in the transparent plastic.

'What the hell are we trying for then? Let's just sleep.'

We collected a mass of firewood, built a blaze of comforting proportions, and lay down close to keep warm in our damp clothing.

Rarely have we tended a fire with such zeal as we did that night, fearful of snakes and wild beasts. Creepy-crawlies found their way down our shirts or trotted across our faces, jerking us awake.

At some time in the early hours, when the flames had dwindled to a feeble flicker, a large animal came crunching through the leaves towards us and we hastily fanned the fire to new vigour. The footsteps halted and after a tense fifteen minutes we assumed that whatever it was had gone. Almost asleep, we leapt upright as the steps started towards us again, but this time the creature took only half a dozen paces before realising that it was making a mistake, wheeled and bolted.

Our smell had sent it packing. We snuggled up in a malodorous huddle and dozed fitfully until dawn. At least the mosquitoes had the decency to leave us alone.

CHAPTER EIGHT

About an hour before dawn, when it's still cave-dark down in the forest understorey, there's a subtle change in the jungle chorus. Whistles, chirps, whoops, trills and cries that have been present since dusk gradually fade away as a new shift comes on duty. Maybe the tree frogs fall silent, or a new bunch of cicadas scratch out a different rhythm, but in a world without bedside clocks the impatient traveller waits for that transition and the end of another interminable night. Quite a while later, when the stars fade and the tracery of branches is just visible against the lightening sky, howler monkeys, parrots, waterfowl and other less subtle heralds of the new day shatter any remaining peace.

Many times that night we shooed the ants from our faces, panicked at rustlings in the undergrowth, thrashed about in the jungle debris trying to extract stones or twigs from under our hip-bones, or lay worrying about a freshening in the breeze that might signal a tropical downpour. Countless times we willed that change in the insect and amphibian repertoire, only to sigh in impatience and try to sleep again. It seemed the night would never end.

In fact, we missed the dawn chorus altogether, waking to bright daylight and uncomfortably hot in our thick clothes. It must have been nearly 8 a.m., but of course we moaned to each other about not sleeping a wink as we left our leaf-mould bivouac and headed for the luxury of camp. Seldom had the garish Brazilian hammocks looked so inviting. We crawled into their soft cotton embrace, tucked in the mosquito nets and promptly fell asleep.

Four hours later I awoke gasping and gagging and yanked up the net to suck in fresh air. I was slimy with sweat, and the rank stink of unwashed skin and clothing couldn't escape through the fine mesh. Although the Tumucumaque was almost totally free of mosquitoes, my suggestion that we remove the nets had been resisted.

'Anything could come slithering or trotting down the ropes,' Heather argued. 'Snakes, tarantulas, big centipedes, or one of those huge ants you made such a fuss about the other day. Vampire bats could suck us dry. No way am I taking mine off.'

'Well I am,' I said. 'Think of those gentle breezes at night, the stars up there through the branches, the space to stretch out. We could even sleep in the same hammock – these are the 'matrimonial' models after all – and do matrimonial things together.'

'Forget it,' she said with a grimace. 'You can be added to that list of pests that the net keeps away.'

I took my net off anyway, and for an hour or two it was bliss; but then a colossal beetle of aerodynamic incompetence crash-landed with a terrifying buzz and crack of carapace on to my sleeping face, making me leap out with a yell. Heather's giggling went on for a long time, and the next night the net was back in place.

The vampire bat *Desmodus rotundas* has the distinction of being the only true mammalian parasite. Brown and furry, with a squashed face, and a wingspan of about 12 inches, it scuttles about on two large thumbs on the leading edge of its wings. The skin is punctured with a downward stroke of its teeth and the victim is unaware of the cut since the bat's saliva contains a local anaesthetic. It also contains an anticoagulant to keep the blood flowing freely, long after the bat has flown away in fact. One vampire bat will consume about six gallons of blood a year but much more blood than that is lost by the bitten victims, so their activities can seriously weaken livestock. It's said that they rarely prey on humans, but why risk it when they can transmit rabies and other lethal infections?

In retrospect we attached far too much faith to our map of the trail. We'd discovered it in the map room of the Royal Geographical Society in London, and we've no idea who made it or when. Despite its sketchy appearance it appeared sufficiently detailed to merit respect, giving the Indian names of many of the hills and their altitude, and some of the information matched that shown on more recent maps composed from satellite photos. So when it showed three hills in the 3 miles between Temomairem and Koulimamopane, we believed it and assumed the fourth would be the Point de Trijonction. Consequently we scoured that insignificant little mountain from top to bottom, raking over the leaf-mould searching for concrete plaques, scanning tree trunks for initials carved in the bark, searching the undergrowth for French litter – empty pastis bottles, Gitane cigarette packets or those little round boxes from Camembert cheeses. Not a thing. Our new mood of optimism seeped away. Had we strayed off course already?

Dropping down into the next valley we established a new camp. The little trickle that flowed through the swamp should have been the Koulimapopane Creek, but looked too small to merit a name. It was time to shift our gear again, so every morning we walked back, picked up a load and moved it across those four hills. After lunch and a short siesta we continued trail cutting. Our progress had been so slow that our once infinite supplies of food were shrinking rapidly and the sacks were emptying fast. We had to get a move on if we wanted to avoid the Maufrais experience of living off the land, and trying to become hunter-gatherers with our limited skills. Those leisurely afternoons dozing in the hammocks became a thing of the past.

'Feel tired and mentally retarded,' I wrote in my diary. 'The lack of stimulation, the dwindling choice of food, the unchanging scenery and the tedium of our daily routine has got to us. My brain has turned to mush, and our only conversations are about practicalities – it's ages since we laughed, clowned or sang. We've become resourceful, we improvise, we're superbly fit, we're quite adapted to this environment, and yet... So much must have happened in the world out there, while we've become dullards, just sweating, cutting, eating and sleeping on a dreary treadmill.'

Our canoe and equipment were now 6 or 7 miles from either river, heightening our feeling of vulnerability. In an emergency it would take an age just to get the canoe and a few essentials to water, before we could even start paddling. When moving gear between our camps in the past we'd more or less loaded up the first things that came to hand. Now we selected items in order of importance: the canoe parts, medical kit, paddles and food first, because our new camp was now slightly nearer the Ouaremapaan than the Mapaoni, and in a crisis we'd be heading that way.

I had a mental image of us toiling slowly up the northern rim of the Amazon Basin like ants slipping and sliding up to the edge of a saucer, where Koulimapopane would be a little decorative crenellation on the very lip. Beyond that the land tumbled away, streams turned and ran north instead of south, and the Caribbean was now nearer than the Amazon River. Cut across two more hills and we'd reach the Coulé Coulé, the first tributary of the Litani, the river that was to carry us back to civilisation. After that stream, the map showed the terrain getting flatter and easier and we expected to reach the Ouaremapaan within a week, this being another, more navigable tributary of the Litani.

The only drawback of being across the watershed was that we were also over the border and into Surinam. The nasty little civil war of the late 1980s had reportedly ended two years before, but with a truce that might not have been to everyone's liking. Gangs of rebels could still be hiding out in the bush, unwilling to surrender their weapons. French Guiana had closed the border with Surinam to stop an influx of refugees, and Surinam had accused the French of supplying the insurgents. We were going to be canoeing down the river that formed this border, with Surinam on the left bank and French Guiana on the right, and the only way we were going to stay out of trouble was if the region was as uninhabited as the maps promised.

The next two hills seemed the same as all those that had gone before, rising up steeply for 200 feet or so from valley bottoms full of palms. Paloulouiméenpeú or 527 were impressive cliff-fringed peaks, but they were the exception. This ancient mountain range had been so dissected and moulded by weathering that Hurault's description, 'a monotonous infinity of hills as anonymous as the waves on the sea', had captured it exactly. Walk in almost any direction and it would look the same: steep hills and wet valley bottoms, crests and troughs.

The Tumucumaque Hills inspired respect for their remoteness and the certainty that any careless move would be the end of us. Lonely, unforgiving, harsh… and spooky too. How could an undisturbed area of rainforest be so empty of life? Apart from that herd of peccaries and the nocturnal visitor of a few nights earlier, we'd seen no sign of large animals. No jaguars or tapir, no deer bounding away in fright. Even the absence of mosquitoes seemed unnatural – an admission that there wasn't enough warm blood around to suck.

After chopping over five more hills from our new camp, we squelched across a wide valley, first up to the top of our boots, then to our knees. We persisted for as long as there was some solidity beneath the peat, but one stride took me into a bottomless jelly that sucked me down to my crotch before I threw myself flat and yelled to Heather to come no further.

I grabbed the stout stick that Heather held out and she calmed my panicked thrashing, encouraging me to twist, tug and roll gently enough to extract my legs without losing my boots. Fifteen minutes later I crawled like some hideous crustacean from the primeval slime and lay gasping on firmer ground.

We then tried several different routes across the valley but they were all too boggy, even in our unladen state. I wearily slashed at the trunk of a palm tree with a machete and the blade bounced off with a steely ring.

'We'll have to fell a couple of dozen of these to make a walkway,' I said. 'Bloody shame we threw the axe away.'

Over the next day and a half we felled thirty-five of those slender trunks, collecting a crop of blisters even on hands well-calloused from paddle and machete, and dragged them into position, gradually creating a path to the other side. Floundering in the muck, repeatedly tripping and falling, we finished up coated with black peat from head to toe and Heather's eyes gleamed out as if through the holes of a balaclava. A few weeks before we might have laughed it off, but our glum faces showed no glimmer of humour. It was too exhausting, and our suspicions that the Indians wouldn't have made their trail through such a valley meant that we might have strayed again.

Safely over to the other side, we hauled our way up a very tangled slope where lianas ruled; weaving along the ground and spiralling around each other like concertina coils of woody barbed wire. Some, with a fibrous russet bark, dripped out a cupful of fresh water when severed. Others produced milky or resinous sap; one dripped a scarlet stream down Heather's back that made me call out in alarm thinking she was wounded.

As lianas can reach 800 feet in length it seemed a shame to slash a way through them, knowing that each cut could produce a few hundred feet of death, but sympathy ebbed away as they sprung infuriatingly from the machete, or when cut sections leapt free and dealt us painful blows. There were inevitable punishments as our chopping and slashing transmitted tremors far and wide. Twice we were forced to make squealing sprints over the hurdles of liana as short-tempered insects pursued us.

Finally making it to the summit, I left Heather dabbing some water on the red swellings on her neck and went for a recce along the ridge. At first it went east, but after several hundred yards it swung north and seemed more promising, until a dense clump of bamboo made progress more difficult. I was just about to turn back when I saw something blue in the undergrowth. Blue is not a colour that occurs naturally in the jungle vegetation, at least not on the jungle floor, and consequently a blue tarpaulin is the chosen colour for making a camp visible to aircraft or passers by. I wriggled through the closely packed stems and prodded out the object from the leaves that almost covered it. It was rusty, but I recognised it instantly, as would anyone who has ever been camping, and I stood there foolishly turning it over in my hand, shaking my head in disbelief. A Camping Gaz cylinder!

It couldn't be real. What a bizarre thing to find in the middle of the Tumucumaque. And what an unnecessary thing for someone to bring, thought my practical mind, in a land where unlimited firewood lay about for the taking. However, here was proof that we were on some route or other, and proof that Frenchmen had been this way – being inconceivable that a Brazilian woodsman would cook on a butane stove.

I took it back to Heather and we examined it together like archaeologists with some rare artefact clawed from the earth.

'This is so weird,' I repeated. 'I couldn't be more surprised if I'd found a jar of Hartley's Strawberry Preserve.'

'It's encouraging, though, isn't it?' she said, with her first smile for several days. 'I suddenly don't feel quite so lonely. Let's push on to where you found it because I think we could be in for a major display of French graffiti!'

Slashing and trampling through the large area of bamboo that had colonized the crest of the hill, we approached the spot. It felt 10 degrees hotter in the bamboo than in the jungle on either side of it, making my trousers sag, heavy with sweat. We flailed at mutuca flies that lanced us through the sodden fabric on our backs, and dust rose from the parched soil; dust that possessed some irritant that made us sneeze and sneeze until our faces were slick with mucus.

It didn't take long to find more French relics. We unearthed a whole rubbish tip of wine bottles and soft drink cans carpeted over by many years' fall of leaves: never have I been so pleased to see an area of natural beauty despoiled by litter. The cans seemed to have lain there for more than ten years, completely rusted through and with only patches of the labelling still visible. One was a Fanta.

'Who could have carried this lot up here?' Heather asked in amazement.

'They'd have had Indian porters,' I reminded her, rolling a wine bottle in my hands. 'Lucky bastards. What I'd give for a good stiff drink.'

There was half an inch of dark liquid that could have been wine still in the bottle, and I had to fight the temptation to drink it.

As always, we'd miscalculated the amount of alcohol to take on our expedition and finished the rum several weeks before. There's an element of embarrassment in buying 20 litres of spirits before departure. All those bottles sitting in the supermarket trolley look much more than two 'moderate social drinkers' (as we like to describe ourselves to our doctors) should need, and yet it's all gone within a few weeks.

On our first expedition together in 1987 we'd also underestimated our capacity, but on the first evening of enforced abstinence Heather remembered we had a litre of surgical alcohol in the medical kit. This had been included to soothe insect bites and clean wounds, but we found it had much more soothing properties if taken internally with a dash of lime juice. We had polished it off within a week, going to our hammocks wondering if this was going to give a new meaning to being 'blind' drunk by morning.

I dropped the wine bottle back on the pile, and chopped slowly through the slender stems of the cursed bamboo, searching for more litter. Suddenly my machete hit something metallic with a clang.

'What the...?'

I examined what I'd taken to be a creeper, and discovered it was a cable. I observed the dent it had made in my newly sharpened blade with irritation.

'It's going to take me ages to file that out,' I whinged. 'I only sharpened it this morning.'

'Ah, bugger your machete, John,' Heather called from ten paces behind. 'What did you hit?'

'A damn cable!' It was all very well for her to dismiss the damage so lightly, she never did any filing. It was going to be me wh—

'What cable?'

I raised my dulled, introspective gaze to hers, and only then did I begin to wonder about the presence of a cable here. In slow motion, with my torpid, unexercised brain working flat out and probably with my mouth hanging open like some drooling village idiot, I followed it upwards and discovered that I was looking up at a 50-foot high metal tower. Four cables radiated out from the top of the structure, and I'd struck one of them.

'Well, fuck me,' I gasped.

'Very eloquent,' said Heather, pushing past to crane her neck. 'Good job it was Stanley and not Harrison out in Africa, otherwise "Fuck me, aren't you Livingstone?" would have entered our history books.'

It looked like an old drilling platform, its yellow paintwork flaked and rusty, but only the shell of the structure, with no workmanlike attachments. What was it doing on the summit of this nondescript hill in the Tumucumaque? It had never been used for drilling, but it might have served as an observation post, or perhaps held an aerial or radar dish. There was a ladder going up the side and I started to climb, but a muscular creeper had got there first that wound and twisted so abundantly through the rungs that I couldn't get past. Also it was rusty and shaky, only attached to the tower in a few places, and I suspected the bolts wouldn't be very reliable. Much as we wanted an unobstructed view of our surroundings, a broken limb from falling off would cause a certain amount of inconvenience.

There was some graffiti written in paint on the tower itself. *'MISSION 1966. ANNECY'* was the only legible one, and it all smacked of military shenanigans again. I've since learnt that French Guiana is used as a training ground for the Foreign Legion; perhaps they were sent off on obscure missions in the Tumucumaque. I could imagine the scene.

'Dumont! Come here!'

'Oui, mon commandant.'

'See this spent shotgun cartridge? See this sack of cement? See this unnamed peak on the map here, altitude 527 metres? Take your platoon there and follow these orders...'

The rocks around us were blackened, and it looked as if this hilltop had once been cleared and burnt off, probably to create a landing pad for helicopters. That would have given the light-loving bamboo its opportunity, and explain the presence of the weighty luxuries of wine and beer, and the tower itself. People hadn't walked in here, any more than they had to 527. Alternatively, this was the bare hill that Jules Crevaux had toasted with his champagne, and the bamboo had grown up later. If so, by leaving behind his empty bottle he'd started a bit of a litter craze.

As I was preparing for bed that night I looked up to see Heather staring at me, her eyes glinting in the orange firelight.

'Something wrong?' I asked, discomforted by her unwavering gaze.

'I'm getting a bit worried about you, that's all.'

'Eh? Why?'

'Do you know how long it took you to take off your boots then? You seem to freeze and go blank for long periods, and at other times you fuss and fidget. Look at your boots.'

'Well?'

'Happy with their position?'

I said nothing.

'Well you should be. You spent three or four minutes placing them neatly together, pulling the tongues up, arranging the laces off the ground, turning them this way and that so that they looked right to you.'

I didn't remember that. I thought I'd just taken my boots off and put them down. It was like being caught talking to yourself, or pulling faces when you thought you were alone.

'You're like that a lot. Fussing about. It takes you bloody ages to light a fire, cook a meal or sharpen your machete. Everything has to be neat and tidy, or done to perfection. You're certainly not like this at home.'

There wasn't a lot I could say.

'Thanks for letting me know,' I said stiffly, and pulled down the mosquito net to block out her piercing stare. She was exaggerating, surely? I had felt a bit tense lately, anxious and plagued by bad dreams, but there was good enough reason for that. I was suddenly starved of nicotine, and we were really out on a limb now with no hope of surviving an accident. I might look a bit blank and vacant too: our activities were hardly *University Challenge* exercise for the grey matter. But it was a bit rich accusing me of fussing when really I was only trying to save our hides. I'd never really worked out whether Heather had a natural sangfroid, or whether she was just lacking in imagination. She coasted along, letting me make the important decisions, seemingly unconcerned for the most part. Maybe she couldn't see the ghastly fate that could befall us if we cocked up?

Actually, what had been irritating me lately was my inability to think of anything coherent or sensible while trail cutting or walking along with a load on my back. Instead of a head full of entertaining distractions to mentally lift me free of the drudgery and pain, my mind had taken another tack. Certain names and words reverberated repeatedly around my head and wouldn't go away. They came at random, from hell knows where. In time with my panting I'd mentally intone Yitzhak Rabin, picturesque, Popocotepetl, Tumucumaque, architrave, Paloulouiméenpeú and anything else I could roll around the tongue. Try as I might I couldn't stop doing it.

I'd casually asked Heather what she thought about while walking to and fro along the trail.

'Oh I think about my family, plan some things for when we get home, remember favourite places, that sort of thing. Why do you ask? What do you think about?'

'The same sort of things,' I lied. If only.

Was the strain of it all making me crack up?

The first rain for three weeks caught us without the tarpaulin up that night, requiring some hasty scrambling through the sodden foliage, tying ropes by the light of our head torches. It stopped just before dawn, leaving the leaves freshly scrubbed and gleaming, heightening the reds and browns of bark, and as the sun rose everything began to steam.

We headed back to the last camp to collect a load, sliding in the mud and wet leaves, having a lot of trouble on our walkway across the swamp. Arriving at the tower we dumped our backpacks and snooped around for more memorabilia. Hidden deep in the bamboo we found a concrete obelisk about 4 feet high, but were wary of going too near as its top was covered with the bulbous mass of an insect nest. Termites or wasps? I approached it cautiously with a long pole, with Heather urging me to leave it alone.

'It might be a bomb!' she appealed.

'What?' I giggled, lowering my lance.

'A bomb.'

She looked deadly serious, but I couldn't muffle my laughter. And she thought *I* was crazy! Nervousness about being in Surinam was obviously getting to her.

'I think your imagination is getting a little feverish,' I spluttered. 'Admittedly the object is round and black, and only lacks a fuse and the word "BOMB" in white lettering on the side, but I think we'll find that it's only an insect nest. Get ready to run like the clappers.'

I thrust the stick through the papery structure and rose on the balls of my feet, ready to put my wife between me and any angry cloud that emerged. All quiet.

I hacked the unoccupied termite nest off the obelisk, hoping to expose an inscription, but there was only a threaded pin set into the centre, making it look as if someone had pinched the plaque or statuette that originally sat there. We also found another concrete slab with illegible writing under loads of root mass and leaf litter, several more empty wine bottles, and the tattered remnants of what may have been a tricolor. Perhaps there'd been a ceremony here years before when the tower was erected; bronzed legionnaires clutching their white kepis, flags flying, the folly toasted with glasses of wine, plaques unveiled by politicians. Such conjecture amused us in that lonely spot.

I made another tentative attempt to climb the tower, leaving the creaking, wobbly ladder to pull myself up on the framework. The metal structure was made of L-shaped angle iron, and I clambered up with growing confidence until I nearly put my hand on a slender snake that was basking in the sun. In fact, the tower was alive with creatures that had appreciated mankind's bizarre whim in erecting such a monument: lizards, beetles and ants scuttled up this giant Meccano set, and buzzing little specks flew in and out of a nest in one of the high forks. I went no higher, memorising the surrounding topography and taking some compass bearings before descending to earth and studying our maps.

This hill had to be Koulimapopane. It would explain the tower as some piece of vainglorious tomfoolery to celebrate the border, and its position in relation to the dominant peak of Paloulouiméenpeú was right. In that case we weren't as near the end of the trail as we'd thought, but barely two-thirds along it, with at least two more weeks in the bush ahead of us.

We accepted it philosophically. At least there was no doubt now that we were on course, and sleuthing around looking for strange French relics had cheered us up. Why the trail map only showed four hills between Temomairem and Trijonction when we'd gone over nine, we couldn't explain.

The mutuca horsefly inflicts a painful stab that raises an impressive lump, but the insect's loud buzz gives a warning and it's quite easy to swat. They harried us all day when trail cutting or carrying our loads, and I watched them settle on the outside of my mosquito net that afternoon, trying to reach the warm blood they could smell inside. Startlingly long proboscises were probed exploratively through the fabric, withdrawn, a scuttle sideways then probed again. I amused myself for a while by pinching the inch-long lances between thumb and forefinger and yanking them off, but began to feel ashamed, torturing flies at my age, and went back to splatting them in folds in the net with claps of my hands. That technique soon achieved some nasty stains and a satisfying body count.

I've no idea what a botfly looks like, but from the size of their larvae I assume them to be mutuca-size or bigger. Presumably the sight of them alighting on your skin would prompt some hostile reaction, so they've developed a rather original technique for distributing their eggs. They capture a female mosquito and lay an egg on its body before releasing it to fly away. So next time the mosquito alights on a warm-blooded animal, the rise in temperature warms the egg enough for it to slide off and hatch into a miniscule worm that wriggles down the microscopic hole left by the mosquito's lance.

This happened to me in 1987 on the crown of my head, in a place where I'd hoped that my hair would still be luxuriant enough to make it impossible for a mosquito to land. Soon I noticed a painful swelling which I assumed to be a boil, but boils don't give an occasional heave as something moves inside, and cause agonizing moments when I'd drop everything and clap my hands to my head, conscious of chewing noises and smacking lips.

I crouched on the ground while Heather examined the lump.

'It's one hell of a spot!' she exclaimed. 'Best leave it alone. It should burst soon.'

'Is that what it looks like?'

'Mmm. More like a boil. Looks pretty inflamed.'

'Can you see any air hole on the top of the swelling?'

'Could be. Or maybe it's just where the boil has been oozing. Hard to tell.'

If I hadn't known about botfly larvae I would have left it alone, but in the Peruvian jungle I once helped squeeze three out of a cat: not that the cat had appreciated our attentions, needing four people to hold it down. I wasn't going to wait for the larvae to finish fattening itself on my flesh before emerging to drop to the jungle floor and hatch into another fly.

I've since learnt that the best way to get rid of one is to get some vaseline and spread it thickly over the air hole, forcing the asphyxiatiating worm to stick its head through. A few more heaps and the worm's far enough out of its lair for you to grab it by the throat and yank it clear. Alternatively it can be poisoned by the nicotine in a smoked butt (lucky creature), but that causes thrashing death throes that hurt the host more than the worm.

'Give it a good squeeze,' I instructed Heather.

She did, and to her horror a repulsive creature, more than an inch and a half long and the thickness of a pencil, slowly slid out. Maggoty-white with a sparse covering of coarse hairs, its walrus-like face was all jaws. A caterpillar from hell. For all I know the botfly could be a gorgeous creature with iridescent wings and antennae like blown silk, but its progeny had left a gaping hole in my head, and would have grown much fatter if it hadn't been implanted in the very thin flesh of my scalp.

As the last sacks were carried over Koulimapopane we had finally left Brazil behind, and somewhere on the computer that registers and controls the comings and goings of foreigners, an alert might soon be flashing. Mr and Mrs Harrison had entered the country, had passed their three-month allotted stay, but had neither asked for an extension nor left the country. Hence they must be illegal immigrants, probably swanning about on Copacabana beach or some such fleshpot. This is a Brazilian department that functions very efficiently, as we know, having been deported twice before for unintentionally exceeding our stay.

Brazil, once a seemingly innocent and joyous land of beaches, samba, football, carnival and gorgeous girls, at least to the eyes of a foreign visitor, is no longer such a carefree place. The rot set in during the long military dictatorship of 1964–85. Potentially the richest country on the continent, the statistics of Brazil's social inequality were stark in the early 1990s. Twenty per cent illiteracy, a housing deficit of ten million homes, an estimated 33 per cent of the population living in poverty, and 20 per cent at a level where they earned insufficient to eat properly. The top 20 per cent of the population earned twenty-six times as much as the bottom 20 per cent. Half of all farmland was owned by 1 per cent of farmers.

Four million of Brazil's 31 million school-age children had never been to school, and 15 million dropped out before the end of the fourth year. Just three million completed their secondary education.

In fairness, the recent government of Henrique Cardoso has taken steps to improve the lot of the poor. Ninety-six per cent of children under fourteen are now in primary school and secondary school enrolment has doubled since 1990, though there are huge variations in quality from state to state. Seven billion dollars has been spent on land reform between 1994 and 1998.

But huge problems still remain. In São Paulo seventy per cent of the children under sixteen are working to supplement the family income, and there are now 1,600 *favelas* (shanty towns) in that city alone, built under flyovers, on steep hillsides, on the banks of rivers and streams. Tens of thousands of children live on the streets.

Not surprisingly, given the desperation of its people, Brazil has now become one of the most violent societies in the world. On our first night in Brazil a few weeks earlier, we'd left our cheap hotel in Manaus to step over the body of a teenager who'd been stabbed to death just outside. A crowd had gathered to stare at the corpse and at the trickle of blood that was making its way down the hill towards the docks. One young couple were nibbling at a takeaway pizza, and a man lifted his toddler to get a better view. No one seemed shocked or even surprised. Violent death is commonplace; the newspapers show gory photographs of the victims of shootings, machete attacks and knifings day after day.

In the larger cities, hundreds of street children have been exterminated by death squads of off-duty policemen, hired, it seems, by terrorised shopkeepers who feel they can extirpate the next generation of criminals by killing them before they grow up. There have been recent indiscriminate attacks on the inhabitants of shanty towns, presumably justified by the same mentality: kill the poor and eliminate crime.

The destruction of the Amazon rainforest has to be understood in this political, social and economic context. The initial motivation was to populate the region by any means, because the existence of that huge and virtually empty wilderness was an affront to the military leaders of a supposedly dynamic and prosperous land. Only by occupying it and peopling it would Brazil stamp possession on her territory.

Later, the government and the elite of the country, helped by the World Bank, the Inter American Development Bank and others, fostered an uncoordinated attack on the forest. Roads were pushed through without first identifying the areas most suitable for agriculture, ignoring the magnificent natural waterways that made roads superfluous. For a fraction of the cost and devastation, navigation could have been improved and a few locks constructed around rapids. Landless people from the south or north-east were then encouraged to take up land in the Amazon with no preparation for the very different conditions that they would find there, while the government subsidised huge cattle ranches that are often abandoned without ever selling a cow.

The poor of the country drift to the Amazon as gold prospectors or in search of a place of their own as the land in the more populated areas of the country is poorly distributed, worn out or mechanised for export crops. Only four per cent of Amazon soils might be fertile, and only seven per cent of settlers successful, but it still offers their only chance of a future.

In 1977, while receiving a conservation award in Washington, DC, the then president of Costa Rica, Daniel Ortuba, head of a country where eight per cent of the territory is designated as National Park (compared to one and a half per cent in the USA), made the following observation: 'When nations have shown little or no respect for the environment and where the natural environment has been ruined or lost in an over-hasty and uncoordinated exploitation of the earth's resources, human relations inside these nations are also likely to be characterised by a lack of respect for individuals and for human rights.' The experiences of Brazil, Indonesia, the Philippines and many other countries seem to support that.

We'd been travelling through an area where the only disturbance to the forest had come from small scale and intermittent gold prospecting, and it should have been reassuring to cross this wilderness area. From the falls of Santo Antonio on the lower Jari, right over the hills and to the Caribbean coasts of French Guiana and Surinam, the forest was still almost entirely intact. But it's unlikely to stay that way for long. The Brazilian military, obsessed with national security, want to defend the border and control drug trafficking that would, in fact, be easier to carry out with a larger population and more infrastructure. Mining companies wish to exploit those inaccessible deposits of minerals that have been identified by survey teams. Ranchers will ignore the lessons of history and persist with creating pasture from rainforest so long as subsidies are available. Dam builders and road construction companies are competing for government contracts.

The pace of deforestation slowed slightly in the early 1990s but is now proceeding faster than ever. Logging is now causing the most deforestation. Western multinationals, banks and loan agencies might have been harassed into a more environmentally sensitive approach, but their place is being taken by Japanese, Korean, Malaysian and Taiwanese companies with no such domestic pressure.

In 1996 Surinam granted concessions to several Asian companies that would allow 12 million acres – 40 per cent of the country – to be logged. Already the Japanese government has offered to fund the completion of the Transamazonian highway from the western Brazilian state of Acre to the coast of Peru, thereby giving easier access from the Pacific Ring.

In 2000 the Brazilian government announced *Avança Brasil*, a $40 billion scheme to push new roads, dams, mines and other projects into the remaining undeveloped regions of Amazonia: a scheme that would leave a bare 10 per cent of primary forest standing by the year 2020. The Northern Perimeter Road across northern Amazonia, which will pass a few miles from the Tumucumaque Hills, will be part of this scheme.

Our trail cutting didn't proceed smoothly from Koulimapopane. On day one we cut 2 miles north-westwards, hit a swamp and came back. On day two we cut 2 miles northwards, hit a swamp and came back. On day three we cut a mile and a half north-north-east and gave up again. Our access to the other river seemed blocked by marshes. Peering at the maps for enlightenment, we noticed that they showed the trail heading north from Koulimapopane for a mile, then making a sharp swing east before recontinuing north. If the trail map alone had shown the kink we'd have disregarded it, as our faith in the thing had reached new lows, but it appeared on all of them.

Having already cut the trail for the required distance north, we chopped our way eastwards along a valley, making the most of the easier terrain, and after a mile felt we'd fulfilled the instructions and turned north again up a hill to its summit and down the other side. Reaching the valley floor, Heather lit a fire to prepare some porridge, and I set off up the hill opposite to spy out the land before lunch. As I reached the top, I noticed something white on the ground and stooped to pick it up. It was a piece of paper with printing on it.

It gives some idea of the devastating effect of jungle travel on the intellect and mental agility that I was at first astonished to find that the little scrap was in English, and seemed to come from *Tales from the Arabian Nights*.

Someone else had been up here and was reading the same book as us!

Then I noticed the cut saplings that lay wilting on the ground, and more shreds of paper, and realised that I had met up with one of our abandoned trails. In effect we were more or less wandering around, if not in a circle, at least in a large arc.

I sank to the ground in weary despair, swearing feebly, bashing my fist to my forehead in dull rage against our incompetence in covering just 15 miles of forest, cursing the extra delay and the tedium of it all. Then I hauled myself to my feet and trudged back to where Heather was preparing lunch, and shattered her good spirits with the news. She took it badly.

'We're lost!' she wailed. 'I knew it! We're just stumbling around with no idea of our route, and all the time our food supplies are getting lower and lower. We'll never get out of here!' She fell on my shoulder and sobbed her heart out.

I patted her back and muttered reassurances. Her reaction took me a bit by surprise actually, and I felt a little pleasurable gloat in seeing her sangfroid crumble. Who was cracking up now, eh? We might have made unfinished trails all over these hills, strewn little paper chases to nowhere, and were still miles and miles from the Ouaremapaan. But I wouldn't call that lost.

Not quite.

CHAPTER NINE

A morpho butterfly danced through the creepers like a windblown scrap of blue foil and a cicada cranked up its imitation of a circular saw slicing through knotty wood, drowning out the midday hum and buzz. And down in the quagmire, a strange tableau: a grubby couple dressed in filthy rags, sitting on mossy logs by a little fire, white smoke hanging in the still air, the woman's cheeks still wet with tears, both sipping black coffee and eating Quaker Oats. Very occasionally I'd really absorb just how isolated we were and what a strange life we led, and this was one of those moments. I imagined us in one of those scenes at the cinema where the camera leaves a close-up of a person's face to soar skywards, rising higher and higher until one can barely make out the figure beneath. Well, a camera leaving our swamp-side picnic would have to climb higher than a satellite before human habitation became visible on the periphery of the screen. I gave an involuntary shiver, and Heather noticed it.

'You scared?'

'A bit,' I admitted.

'What are we going to do?'

I couldn't think of an answer yet. Any attempt to get out of this mess would require more energy and stamina than I seemed to have left. I just wanted to stay put for a couple of weeks, swing in my hammock, eat well and summon up new reserves.

'Should we go back?' she asked.

'Think how long it would take to get everything back to the Mapaoni, and how little water there'll be in it now. The chances are that Abel and his gang won't be working near Molocopote any more, so we'd have to paddle all the way down the Jari...'

'I'll take that as a "no" shall I?'

'We'd have to travel a lot less distance to reach villages over in French Guiana than we would in Brazil, is what I mean.'

'But we're wandering around pretty confused, aren't we?'

'Right, but we've passed what definitely must be Point de Trijonction, and that's over halfway along the trail. The Ouaremapaan can't be more than six or seven miles away.'

'We seem to progress in lurches: landmarks like Temomairem or Koulimapopane appearing after days of uncertainty, and then we stray straight off course again.'

She was quiet for a moment, long enough to hear the manic buzz of a mutuca fly and the smack of a swatting hand.

'We're not going to die out here are we?' she asked quietly, eyes quartering my face for a glib, bullshit response, the slight tremor of her mouth and the forced casualness of the tone bringing a lump to my throat. I gave her a hug and shook my head vehemently. Things weren't going too smoothly, we'd wandered a bit off course but that was no cause for such talk. We'd find our way out soon enough. I was fairly sure about that.

'No, we can't do that,' I assured her. 'Think of the disgrace. No one would understand what we were trying to achieve and they'd think it a really dumb way to die.'

'And they'd be right.'

'Indeed.'

I imagined people's reaction to the news that we'd disappeared in the Tumucumaque.

'The where?'

'The Tumucumaque Hills in the north of the Amazon.'

'What were they doing there?'

'I don't really know. Trying to cross them with a canoe I think.'

'Cross mountains with a canoe? Were they nuts? Was he some sort of Fitzcarraldo loony?'

'It seems so. My sympathies go to his wife. She probably followed him out of a misguided sense of loyalty, poor creature.'

And that would just be the kind ones. Look at all those cruel comments made against Raymond Maufrais after his disappearance. Tabloid columnists would pontificate about our recklessness and irresponsibility. My mother, in spite of promises extracted in the past, might squander her savings funding expeditions to look for that greasy spot of jungle floor where we had expired. No, we had to get ourselves out in one piece if we were to avoid that sort of posthumous humiliation. People might think us stupid and reckless if we succeeded, but we couldn't give them the opportunity to crow about our demise.

So there you have it. My survival instinct and my sense of self-preservation are motivated by pride, and the fear of some unkind column inches.

But first, if we were going to engage in a struggle between Life and Death, we needed a little siesta. It would have been all too easy to panic and go slashing off searching for that elusive river, but we chose the tough option of heading for our hammocks and sleeping right through to the following morning. When in doubt, do nought.

We decided that many of our troubles were caused by attempts to follow the maps too slavishly, so after breakfast we opted to ignore the supposed kink eastward in the trail and just chop north-east. The Ouaremapaan ran from east to west across our path so we couldn't miss it.

Oh yes we could. It took two days to discover that the Wayana Indians know best, and that they don't make lengthy detours to the east without good reason. Our bearing took us through wide valley bottoms that sucked the boots off our feet and the hills gradually diminished in size. Soon we were standing on the edge of an area of swamp bigger than the ones crossed by the

Mapaoni. We'd have to go back. Another waste of time, and another truncated trail.

'What have you done with the rest of the food?' Heather asked, searching in one of the blue sacks for the predictable stodge for our dinner.

'Nothing,' I replied. 'That's all of it in front of you.'

'It can't be!' She threw out 8 kilos of rice, one of beans, two packs of spaghetti, six dried dinners, one packet of Quaker Oats, two litres of cooking oil, the salt and coffee. 'You mean to tell me that's all we've left?'

'No, that can't be right. We must have left some at Camp Two with the rest of the gear.'

'I thought we'd decided to move up all the food and leave the rest for later?'

'We did, but we must have overlooked a sack.'

But we hadn't. A trip to Camp Two proved it.

I looked at the meagre pile of food in dismay. How had we passed so quickly from abundance to scarcity?

'There must be another sack around somewhere,' I said.

'Well there's not.'

'Sure we didn't mislay a sack somewhere along the trail?'

'You know how careful we are.'

'Even so, I'd better head back tomorrow and make sure.'

So we wasted a day while I retraced the trail all the way to the banks of the Mapaoni, shotgun over my shoulder, pockets stuffed with ammo. Any stroppy peccary was going to get it this time. Even with such minimum baggage it seemed a long hike, up and down all those hills, squelching through swamps, following the scraps of paper and the prone saplings that grew browner and more desiccated the further I went.

Four hours later I lay in the remnants of the Mapaoni, struggling to find water deep enough to cover my body. It had dropped nearly 3 feet since I'd been here last.

I tilted my head back, closed my eyes, breathed in and out gently feeling my buoyancy increase with each lungful, a pleasant lethargy and sleepiness creeping over me, the cool water soothin—

'Ca-Ca-Ca-CAAAA!' yelled the caracara. 'Ca-Ca-Ca-CAAAA!'

'I'll give you something to fucking caaaa about!' I shouted, leaping to my feet and loosing off a couple of shots in its direction, but it was just out of range and carried on jeering at me as I got dressed again and pulled on my boots.

Turning my back on the sunlit Amazon tributary, I parted the bushes and paused to let my eyes adjust to the gloom at the site of Camp One. In the leaf mould at my feet I saw several substantial dog-ends from tobacco-rich days of the past and pounced on them with glee. If I'd had a light I'd have smoked them there and then, but I didn't, and a maturer, healthier, priggish little voice eventually encouraged me to grind them up in my hand, drop them on the floor and walk away.

I strode back towards the Caribbean-bound streams on the other side of the watershed, searching all the while for that mislaid sack of provisions. The walk back was much more complex because I kept straying up cul-de-sacs and sections of trail that had been abandoned in past moments of confusion; finding my way suddenly ending in a frustrating wall of greenery like some unkempt maze. God help anyone who attempted to follow our path from the Mapaoni; it was a Hampton Court of misleading alleyways. It became a race against time as the shadows lengthened, but I made it home in the twilight, lathered with sweat, parched and hungry.

'That's one of the engineering marvels of the twentieth century,' I said after a good gulp of spring water.

'What?'

'That trail. Mile after mile of it, up and down and round and round. Impressive stuff.'

'No lost sacks though?'

'No. That really is all the food that's left.'

'If we were in an inhabited area I'd assume that some food had been stolen, wouldn't you?'

But our appetites were enormous, and Heather monitored our consumption in one day as nearly a kilo of rice, a quarter of a kilo of oats, two dried dinners plus coffee and sugar, so if that was typical we had to look no further for our thieves. Unless we could start supplementing our diet with fish or game, our food would run out in two weeks. I made a sling for the shotgun and carried it across my back, ready for any chance encounters.

One item we were grateful to have plenty of was salt. Our bodies seemed to be crying out for it and we were slinging vast quantities over every plate of food. On past jungle trips I'd occasionally tested my need for salt by adding a tablespoonful to a litre of water. If it tasted too pungent to drink, my balance was about right. We tried the same test at one of our camps in the Tumucumaque and the mixture tasted almost sweet – even with two tablespoonfuls per litre we managed to drink it.

Allowing ourselves only one more week before we gave up and returned to the Mapaoni, we searched over a large area for a ridge of high ground that would swing us eastwards. We moved fast, signposting our way back to camp with gashes in the tree bark. On the second day we reached a hilltop that seemed no different from all the others, and we expected the flat summit to end soon and drop down into another valley. But it continued in a ridge that was still proceeding east an hour later, and in the fading light I trotted ahead to discover that it then began a slow swing northwards. This was more like it.

Next morning we felt optimistic enough to hack open a good path as we returned along the ridge, and five hours later we sat down for a rest, practically having to prise our hands off the machete handles. They'd seized in a grip and lay curled in our laps like claws.

An extraordinary caterpillar was chomping its way through a leaf nearby, looking like a piece of discarded candyfloss. Silky pink hairs 4 inches long extended from its head, swept back like some 1960s bouffant hairdo. It was all show. Through the hairs we could see that it had a small body, and shaved of its finery it would become a 1-inch white maggot. Mind you, those luxuriant hairs might pack a painful punch. Some hairy ones have a poison that leaves the skin irritated for a month or more. One Amazon caterpillar, *Lonomia achelous*, has a poison that interferes with blood clotting. *Premolis semirufa* can cause such deep inflammation around the joints that it leaves the victim permanently disabled.

I actually felt interested and curious enough to take a photo of this specimen, and while I messed about with the flashgun Heather was examining a sapling that grew lopsidedly beside where she sat.

'Look, it's been cut!' she said excitedly.

Big deal. I'd chopped at several hundred similar saplings that day, so why should she find that one so fascinating?

'No, it looks like an *old* cut. Someone chopped it years ago.'

I ran over to look. The small tree had a machete cut in its trunk that had almost severed it, causing it to heel over at 45 degrees and rest against a neighbour. There it had been left, new bark almost covering the wound, the tree surviving and growing at this new angle.

Eagerly we searched the surrounding area for more, but without any luck. The cut had been a very old one, and had only survived because the tree hadn't died. Any other cut saplings would have rotted away by now. However, it was proof that someone had been there, and we were even more reassured when the ridge swung to slightly west of north, as the map showed. What was represented as a slight eastward kink on the maps was in fact a swing of 2 miles or more. Then, as if to confirm it, I found two more severed stumps of cut saplings.

The cut portions had disappeared long before and the stumps toppled and crumbled with the merest push, but how we conjectured around these human traces! The slope of the cuts went down across the trunk with the point of entry of the blade being on the top right. That meant, in the usual way of handling a machete, cutting across the body, that the cutter had come from the opposite direction. Our cuts were the reverse. I was very smug with this piece of detective sleuthing until Heather ruined it by arguing that I was assuming too glibly that the cutter had been right-handed. Damn.

We weren't quite out of danger yet, but from now on we were going to cut due north until we reached the river, unless something serious got in our way. Before that, we still had to collect gear from the last camp and carry it up two very large climbs and several smaller hills over a distance of 5 miles each way. We attempted it the first time without taking any food and ran out of energy on the way back, having to abandon our loads a mile from home to reel the rest of the way, exhausted and sick from hunger. For the other trips we packed some cooked rice.

The final push to the Ouaremapaan could now begin. We took the tent, and the first day's cutting took us over five hills, four of them quite small, but through thicker patches of vegetation than usual. We camped beside a tiny stream, and were awake early, packed up and eager to be off, climbing one more hill before picking our way across a wide valley bottom with growing excitement. The river we'd taken so long to reach must be near. It couldn't be far… little bit further… where the bloody hell was it?

This was evidently the floodplain of a large stream and the high-water silt and debris were still visible in the bushes, but we chopped on and on, approaching the base of the hill that formed the other margin of the valley, until there couldn't be anywhere left for the Ouaremapaan to be. Surely we hadn't strayed off course again?

But then we parted some bushes and found ourselves standing on the lip of a steep bank. There it was beneath us, whispering past, clear and so enticing. A grey wading bird hauled itself into the air with slow flaps, mouth gaping in shock, releasing a jet of diarrhoea, neck kinked like a U-bend.

The stream was surprisingly wide, about double what the Mapaoni had been where we left it, but very shallow and sandy. We stripped off and gingerly entered the sparkling cool water. Gingerly because Edgar Maufrais wrote that the Wayana Indians fear this river for its numerous stingrays and electric eels. We prodded the firm yellow shingle and waded cautiously to a patch of sunlight and lay back in the current.

'We've made it,' Heather gloated, putting her lips to the surface and slurping a long drink. 'We've finally made it!'

'Maybe this isn't the Ouaremapaan,' I said in a deadpan lugubrious tone. 'After all, where's the proof that this really is the right river?' I burst into laughter at Heather's expression.

'I wouldn't put it past you to be serious,' she taunted, trying to duck my head. 'Old doom and gloom John.'

'That's rich coming from you, who a week ago thought we were done for.'

'I did, I really did. How things can change in just a few days.'

We lay back, enjoying the warmth of the sun on our faces and letting the current sweep away the worst of our dirt to pollute downstream. Our celebrations were muted because we hadn't hit the river at the waterfall of Icholi Epoyane, and any river travel was going to be short-lived. Assuming the falls were below us, we'd only go a mile or two before everything came out, and the canoe folded up again. We knew from Edgar Maufrais' account that there were rapids below the falls that had to be skirted on foot for another 2 miles before quiet paddling waters were reached.

Ah, what the hell. Ribs and shoulder blades stuck through the milky whiteness of our grimy skin, showing we'd lost well over a stone each. We were skinny and exhausted, but otherwise fit and healthy.

Little fish inhabited the shallows, and moulding damp *farinha* around a tiny hook, I caught three to use as bait, killing them with a sharp flick of my finger to the head. Putting one on a large hook I cast into a spot where the water was deep enough to hide the bottom, tied the line to a bush and went to help make camp. Before we'd even got the tent erected, the bush started shaking and we had a traira for supper. Only about one and a half pounds, but a perfect size for our frying pan.

CHAPTER TEN

Three-quarters of the way along the trail to the Tamouri River, Raymond Maufrais finally conceded that he'd better leave the forest and return to civilisation. This change of heart could have been prompted by any number of factors: his crumbling equipment, the onset of the rains, his chronic dysentery, or a realisation that he couldn't hope to feed himself from the forest and that he'd embarked on an impossible exploit. He might have had a premonition that he'd die if he didn't give up.

Actually, the only reason he gave for wanting to get out of the jungle was to visit a camera shop:

> ... the shutter isn't working properly. It takes no account of exposure speeds. Blast it! I can't take good photographs till I've had it repaired. So I must get to the Oyapok, and from there go to St Georges, whence I can do the necessary by aeroplane. Then I'll go on to the Tumuc Humacs. I hope this won't hold me up for long. It's an infernal nuisance anyway.

His hunting produced erratic results: moments of glut where he shot a spider monkey the size of a three-year-old child, a curassow and a tortoise in one day, followed by a ten-day stretch where he could only find a snake, two little lizards and one small tortoise.

Arriving at the Tamouri, he needed to build his strength up to construct a craft to travel in and get downstream:

> I found nothing in the woods. Everywhere's deserted. The water is low in the creek and it doesn't seem to have many fish in it. I tried fishing with seeds, worm and insects, and it was useless. Dry lips, swollen tongue, violent stomach pains, an immense desire to masticate something. A palm heart calms me for a few seconds. Palpitations. Always out of breath. When I got out of the hammock I was dizzy again. Unless I eat tomorrow I shall die. I shan't even have the strength to hunt any more.

This is the classic survival trap. Weak, hungry and sick, explorers search desperately for food, but what they find never even replenishes the energies expended in the hunt. What was a temporary, overnight camp becomes more and more permanent, and the poor victim knows all too well the danger that he's in:

> At night the usual row starts up at full blast, and the storm howls, and the dead trees begin to fall. I fall asleep and dream and wake up with a start and know that I'm mortally afraid. I feel so far from everything, lost, alone, without the strength to keep going. I know that I'm ill. Terror takes over; my hammock is drenched with rain, the awning fills like a pocket as the water pours down, and my blanket is soaked by overflow. I long to cry. Very quietly I call out: 'Mummy!'

A jaguar growls, and an alarmed Bobby scratches at my mosquito net. I take him inside the hammock with me. It comforts me to have him there.

In the morning I gathered all my strength and went out hunting. A lot of doves flew off at 15 yards and I chased them. No good though. The rifle shook in my hand and I couldn't look into the upper branches. Bobby feels ill and is turning nasty. My ankle's swollen. I feel bad.

Two days later he wrote:

I killed Bobby this evening. I was just strong enough to cut him up in front of the fire. I ate him. I was ill afterwards: my constricted stomach caused me agonies of indigestion. I suddenly felt so alone that I realised what I'd just done and began to cry. I was angry and disgusted with myself.

It's all too easy to sit back in comfort and analyse where Raymond went wrong, but he wasn't thinking straight by this stage. He started to construct a raft – a totally inappropriate craft for a congested rainforest creek – and one whose construction required huge amounts of energy that he didn't have. With a puny hand axe he felled trees and cut them into 10-foot lengths. They floated, but many were needed to support his weight and his equipment too. All the time with his empty stomach flapping against his spine:

I've eaten nothing since yesterday morning, except three little birds and three tiny fish which I caught by a miracle and ate raw (bones, intestines and all) to give my stomach a little extra load. I can't go on. Hunted all this

251

morning, and drew blank again... Blank, blank, blank... Forest
and river are dead, completely empty. I feel as if I'm
in an immense desert that's just about to swallow me up.
I get weaker every day. I sometimes wonder how I'm
still alive.

I thought of Bobby and realised how necessary to me
was his silent companionship. There's nobody in camp now
to welcome me in the evening. No more barking, no more
eager licking... I'm alone. Poor Bobby!

I dived again in the woods — my last hope — dived
deeply; grubbing about in old tree stumps, exploring every
hole, turning every leaf, hoping for a snake, a tortoise, a
lizard — anything that's alive.

Raymond's diary obviously wasn't intended for public
consumption. If he'd returned safely he'd have edited out the
more emotional sections. But it's in these passages that he reveals
his warmth and sensitivity, so different from the brash arrogance
of his public face. Miraculously, in spite of all his suffering, he
was still attracted by the excitement of his adventure and curious
about his surroundings. Even while desperately searching for food,
he appreciated the beauty of the rainforest that was imprisoning
him and found time to sit down and write about it:

The forest is ghostly — full of thick mist in which the big
lianas loom. The beauty of it! I heard only the shrill sound
of the thousands of grasshoppers and the 'whoo hoo hoo'
of a night bird. It was overwhelming, annihilating — the
grandeur of dawn in the deep forest.

And at my feet the undergrowth was lacy, web-like. Snowy-white, it was like the snow crystals that form on the windows of a house, and so fragile that I hardly dared touch it for fear it would break. There was also a mushroom, tall and white, with a curious beige hat on its top and a fuzzy white fringe that vanished at the merest puff.

And so I forgot my hunger in watching these pretty things. One day I shall enjoy reading this notebook — smiling at the record of my trip, and delight at having overcome my discouragement.

The inevitable happened when he launched his raft and set off downstream. He had to move rocks from the shallow riverbed, and spent three days cutting one fallen tree out of the way. Then the raft fell to pieces and he'd only gone 300 yards:

It's night now but I can't sleep. If only I could get away! I must get away: this empty corner of the bush spells doom for me. The longer I stay here the weaker I become. I can't possibly go on foot, with my feet crippled and bare and my knapsack falling to pieces... I mustn't die of hunger. I've got to eat; nobody else is going to feed me... I'm alone, and I've got to work this out for myself. I'll kill, and I'll kill to eat. I want to live, to get back to the people I love, and the crowds in the streets, and the streets themselves, and my own home. I want to live — not end my career on the banks of the Tamouri like a weakling or an incompetent.

So then he came up with the idea of walking and swimming his way down the creek. It would be tough to walk along the banks because increased sunlight makes the vegetation thicker, and anyway Raymond's feet and ankles weren't up to the task. I imagine the Tamouri must be similar to the upper Mapaoni with a few deep sections and lots of cluttered shallows, and Heather and I can vouch that wading and swimming such a creek is certainly quicker than canoeing it. Raymond reckoned he could cover from 5 to 7 miles a day.

But once again he made surprising choices of equipment to take with him:

> During those ten days I should certainly have nothing to eat, since I couldn't possibly take my rifle along.

Why on earth not? Even on deep sections it's possible to swim and hold it aloft, or make a little buoyant bag to float it upon. As long as the ammunition is kept dry in another container it doesn't really matter if the rifle is dragged along the riverbed. The only clothing he took were his shorts, condemning himself to some icy nights in the rain:

> Get through or die: that's what it amounts to. And get through I will! I thought of writing a letter to my parents and leaving it in my bag in case... No, there's no point, since I'm going to get through. Their love and my faith will work the miracle. I could never make them miserable by failing to come back.
>
> And yet for a moment — because of the ice-cold night — the idea terrified me. It will soon be dawn, and I imagined myself tomorrow at the same time, asleep on a rock with no shelter.

I'll soon be seeing you, my dearest parents! Trust in me! I'm leaving this notebook here and only taking the little pad with me. This notebook is yours: I thought of you as I wrote it, and soon I shall put it in your hands.

I promised to come back; and come back I will, God willing.

That last entry was dated Friday 13 January 1950. Not an auspicious date for the superstitious.

'Even if I were to live for a very long time indeed, I would hardly ever forget 7 July 1950,' wrote his father, Edgar Maufrais, several years later.

That was the day on which, hurrying to my office in the Arsenal Maritime at Toulon, I first learnt of the disappearance of my son Raymond.

On my way, I met one of the girls employed in my department, and she asked me, 'Is it your son the newspapers are talking about, Monsieur Maufrais?' In my hurry to get to the office I had omitted to buy the morning newspaper. 'I don't know,' I replied. 'Why?'

She was obviously taken aback at my ignorance and I saw her go pale. To avoid further questioning on my part she said quickly, 'Oh, nothing. Nothing.' And she went away rather abruptly.

When I got to the large office in which I work I found most of my colleagues already at their desks, and I asked one of them to let me have a look at his newspaper. He excused himself, saying that he hadn't bought one that morning. And in all their faces, although they tried to avoid catching my eye, the sympathy was unmistakable. I was startled and already ill at ease.

Just then another colleague arrived and I could see that he had a folded newspaper with him. 'I'm terribly sorry,' he said when I asked him to let me see it, 'but it's yesterday's.' I didn't believe him by this time and without more ado just took it from him. On the very front page was a report that my son had disappeared and that only his kit had been found on the banks of the river Tamouri. At first the letters jumbled up before my eyes but I managed to read through to the end. It was believed my son had been the victim of Oyaricoulet Indians.'

The first thing to do was to get back to my wife before she learned from the neighbours what had happened. I must have been pale when I entered our little flat, for my wife immediately asked me if I were ill. But then she spotted the folded newspaper I carried and she exclaimed at once, though her voice trembled, 'Is there news of Raymond?' For the moment I hadn't strength enough to reply and I looked first at the photograph of our son smiling out at us from the chimney piece and then at my wife who stood there and waited for me to speak. Then I told her the truth, as mercifully as I could, but she fainted away.

Even with Raymond's diary in his possession, Edgar refused to accept that his son was dead. He argued that the search parties should have found some trace of his possessions, or even his body caught up in the undergrowth, revealed by the lower water level. In fact, one last trace had been found nine months after his disappearance: a crude shelter 3 feet high, thatched with palm leaves, more than 15 miles downstream from where he had abandoned his kit. So Raymond had succeeded in travelling for three days or so, past the most difficult reaches of the Tamouri and was by then only 8 miles from an abandoned Indian village crammed with papaya, pineapples, bananas and sugar cane.

Edgar preferred to think that Raymond had survived, 'perhaps a prisoner in the hands of one of those mysterious tribes whose existence in that neighbourhood he had always suspected'. The French newspapers liked that scenario too, even fabricating the myth that Raymond's life had been saved through the intervention of some dusky Pocahontas.

Although fifty-two years old, Edgar wasn't daunted by the prospect of going to look for his son in the South American jungles:

> I had already been through two World Wars, been a prisoner of war for two years, fought side by side with my son in the battles for the liberation of France and been both sick and wounded. After all that, I didn't see that the jungle need intimidate me.

He was to spend the next twelve years searching; covering 12,000 miles of some of the remotest spots on earth, showing a well-thumbed photo of Raymond to everyone he met, even learning to play some of Raymond's favourite tunes on the harmonica so that if he was being held captive in a village hut he'd hear the music and cause a commotion.

Some newspapers claimed the whole thing was a giant publicity stunt to increase sales of his books. Once enough media attention had been whipped up, father and son could contrive a touching and lucrative reunion. The reverse was true. Edgar lost his salary, spent all his savings and any royalties from Raymond's books, and ended up perpetually short of money. A group of friends and supporters in Toulon organised by one of Raymond's schoolteachers, The Association of the Friends of the Explorer Raymond Maufrais, raised funding and exists to this day in Toulon Town Hall.

Perhaps Raymond's mother deserves most sympathy. She lost a son and then, for most of the next twelve years, she lost her husband too.

Edgar left travelling to the Tamouri River until his eleventh expedition. He figured there'd been enough search parties in the area, and Raymond was more likely to be over the border in Brazil:

> Searching around in the undergrowth where Raymond's shelter had been, I found a screwdriver. It was rusty now and the wooden handle was missing, but it was probably the one I had given him before he left France. Tears which I could no longer hold back ran down my face, now covered with several days' growth of beard.
>
> I realised too, that only because I was his father could I still hope that he had been picked up by some unknown nomadic tribe, for after what I had seen with my own eyes any reasonable person would have to say to himself that the boy had only one chance in a hundred of getting out of that hell alive – and that he had not been lucky.
>
> In the course of my search I was spared nothing, neither outrageous accusations nor calumnies which were particularly painful to me as a loving father, nor sensational 'revelations' purporting to prove that all my efforts were aimed at nothing but advertising my son's books. And not only I suffered from these things, but my wife too was shocked and hurt.
>
> But all that is nothing – neither the praise lavished by professional explorers on my exploits that they describe as miraculous, nor the worst outrages, nor the hardships and privations of the jungle. They are nothing because my main objective has not been attained – the finding of my son.

Edgar gave up his search in July 1964 after eighteen expeditions. He died ten years later, bedridden in a home for ex-soldiers. Marie-Rose Maufrais hung on until 1984 in another nursing home, losing her memory in her later years. Her few personal effects were offered for sale by auction in 1986, as there were no surviving members of the family.

CHAPTER ELEVEN

We might have reached the banks of the Ouaremapaan but unfortunately the bulk of our equipment was still six hills behind us. Twice a day we trekked back to fetch it all.

Dumping my rucksack, whose straps and padding were so saturated with sweat that they dripped, I squatted beside Heather who lay in a twisted sprawl with her pack still on, gasping like a beached fish. Concerned by her pallor, I scooped a cupful of water from the river and held it to her mouth. She drank, spluttered, and drank some more. Finally she opened her eyes.

'Well at least we've got all our gear over to the Ouaremapaan,' I said cheerily, peeling off my sodden shirt. 'Only thirty-six days after leaving the Mapaoni. Thirty-six bloody days, can you believe that?'

'Stop twittering. Make some coffee and catch some fish,' she ordered, and closed her eyes again.

'Sure thing, Miss Heather. Coming right up.'

We'd used up all the bicycle tyre inner tubes, so I sliced a section off a broken flip-flop to ignite the kindling. By now it had become a ritual where I strived to construct a blaze using as little rubber and wood as possible. In the past my fires had been messy, unstructured piles; now they were orderly affairs with large logs laid out in a star shape, gradually moved into the centre as the flames consumed them. It took time to find the right size of logs that weren't too damp and crumbly from termite attack, but it was worth it. By now I had to find my pleasures wherever I could, and this blaze was catching nicely, little orange flames peeking round the edge...

'Dammit John! Can't you just make a quick and ordinary fire like everyone else?' Heather had sat up and her face was contorted in anger. 'And if you must be so obsessive can you spare me the bloody commentary?'

'Commentary? What do you mean?'

'You don't even know you're doing it, do you? You're more nuts than I thought! You've been muttering to yourself while you build your prize-winning conflagration. "Oh, that's a fine dry log",' she mimicked in a sing-song sneer, '"That'll burn slow and sweet. You'll do nicely my beauty." That sort of crap.'

Had I really? She was exaggerating. It was probably envy. You should have seen her chaotic fires: twigs, sticks and logs all piled haphazardly together, producing leaping flames that you couldn't even approach, let alone cook upon. And so inefficient! All that wood, *whoomph*, reduced to ashes, literally gone up in smoke. It hurt me to watch her.

Once the kettle was hanging over the fire I moved away and started fishing, landing a small traira within five minutes, and after a further fifteen minutes, two more. Eat your heart out Raymond Maufrais! Soon we were lunching on fresh fish, so perfectly baked on my controllable campfire that it might have been cooked in an Aga. Heather's fires would have produced 'fish in charcoal': super-fresh fillets of traira, lovingly scaled and boned, lightly seasoned, and then coated in 2 inches of black crunchy carbonaceous residue. Sketch with it first! Search for the little white bit in the centre!

Straight afterwards Heather withdrew to her hammock and yanked the mosquito net down behind her. I sat on the watertight drum reading my book, but soon began to feel uncomfortable. She was probably asleep behind the obscuring screen, but alternatively she might be observing and analysing my every twitch and mannerism. I escaped to the river where I tried to read and soak the fatigue away, head comfortably supported on a fallen branch, but I found myself worrying about neuroses, compulsive disorders and the rest. Was it possible to crack up and hardly be aware of it? Were my quirks and foibles an understandable reaction to the strain and precariousness of the past weeks, or was I really going mad?

'What's that?' Heather's anxious whisper behind me snapped me out of my worries.

'What's what?'

'Someone's coming! Listen!' Stealthy footsteps were approaching on the other bank, scrunching in the dry undergrowth. A twig snapped with a crack. I quickly hid under an overhanging bush as someone forced his way through the dense foliage. Heart thumping I peered through the leaves, wishing that I had the loaded shotgun in my hands, certain it was going to be a cigar-smoking guerrilla in battle fatigues, beret pulled rakishly over one eye. The screen of vegetation parted and not one, but four hairy faces peered through, nostrils flaring and ears waggling for danger.

We let out our breath as the family of capybara squatted down and relaxed in the sun, cyclids drooping into a doze, and I knew I should kill one. Our food was almost gone, and here was an opportunity too good to miss. They didn't even stir when I waded ashore, loaded the shotgun and squatted down to aim at one of the youngsters. Fired from 6 yards the lead shot would hardly have started to spread, smashing through the brain in a lethal clump, probably severing the spinal cord. Death should be instantaneous.

I breathed slowly in and out, in and out, in and out, drew in a final lungful and held it, the wavering sight now steady on the chocolate brown face that twitched slightly in the excitement of some dream, my finger beginning to press the trigger. And then a fly settling on the capybara's nose made it sneeze and open its hazel eyes and I couldn't go through with it. I lowered the gun and uncocked the hammer. It would have been a massacre of the innocents, a betrayal of trust, and I'd have been upset for days. All the joy at reaching the Ouaremapaan would have been washed away in blood.

I turned my back on the river, and found Heather watching me again.

'Why are you always staring at me like that?' I snapped.

'Like what?'

'Here,' I said, holding out the shotgun angrily. 'You shoot it if you like.'

'I don't want to kill it,' she answered coldly.

'No, you never do.'

'I can't shoot.'

'You've never even tried. Hunting for the pot is John's job isn't it? You just enjoy eating the victims.'

'Why are you getting so angry?' she asked in that way calculated to get me even angrier.

'Because I'm getting tired of shouldering all the responsibilities and tough jobs all the bloody time, while you just tag along criticizing me for being obsessive, indecisive, cautious and barmy!'

'And obviously paranoid as well,' she added.

'Oh stick that on the list too!'

'What?'

'Paranoid! According to you I'm neurotic, obsessive and manic already. Why not add paranoid to the list?'

'Is that how you feel?' she asked calmly, but with no trace of sympathy.

'I honestly don't know,' I muttered, turning away to find a job to do. I'd said too much already.

The dopey capybara slept through all the hammering as the bent and battered canoe frame was persuaded into position with me swinging the mallet with unwarranted violence. Our scent meant nothing to them and that was as it should be. If the wildlife had suddenly been terrified of man we'd have concluded a bunch of mercenaries must be in the neighbourhood, and all the hazards of the Amazon – snakes, peccaries, electric eels, piranhas and the rest – are but nothing compared to the nightmare of running into a group of bush-crazy, over-armed, oversexed adolescents, tanked up on booze and dope, tempers inflamed by crotch rot, catching you in their territory.

We'd left Molocopote airstrip with seven sacks of food: now just 2 kilos of rice and one of beans remained, so the canoe floated in less than 4 inches of water even after we climbed in and pushed off downstream.

We luxuriated in the intermittent sunshine on the little creek, in the novelty of going with the current for the first time, in the relief of making progress without walking crushed under huge backpacks. The current alone was nearly walking pace. Only seven fallen trees forced us to unload in the first mile; no hardship with our reduced supplies, and the river was usually 4 or 5 yards wide, which for the beginning of November was much better than we had any right to expect. Later, the difficulties increased as the river grew rockier, slipping between large boulders where the canoe couldn't follow. Then there was a small rapid and a long stretch of shallows where we ran aground and had to haul the craft along against the suck of the shingle for the rest of the day.

We never reached the waterfall that night but camped in a beautiful spot with a small beach and flat rocks to sit upon, amenities we never made much use of as a wave of tiredness engulfed us, so overwhelming that we retreated to our hammocks without bothering to cook. Ever since the rapids on the Mapaoni our days had been full of exertion and drudgery and it all seemed to catch up with us that night.

Thirteen weeks to the day after leaving Molocopote we arrived at the waterfalls of Icholi Epoyane, hearing their roar as we approached at a snail's pace, unloading over rocks and fallen trees, in no danger of being swept over the drop. Anyway, the river was only occupying a tiny portion of the rock shelf that it splashed over at 45 degrees before tumbling vertically the rest. It was a charming place of open rocks blessed with sunlight, rainbows dancing in the spray, butterflies lapping up moisture from the wilting Podostemaceae and the many bushes in flower.

Beside the stream were water-filled blow holes created at high water by the swirling action of rocks and pebbles, and after jabbing into their depths with a paddle to check for unwelcome occupants, we stripped off and climbed into these sun-warmed baths to perform forgotten tasks of toiletry like washing hair and cutting toenails. I clipped my beard to a designer stubble and Heather even shaved her legs. Anyone would have thought it was a Saturday night and we had somewhere to go. Then we soaped, bashed and thrashed the life out of our clothes until glimpses of their original colour could be discerned through the stains, and spread hammocks, mosquito nets, blankets, backpacks and boots out to toast in the sun. Everything had been damp, mildewed and unaired for too long, ourselves included.

I looked up from these chores to glimpse a couple of curassow moving in the jungle nearby. I thought of sending Heather off to do the deed, but we'd spent at least an hour without exchanging a cross word and it would be a shame to shatter such matrimonial bliss for the sake of a little point scoring. I grabbed the gun. Any nonsense about curassow in pairs being sacrosanct was a sentimental legacy from fatter days long before. These two took one look at the murderous glint in my eye, peet-peeted frantically and took off like snipe.

Dragging firewood out on to the rocks we did our cooking in the open under the bright stars of the tropical night. A full moon threw enough silvery light for us to walk around without torches, our shadows preceding us. Unfortunately, the hammocks had to be hung 50 yards away due to the absence of stout trees near the falls.

In the morning we donned our fresh clothes, forced feet into bone-dry boots and headed off to attack the last section of trail. It wasn't long before my shirt and trousers had completely lost their newly laundered look and only a couple of small dry patches remained.

Edgar Maufrais had commented that the going was dangerous, and he was right. The ridge was less than 3 yards wide, and only the trees and vegetation stopped it feeling exposed and frightening. Far down on the left we could hear the roar of the rapids. We'd discussed staying on the river, thinking that any canoeing difficulties would be preferable to more backpacking in the forest, but we hadn't dared risk it. It could prove to be much harder work than opening a trail to cover these final 2 miles.

Incidentally, Edgar Maufrais had taken just five days to cross from the Mapaoni to the Ouaremapaan. That could have made us feel inadequate, but he and his Indian guides had only carried a small pack each, they knew where they were going, and they had no trail to cut or canoe to carry. So what the hell took them so long?

As soon as the river valley sounded peaceful, we left the ridge and traversed down steeply, the vegetation dense and stubborn all the way. Those sweet little red wasps even laid a farewell trap: hiding their nest under a large leaf so that they could give me seven stings and Heather four, bringing the grand total to sixty-eight since we'd started counting on the upper Mapaoni. We were going to miss the little bastards.

Sunlight gleamed through the bushes, and with a few last chops we broke through to the riverbank and our trail was complete. I stuck the machete into the sandy soil and straightened my back, removing the elasticated bandage from my swollen elbow and flexing the inflamed joint. It could rest at last. More than 25 miles of trail had been opened through these hills, many off course and abandoned, and it had taken three times longer than expected, but we'd made it. I tried to give Heather a celebratory hug but she quickly wriggled out of my embrace.

'Get away, sweatball,' she said, with an attempt at a laugh.

'Oh that's nice,' I said, hurt by the expression of disgust I'd seen flit across her face.

'Well look at you!'

I glanced down at the sodden fabric of my shirt, conscious of droplets running down my face and plopping off my chin. My arms shone with moisture. In contrast, her clothing had just one large wet patch that I'd planted on her shirt front during our brief embrace, and tiny damp patches under the armpits and a thin line between the shoulder blades of her own making. Her face was almost dry.

'Pretty clear proof who's been working hardest,' I said, dumping my packload into a waterproof sack and heading back to the falls, but I knew it wasn't true. She never sweated much. The ice maiden had coolant in her blood.

Shortly after dawn I swung my legs over the side of the hammock, pulled the net up and peered sleepily out, blinking myopically about me. The roar of the falling water obliterated most sounds, but a faint tweeting was familiar enough to make me moisten my contact lenses with a bit of spit and stick them in place.

A smeary clarity brought some order to the blurry mass of foliage, and I reached down for the shotgun, checked it was loaded, then searched the vicinity for the curassow. There it was on top of a bush less than 20 feet away. The blast of gunfire a couple of feet away from her ear made Heather leap awake with a jolt, and the bird was dead before it hit the ground.

Meat and blood! I plucked its warm carcass, frying up the heart and liver with some rice, then cut the rest into portions and put them into a large pan of water to cook while we were away. It was bound to be tough, boiled up in river water without being able to control the heat to a gentle simmer, but it couldn't be helped.

I once asked a Brazilian prospector who'd just shot two macaws, about the best ways of cooking them.

'They can be pretty tough unless cooked properly,' he warned me.

'Do you roast them?' I asked.

'No, that makes them tougher still. I put them in a pot of water with some salt and pepper, and a six-inch nail.'

'A six-inch nail?' I queried.

'Yes. That's important.'

'OK. If you say so.'

'I simmer it slowly until the nail is soft, and then the parrot is ready to eat!' he said, dissolving in such fits of mirth that he fell off his stool.

A collared peccary, a small and solitary version of the pig family, crossed our path, standing and gawping in porcine bewilderment until we were only five paces away. An easy shot, and if the curassow stew hadn't been cooking back at camp I might have brought myself to do the deed. I doubt it though: my killer instinct had gone on holiday, and the way the little chap cocked its head and wrinkled its pink piggy snout was really most endearing.

Somewhere along the way we must have brushed against a nest of ticks because scores of them had buried their heads in our flesh. A couple had swollen to the size of peas, taut and russet with blood, but most were too small to burn off even if we'd had a cigarette to waste on them, and doctors don't recommend it as the pain makes the ticks regurgitate harmful bacteria. Having lost our tweezers, we could only scratch at the itching they produced, breaking their heads off to remain festering in the skin. Actually, in a rare exception to the norm, the ticks of Amazonia are more benign than their European and North American relatives. In those parts of the world, sheep or deer ticks can cause Lyme disease which may progress to complications involving the joints, or the cardiac and nervous systems. Amazon tick bites just itch or become infected.

The stew was ready and we sat gnawing at the bones in the sunlight, loosening our teeth, feeling morale and strength returning. Psychological probably, but it filled us with so much zip that the next morning we were packed up and on the move at the crack of dawn. By eleven we'd reached the end of the trail, and two hours later the canoe was assembled, all the sections were wired together for permanence, our equipment was loaded, we'd brunched and were ready to climb aboard and begin the third and final section of our adventure – more than 200 miles downstream to the small town of Maripasoula in French Guiana, with thirty large rapids on the way.

It promised to be exciting and fun, two underused adjectives in the previous weeks.

We'd crossed the Tumucumaque in forty-two days, twice as long as expected, and I realised how lucky it was that Peter Strub and I hadn't left the Mapaoni in 1983. We would have killed ourselves attempting to carry a rigid 18-foot canoe weighing 80 pounds across those hills, trying to live off the land all the way.

We pushed out into the river, and for the next three hours we clambered over fallen trees or negotiated log-jams where the current had piled driftwood into shallow water. On other rivers we'd have hopped out and waded briskly through, but we shuffled along, prodding the sand ahead of us with our paddles, alert for stingrays and electric eels.

Electric eels average 4 or 5 feet in length. They can emit shocks of 500 V at frequencies of 400 a second, at an average wattage of 40: quite enough to stun you. Their eyes are apparently useless because of cataracts (which may be the result of the eel's own electric discharge or those of its neighbours) and they locate prey by small pulses of low voltage that act as radar. They surface to gulp air every three or four minutes.

Alexander von Humboldt said the Indians on the Orinoco drove horses into the water to exhaust the eel's electricity, before handling the eels with impunity. However, more recent experiments have shown the eels are able to emit electricity all day, only needing five minutes to completely recover from twenty minutes of heavy discharge. The swift flowing, shallow and clear

Ouaremapaan didn't look like their usual habitat quite frankly, but the Wayana know best.

I was equally concerned by the *aimara*, a large fish that Raymond had described thus: *Its teeth are pretty little daggers that cut clean through whatever comes in their way; that's why it's a mistake to trail your feet or hands, and an even greater one to bathe in the upper creeks.* Could this be the traira? From his accounts it sounded like something much larger and fiercer.

By afternoon my fair skin, so inadequate in pigment for the life that I lead, had begun to smart with sunburn, and we camped early.

It didn't take long to finish off our food supplies, leaving just coffee, salt and a litre of oil. That was it. Whenever Heather irritated me, I reminded her of how much worse off we'd be if we'd followed her great plan to jettison 8 kilos of rice at the start of the trail, an idea that I had so rightly resisted. I could tell by the tightening of her lips that she wanted to grab the machete and hack my smug head off.

Shaking the last grains of rice into the pot rather focused our minds on the precariousness of our existence, still ten days from habitation, so when we saw a spectacled caiman (one of the Amazon alligators) lying with just its eyes and snout showing in the shallows, I shot it without too much soul-searching. It was a small one at about 4 feet in length, but we dragged it ashore and cut its head off with the machete just in case it wasn't as dead as it looked. For an hour we busied ourselves making camp, then I grabbed the sharpest knife and went over to start skinning the creature. It had gone.

Following a rather obvious trail of footprints on either side of a furrow made by the dragging tail, I found it 30 yards away, ambling headless up the sandbank.

It struggled strongly when picked up, so I opened its belly and removed all the guts just to make sure it really was dead. Then, taking the knife, I located a soft spot in its armour and pushed the tip in to start removing the skin. Immediately the caiman's leg scrabbled at the knife and knocked it out of my hand.

'Must be a muscle reflex,' Heather said. 'Try again in another place.'

I did and the same thing happened. A different scaly foot kicked the blade away.

'It can't be alive,' I protested. 'It's got no head and its heart and other organs are floating away downstream. It must be nerves.' Our own nerves were a little shaky.

'Let's make coffee and leave it for a while,' Heather suggested. 'It'll quieten down soon.'

It didn't. Even after forty minutes it still cringed from any contact with the knife, and by trying to remove its skin we were only prolonging the agony. Best to cut it into sections quickly and worry about getting the skin off later. Placing it on a log I quickly hacked it up into eight pieces with the sharp machete.

As we looked down at the blood-spattered ground and the pieces of caiman still twitching and scrabbling in the dirt, we were close to tears.

'Is this what 'back to nature' is all about?' Heather asked in a weak voice.

'I guess so. It's how I feel every time I shoot something. I'm really looking forward to going to Sainsbury's and buying my meat cellophane-wrapped, with someone else doing the dirty work of killing and butchering somewhere well out of sight.'

Nevertheless, the caiman provided us with quite a feast. Its meat is rather soft and fishy, so we constructed a platform of sticks over a smouldering fire that by morning had given the meat the colour of a pub ceiling and firmed up its consistency.

By the end of the next day we'd got two-thirds of the way down the Ouaremapaan. The tangles, log-jams and fallen trees didn't make it easy, and occasionally one of us would even grumble a little, to be rebuked and reminded how much worse things had been inland. A tapir mother and calf were wallowing in the stream, hardly bothering to get out of our way, the calf still with the brown colouring and stripes that showed it to be less than six months old. This is excellent camouflage in the dappled sunlight of the forest and helps protect it from jaguars. Later, the sheer bulk and strength of the tapir makes it a handful for the cats to tackle. If one leapt on its back the tapir would career through the undergrowth and probably sweep the jaguar off before it could penetrate the tough hide. The skin of the neck is thick enough to make sandals from.

Once we entered the Litani we were back on wide, open river again. This was as wide as the Jari had been at Molocopote, and the good times had truly returned at last. No more fallen trees or tangles: just a sunlit expanse of meandering river with the current helping us along. The rapids began 50 miles downstream, and the only aspect of the Litani that marred our enjoyment was the muddiness of its water. We'd grown accustomed to crystal streams where the riverbed was visible, but this one was grey-white and opaque.

When we stopped to grill a piranha luncheon I saw an Indian emerge on to some rocks downstream. I'd been looking across, wishing I'd seen that spot before I'd opted for this muddy spit of land to have our break upon, when I saw movement at the edge of the trees. An Indian wearing a red loincloth came slightly out into the open, looked across at us and waved. I waved back.

'There's an Indian over there,' I said to Heather.

'Where?' Her head jerked round.

I showed her. 'Can't see him,' she said.

'Another one has joined him, looks like a child, quite a lot smaller.'

Heather seemed unable to see anything and I repeatedly showed her the spot with growing exasperation. Now and again I waved and the Indians waved back.

'After lunch we'll call over there for a chat,' I suggested.

'I think you're seeing things,' she said, and went to fetch the binoculars from the canoe.

'You are! There's nothing there!'

'Don't be daft. Give them here.'

I raised them to my eyes, and the two brown-skinned Indians in loincloths sprung into close-up – as a bush with some red flowers at waist height.

When lunch was over we paddled across anyhow, and the clump of trees behind the idyllic foreground held many signs of previous campers. No deodorant sprays or Camping Gaz cylinders here, but an empty bottle of rum from Martinique, a box that had held a dozen French 12-bore shotgun cartridges, and an empty can of two-stroke oil from the USA. This was definitely white man's trash we decided, and it looked no more than a year old.

'Maybe commercial jungle tours come into this area,' suggested Heather.

'It'd be a good place to come, but I thought this part of French Guiana was closed to everyone except the Indians.'

'We're still in Surinam,' she reminded me, and we would be for another two days. After that, the right bank would become French Guiana, but not in the opinion of the Surinamese. They claimed territory as far as the Maroni River further to the east.

Feeling tired and sore we decided to go no further. After a short siesta I set out to catch something tastier than piranha for supper. An hour's spinning caught nothing so I baited up with dead fish and took the rod down to the end of a rocky peninsula where the current swept strongly by before swinging back upstream in a large eddy. The bait sank to the bottom and I waited. One minute, two minutes, five minutes went by, and a fisherman in the Amazon gets impatient with such delay. 'Come on,' I grumbled, and something heard me because a foot of slack was slowly removed from the line. I struck, and felt a solid resistance before the line sprung back, minus hook and wire trace.

'Blast it!' Sunken tree or rocks.

Tackling up again I cast in a different spot, but the same thing happened and another hook and trace were lost. I searched for a new area that might have less underwater snags, but I couldn't understand why I was losing the hook each time. If I had hooked a snag the line would only break if I tugged with all my might. Could it be a fish?

This time I made up a trace 2 feet in length so even if something gulped the bait down, the line would still be clear of the teeth. I also put the rod aside and searched for some nylon cord that had a breaking strain of about 200 pounds. Unfortunately the longest length was only 15 yards, so I had to cast in close to shore and wind the rest around my hand.

'Right then. Let's see what you are.'

The slack jerked and vanished and I struck hard, feeling a solid motionless weight. It had been a sunken log or rock after all. I tugged hard in an attempt to free it, but as I did so the riverbed began to move, fluidly, slowly and unstoppably. I tried my best to hold on, but the cord was cutting into my hand, and I was literally pulled off the wet rocks into the shallows before I was forced to let go. The end of the white cord snaked along the surface before it disappeared into the depths, pulled by a fish of 150 pounds or more.

We'd never seen any electric eels in the Ouaremapaan, but the murky Litani seemed full of them, thrusting their conger-like faces out to gulp air before sinking down again. They were thicker than my arm and quite put us off our evening wash. Strolling along the shore, I saw one rise and I cast the spinner at it out of curiosity. It was an accurate shot, and the eel grabbed hold. I heaved and the eel writhed and twisted and pulled back with great strength, but I was winning and it was coming to my feet. What on earth was I going to do with it? I wondered. I was curious to see one out of the water and photograph it, but it was going to be a handful. Suddenly the hook pulled free and the eel escaped, and for once a fisherman was relieved to lose his catch.

After an afternoon of such sloth, we got on our way early next morning and paddled long and hard as the fleshpots of Maripasoula were beckoning. Many times in 1983, and over the past weeks, conversation had turned to Maripasoula and the joys it might contain. The maps didn't say much – it had an airport, a hospital and it was the administrative capital of the region and the biggest town in central French Guiana – but we had great hopes for it. There would be unpretentious restaurants with checked tablecloths, serving food that combined the best of tropical ingredients with metropolitan culinary flair; refrigerators crammed with icy beers; bars with terraces placed to catch the breeze from the river. On a more sombre note there would also be policemen and one or two embarrassing questions about the absence of entry stamps in our passports and our presence in a prohibited zone, but we'd worry about that after a cold beer or two.

According to one of our maps printed in 1951 we passed the sites of old Indian villages, and when we were confident enough of their position we stopped to scavenge for fruit. Even to our untrained eyes we could tell that these stretches of riverbank had been felled at some time; the jungle was as high as elsewhere but the variety of trees was absent, dominated by light-loving ones, especially cecropia. We pulled ashore and slashed our way inland hoping to find juicy oranges, papaya, bananas, cashews or pineapples, but came away empty-handed each time. All we found was an urucu bush, the source of an important pigment for most Indian tribes. It comes from the thin covering of the seeds that are washed and crushed until the pigment settles to the bottom of the container. Later this is dried, mixed with animal or vegetable oil and made into balls or cakes, then used to decorate the body and hair and to colour cotton thread and ceramics.

Once, on the river Teles Pires in 1980, Andrea Bettelli and I had also stopped at an abandoned Indian village, where rotting huts leant drunkenly and lizards scuttled noisily out of our path.

We found papaya, cashews and some familiar plump green vegetables on a vine that grew along the ground. Marrows.

That night we cut one into sections and placed it in boiling water while we prepared a white sauce and grilled a large fish. But when we came to eat the marrow we found it fibrous, tough and totally inedible.

'Maybe it needs more cooking?' I suggested doubtfully. It had already boiled for fifteen minutes.

Andrea had cut open another one and was examining it closely.

'Look at this,' he said. 'See all these seeds? If I shake them all out, what does it remind you of?'

I looked at the hollow recesses on three sides of the centre, and the Shredded Wheat-like fibres that lay encased in the flesh. It was familiar, but I couldn't quite place it.

Andrea had the explanation. 'John my friend, we've just tried to eat a loofah!'

Amazon tributaries come in four degrees of clarity: opaque like the Solimões, Amazon and Branco; dark and tannin-rich like the Negro that writers have described as either the colour of 'milkless tea' or 'good bourbon' depending on their drinking preferences; greeny-black like the Jari where visibility is 3 or 4 feet; or crystal clear like the Tapajós used to be until 100,000 gold prospectors began work upstream.

Generally, the difference in colour is explained by the age of the mountain ranges the tributaries flow from; those from the relatively young Andes carrying much more silt than those originating in the ancient Guiana Shield or the Brazilian Shield of the northern Mato Grosso. What is harder to explain is why the Branco and the Negro, both flowing from the Guiana Shield, should be so different in colour, or why the Litani should have been so murky when the Mapaoni had been green-black, and the Ouaremapaan so clear.

Whatever the reason, it was an unwelcome development. The rocks and pebbles on the foreshore were coated in a layer of mud that dried into a flaky crazy paving as the waters retreated, or left a slimy zone where we would need to step out of the canoe. Bathing ceased to be a pleasurable romp in clear water where the sandy bed could first be checked for hazards, and cooking and drinking had to be done with a liquid that looked like used washing-up water. It was probably as innocent of germs as the Mapaoni water that we'd drunk untreated, but it looked unappetising.

We always pursued the policy of treating our water depending on the number of people who might be using it as a toilet upstream. On the Amazon for example, we filtered and then purified with iodine. On rivers with a village or two we used iodine alone, and once past those villages we drank it straight from the river. However, on some of the western Amazon tributaries these guidelines wouldn't guarantee a safe drink these days.

One of the less publicised effects of the cocaine business in the highlands of Peru, Colombia and Bolivia is the disastrous repercussion on the environment. In Peru, an estimated 1.8 million acres are planted with coca, and 15 per cent of all rainforest destruction in these countries is for coca cultivation. Huge amounts of toxic waste are dumped in the rivers and streams. Buenaventura Marcelo of the National Agrarian University in Lima estimates that the following chemicals, used in the processing of cocaine, are dumped in the Amazon headwaters annually: 15 million gallons of kerosene, 4 million gallons of sulphuric acid, 16,000 metric tons of lime, 3,200 metric tons of carbide, 1.7 million gallons of acetone, 1.7 million gallons of toluene, and even 16,000 metric tons of toilet paper that is used in straining and filtering.

This lethal cocktail is much diluted in the colossal volume of the Amazon's flow that averages 170 billion gallons of water an hour, but it's added to in every large town and city with more industrial waste and untreated sewage. The local people regard the world's mightiest river as little more than a convenient drain that will cart off the rubbish, at least around the bend before it washes up on shore again. Dozens of throwaway plastic cups, bottles and tin cans bob in the wake of each riverboat, as well as the diarrhoea of the travellers who then grab a drink from the water containers that are refilled from the river.

The Litani was certainly unpolluted from chemicals or human sewage and strangely, as we journeyed downstream, it became gradually clearer, until by the time we reached the first rapids it looked even cleaner than the Mapaoni. Either heavy rainstorms had temporarily stirred up the silt or it had been a local phenomenon in the headwaters.

Pristine rivers and streams are becoming harder to find in Amazonia because there are few that aren't worked by teams of *garimpeiros* with their dredgers and high-pressure hoses. It's estimated that 500 tons of gold have been extracted from the area in the last fifteen years, and for each ton of gold, twice as much mercury has been lost into the environment. Although the sale of mercury is supposed to be controlled by the Brazilian government (all importers and dealers are licensed and its use restricted), in reality there are few controls. Once the mercury has served its purpose in separating the gold from the cassiterite, the amalgam is heated and the mercury vaporises off to be brought down to earth again by rain. Drops of mercury falling into the rivers wouldn't be a problem as metallic mercury passes out of living tissues, but bacteria can transform the rain-borne vapour into methyl mercury that can be easily absorbed. It then makes its way up the food chain from plankton to insects to shellfish and to ever larger fish until eaten by man.

The effects of mercury poisoning can take many years to manifest themselves, but in the Japanese bay of Minamata, where families ate fish contaminated with the mercury waste from a photographic factory, the effects were devastating. It attacked the nervous system, leading to loss of feeling in the extremities, failing vision, and then paralysis and death. But Minamata was a tiny area compared to the goldfields of Amazonia, and the discharge of mercury much smaller. Since the effects can take a while to appear it seems that a deadly legacy has been left for future generations. Already the mercury levels in the blood of fishermen and their families living in remote areas are a thousand times greater than one would expect. Even if mercury was banned now, or the miners forced to use a simple retort that would reduce the emissions by 95 per cent, the damage has been done. Several centuries ago there was a gold rush in the state of Minas Gerais, and scientists think that mercury used then is responsible for the high levels of mental retardation found in that area now.

The first of the rapids was upon us in no time at all, and I approached it with the same flutter of apprehension that I feel when gliding towards any unknown white water. Heather seemed indifferent, and I still couldn't work out if this was due to that natural coolness, or a confidence that came from an abnegation of responsibility. Old hubby was in the driving seat – he would sort it out. I stood up in the stern as we drifted nearer, peering ahead, attempting a snap judgement if this rapid required a portage or not.

Heather laid her paddle across her knees and scooped a mouthful of water from the river, seemingly unconcerned by the quickening current and the noise ahead. What was going on in that head of hers? She was probably berating me for fussing and fretting again.

The stream was compressed into one channel between an expanse of rock, but there was a central V that avoided all the rocks, so we could paddle safely through with a little bouncing in the choppiness.

'Huh! Call that a rapid?' we sneered. 'In Brazil that would be regarded as mere bubbles!'

One day on the lower Jari, Mark and I had been making our way up a rapid when a boatman drew up beside us, tweaking the throttle of his powerful outboard so that he could hold his position in the current and sneer at us for our slow progress.

'I saw you two weeks ago, down by Veriverina! Is this as far as you've got?'

We felt at an uncomfortable disadvantage peering up at him from our position chest-deep in the river.

'Well it's been pretty difficult going,' I protested. 'There's hardly been a calm stretch for weeks.'

The boatman lit a cigarette and kept it dangling from his lower lip. We were obviously supposed to be aware that we were dealing with superior manhood here.

'The Jari's one of the easiest rivers I know,' he said provocatively.

'Oh yeah?'

'Sure.' He squinted through the smoke of his Hollywood.

It was tiring holding our footholds in the current with the weight of the canoe tugging us off balance.

'What's the creep saying?' asked Mark the linguist.

'That the Jari is a doddle of a river.'

Mark made some comments about the man's ancestry and character in English that at first I was relieved that he couldn't understand. After the boatman's next utterance I wasn't so sure.

'You should see the Paru! Now those are real rapids. Good job you two aren't on that river or you'd never get anywhere!'

'Oh come on. You're saying that this river is *easy*?'

'Sure. It's got a few large falls, but most of the other rapids are long stretches of bubbles.'

Our innate sense of courtesy was exhausted. Rudely turning our backs on him, we got on our way.

The next five rapids on the Litani proved just as easy as the first. No need to disembark or even scout them out, just an exhilarating swoop down with a little water splashing over the side. Only when we glanced over at the bank did we realise the speed we were doing, and let out yells of excitement. We deserved a few thrills after the tedium of the hills.

The next falls were a little more complicated in that they disappeared around a bend and we didn't know what might lie around the corner. It would have been prudent to tie up the canoe and trek across the rocky expanse that resembled a platform at low tide to check things out. But we felt that blasé fatalism of the chronically tired. Too much bloody effort. *Que sera sera* and all that. So we lined up nicely for the section of the rapid that we could see, and leant on the paddles to create some speed to steer by.

Much of the river poured down a gap between two jagged boulders and the canoe swooped down that to smash through a back-curling wave at the bottom. Without a spray cover the nose of the canoe dug in, Heather's knees disappearing under water briefly before the bow shook itself free. The weight of twenty gallons now sloshing around our feet made the canoe too heavy to manouevre quickly.

The bend still hid what lay ahead, and I was having second thoughts about facing it unseen.

'Head for that eddy!' I yelled with the tyranny of a cox on a Roman galley. 'Paddle left! LEFT for Christ's sake! Harder!'

Meanwhile I ruddered, backpaddled, heaved so hard on the paddle that the wooden shaft bowed, but to no avail. The last refuge swept by and we were committed to face what lay around the corner.

The river had that oily, surging smoothness that usually indicates that there's trouble ahead. No waves, breaking crests or rocks to avoid, just a rush between high rocky banks where there was nowhere to land. I yanked a cooking pot from the sack and busied myself trying to rid the canoe of some of its fateful burden, frenziedly scooping out 2 or 3 litres at a time, but before it could make any difference I heard Heather shout.

'Oh shit, John, look! LOOK!'

I looked up, and the sight made me toss the pot aside, grab the paddle, and backpaddle frantically in useless panic. Forty yards ahead the river just disappeared over a line of falls: it was as if there was a crack in the earth's crust and the Litani had tumbled into it. I stood up and tried to make a snap assessment of the options. There seemed only one place where the water flowed down a chute rather than plunging vertically, but it was going to be hard to make the 15 yards to the right to reach it.

Heather couldn't see from her seated position, but there was no time to explain.

'HEAD RIGHT! Paddle like hell or we're dead!'

The muscles on her back writhed as she paddled furiously, while I turned the bow round until we faced slightly upstream and attempted to traverse across the river for the necessary distance, now being swept down sideways towards the noisy chaos that lay ahead.

We inched across the stream, inches becoming feet, feet becoming yards. One yard, 2 yards, 5 yards, 10 yards. It felt as if my eyeballs were going to pop out and go skittering away; with each haul on the paddle my bum rose off the seat, and the paddle shaft slipped in the sweat of my grip.

'Turn John, TURN!' yelled Heather, as we rushed sideways at the falls, now only 10 yards away. 'Turn now, or it'll be too late!'

But I could see that turning now would only send us down the chute along its turbulent edge, where water heaved over submerged boulders and toothy strata.

'Two more yards across, and we can turn,' I gasped. 'Keep pulling!'

One stroke, two, three. Maybe enough. There was no time for any more.

'TURN! DRAW STROKE LEFT!'

I felt a moment of pride as Heather reached the blade as far out to the left as she could and heaved it back towards her, dragging the bow toward the paddle. What a team! Meanwhile I reached back and did a colossal backpaddle that lifted me to my feet, and our combined efforts spun the craft around 90 degrees in two seconds. Just in time. The bow had just faced forward when it tilted down and we went screaming down the chute, bang in its centre on a perfect line, as if this whole caper had been planned and prepared for. We would make it.

But we didn't. It was the weight of water in the bilges that did it for us. Otherwise I think we'd have driven through the waves and emerged waterlogged but afloat, but the canoe couldn't rise and dug itself in. My last coherent recollection was of a wave engulfing Heather, passing clear over her head and sweeping down the canoe towards me. Then I was knocked backwards out of my seat into a tumbling madness where I was buffeted, upended, twirled and spun; all the time trying to hold on to the breath in my lungs.

I felt strangely lucid and calm. Was I going to drown? Where was Heather? Why on earth hadn't we brought life jackets – people even wear them when canoeing the stagnant canals of Britain. Occasionally I peeped out through slitted eyes to see if there was anything to see, anxious about having my last set of contact lenses washed away. It all looked foamy and seltzy and sunlit bubbly, so I closed them again. I even tried to obey the instructions to point my feet downstream so they, rather than my head, would make first contact with the rocks, but where the hell was downstream in this wash cycle?

Gradually the violence of my spinning slowed, and my head was thrust briefly above the surface where the sunlight on my closed eyelids encouraged me to risk a quick gasp of air before I was sucked down again. The turbulence was dying away and I soon rose again. I looked around and found myself bobbing in the midst of some of our possessions: a garish yellow watertight sack, a red and white drum that held the cameras, a water container, paddle, straw hat and even a backpack kept afloat by the air trapped inside. Heather? Where was she? I swivelled around anxiously, and felt much better when I saw her wading towards a small sandbank 30 feet to my right. Between us, the gunwale outline of the almost submerged canoe peeked above the surface.

I swam over, my legs and arms wobbly from the shock, relieved that Heather was safe and that we still had a canoe, at least one paddle and some gear. Thankful too that we'd capsized at the end of the rapid, with calm water below where our drifting equipment could congregate.

'You OK?' Heather asked.

'I'm OK,' I replied. There seemed little else to say. We'd been foolish and we'd been punished. *Que sera sera* and all that. We waded and swam to fetch the bobbing items, and then hauled the canoe to the shallows and rocked out much of the water. Only the spare paddle, a machete and the shotgun, items that we wedged between the frame and the fabric every day, were still inside.

The yellow sack with the cooking pots and utensils was snagged in an overhanging bush 70 yards downstream, but as soon as I grabbed it I knew from the weight that a lot was missing. Sure enough the two large pots, including the one that I'd been using to bail out water, the kettle, a plate and a mug had gone. We were left with a frying pan, a kettle, one small pot, one plate, one mug and one spoon.

Once all the flotsam had been gathered and spread out to dry, we could appreciate what was missing. The fishing rod, a machete, a collection of clothes and towels that had been drying on top of the load, and some trainers and flip-flops that had been loose under our seats were all gone.

Back in England we had thought it a good idea to pack a mask and snorkel, hoping that the streams would be clear enough to explore underwater. Some of them had been, but our days had been too full to have time for such frivolity. Nevertheless we hadn't thrown them away. We were heading towards the Caribbean and once we reached Maripasoula we intended to fly to a Caribbean island and have a vacation in the sort of place where snorkelling would be fun.

Putting on the mask and snorkel, I walked up the sandbank and rocks to the base of the falls, entered the water and swam as near to the edge of the chute as it was prudent to go, then let the current pick me up and float me face down through the pool, where I occasionally glimpsed an item lying on the riverbed and could dive and grab it. By drifting over a different section each time I retrieved two shirts, a towel and one trainer. I glimpsed the fishing rod and one of the large pots, but they were too deep to reach.

Wading ashore up a narrow cul-de-sac inlet of water I disturbed a shoal of fish that had sought out the sun-warmed shallows to bask. Suddenly the surface erupted in dozens of bow waves as large fish rushed towards me to avoid being cornered by my advance, scaly flanks bouncing and brushing my bare legs. I squealed in fright. After years of pooh-poohing the piranha threat I was going to be taught a lesson.

'What's up?' called Heather.

'Piranha!' I yelled, splashing frantically for shore, one 5-pound fish colliding with my shin, probably removing a chunk of flesh. The pain would come soon.

I reached dry land and glanced anxiously at my legs. Unwounded, just a few pink marks that were fading already. In the empty inlet was a cloud of sediment and some lapping waves. I turned sheepishly to face Heather who was panting across 70 yards of sandbank to my rescue. This was going to join 'Don't shoot! Don't shoot!' in her fund of jungle anecdotes.

We had to hurry and dry our equipment while the sun was still high.

'It could have been a lot worse,' Heather said as we turned the sandbank into a gypsy encampment of colourful chaos.

'Definitely,' I agreed. 'Good job we're near the end of the trip. Imagine if we'd had to go the whole time with no fishing rod, only one machete, just one small saucepan, one plate and one mug to share. Cooking's going to be a real pain.'

'Good job we've got no food to cook then,' she replied with a grim smile.

When the sun was descending below the high trees we paddled over to a section of the riverbank that promised to make a reasonable campsite, and after putting up the damp tent I left Heather lighting a fire and returned to the sandbank to pack away the other gear.

Most of the clothes were still too wet, so I piled them together and left them out, hoping we'd be spared a rainstorm. Likewise the books that had swollen and thickened, pages clumped together, tearing if I attempted to separate them. Our diaries had fared better, being kept in the sack of hammocks and bedding, and only the page ends were damp. Mine had an orange cover and spiral binding: 'Nairobi Safari Club' was printed in an oval in the top right-hand corner around a pith helmet and pair of binoculars. Heather's had been bought in Santarém. Its cover showed the back view of a pair of jeans adorning a pert feminine bottom. 'Blue Jeans Party' was stitched across the pocket.

Call me a low-life ratbag, but a companion's private diary presents a temptation that I don't seem to have the common decency to resist. Heather was 60 yards away across the water, and here were her jottings and honest descriptions of our journey together.

'No,' I told myself firmly, and placed the diary in the bag with mine, busying myself tidying up more gear, trying to distract myself from temptation.

Back in 1983 when Mark had burnt his foot and we'd camped for ten days in a growing atmosphere of tension and recrimination, I had yearned to see his diary. Other forms of communication had deteriorated into surly exchanges and grunts, and the claustrophobia of our little camp pushed me to spend hours fishing or to depart on long hunting forays into the jungle. It would be very easy for him to read my diary, I thought, and at first I'd hidden it away, not wanting to reveal my anxieties. Later I thought it could work in my favour, and began writing entries expressly for him to read.

I was afraid he would pull out of the expedition, so I expressed disappointment in his stamina, will-power and basic manhood, hoping to sting an Australian macho into proving me wrong. Of course I praised his strengths too, pampered his ego, admired his qualities, but the tone was always slightly disappointed, as if I'd hoped he'd perform rather better. I then slammed the notebook shut, placed it somewhere visible, and left on my long excursions. I was assuming that Mark shared my weakness for an unguarded diary, but for all I know he might have been of better character. I don't think so though, because once I yanked a hair out and placed it within the pages, and later it had gone. Those James Bond films weren't a total waste of time it seems.

Meanwhile, I had no opportunity to get my hands on his journal. He only hobbled out of camp to relieve himself, leaving me no time. Until one morning when he decided that his burns might benefit from a session unwrapped from bandages, letting air and sunlight dry out the suppurating flesh. He paddled out to some rocks in midstream and I was on his diary in a flash, flicking through until I reached the entries for the last few days. They told me nothing that I hadn't guessed already. He was worried about continuing without fresh supplies. He was growing tired of jungle life, and he knew that I needed him because I couldn't continue on my own.

'John only wants me to stick it out so that he doesn't have to go home too. Sometimes he tries to be nice to keep me sweet, but I think he despises me. He's incredibly stubborn and pig-headed. He argues for pushing on with no thought for our safety. "We'll get through, don't you worry" he assures me, but I can't share his blind faith.'

There was one other entry that stung a little:

John likes to think that he's an easygoing sort of guy who'd rather share the decisions democratically than go around giving orders. The truth is he might as well bellow out an order than go through the charade of asking what I'd like to do, because he ends up ignoring my suggestions anyhow. We always end up doing exactly what he wants.

Ouch. As Aesop told us, 'Listeners never hear good of themselves.'

Everything was now packed away, or heaped into piles for drying the following day, and I should have paddled away from temptation. Instead I opened Heather's diary and furtively leafed through the closely written pages, trying to decipher her scratchy handwriting, my back turned to the section of jungle through which campfire smoke was filtering.

'He's been so creepy lately...' I glimpsed, as my eyes shot hurriedly down a page dated two weeks before, and I skidded to a halt.

'John is getting quieter and quieter, and he's been so creepy lately that he really gets on my nerves. I don't know whether it's due to strain or what, but he's started behaving like a crank. Everything he does is pedantic and ritualistic – his firelighting, machete sharpening, cooking; just the way he performs a simple task like adjusting the straps of his backpack. Everything takes him hours until I want to scream in frustration.'

Over the page.

'I don't know whether we'll stay together after all this. We've been through a lot but maybe I've just learned more about him than was good to know.'

The cow! I bring her out here, guide her through it all, protect her every step of the way...

'He can be such a prick. Sort of pompous, but weak and vacillating. Then he fusses around, grows super-cautious, patronises me, acts like a real wimp...'

Wimp! Me? Cheeky fuc—

'JOHN!' A call from the jungle behind me made me drop the book with a guilty start.

'Coming!' I called, shuffling the notebook back in the bag, pretending to be busily arranging some clothing, all the time reeling from the shock of what I'd just read. The cheek of it! What the hell did she know about safety, prudence, and expedition survival?

I arrived back in camp, drank the coffee she offered and made some excuse to go straight to the tent. Pulling off my boots, I started to place them together outside the doorway, but then remembered what I'd read and tossed them casually down. One even landed on its side, open for any insect to slip inside, and it needed real willpower to leave it alone and not place it neatly side by side with its fellow, toe to toe and heel to heel, tongue stretched up, laces tucked nicely inside.

CHAPTER TWELVE

'What are you sulking for now?' asked Heather as I shuffled around folding up the tent, moving lethargically like a toy with its clockwork winding down.

'Nothing,' I mumbled, stuffing the bedding into a sack, actually wanting to shout, 'What the hell do you mean by calling me a wimpish prick?' It was bad enough learning some unpalatable truths from reading someone's diary, but it was still inadvisable to challenge the writer about them.

'Well, cheer up for Christ's sake. Come and have your coffee.'

I sat down on a drum and sipped from a large plastic mug, trying not to think about food, because there was none. The capsize and its aftermath had left us no time to fish or put out night lines, so yesterday's lunch had been our last meal. The wind constantly changed direction, repeatedly enveloping me in choking smoke almost as acrid as the much-mourned Brazilian tobacco. I leant to either side, shifted the position of my seat, but it always found me out, and somehow only Heather's little segment of fireside remained smoke-free. My streaming eyes started my nose running in sympathy, and having no handkerchief I pinched one nostril shut at a time and snorted two good blasts of snot into the surrounding undergrowth.

'Oh, don't be disgusting!'

'What?'

'Not at the dinner table!'

I swear it. The dinner table. 'Would you prefer it if I blew my nose on the tail of my shirt? Stop getting so uptight – we're in the jungle, not some Cheltenham tearoom.' I swayed away from another smoke cloud, inadvertently letting out a little fart.

Heather wrinkled her nose in disgust. 'You're like a little kid.'

'It was an accident.'

'Come off it. I saw you lift a cheek the way you boys like to do.'

'I was swaying away from the bloody smoke and it slipped out! Change places with me and my nose might stop running.'

'You can have my seat because I'm not sitting here watching your disgusting habits any longer.' She grabbed a towel and scrambled down the bank to wash.

I sat down in her place and breathed a couple of lungfuls of clean air. The wind immediately swung 90 degrees and I disappeared from view.

Our equipment was drying nicely on the rocks in the morning sunshine, but needed a while longer. I distracted myself by trying to spear fish in the shallows. I'd sharpened a slender pole and notched barbs above the fire-hardened point to grip my squirming catch. By moving slowly along the rocks I could see fish with the help of my Polaroid dark glasses, and moved into position for the thrust. But refraction made the whole thing impossible. Either the fish darted off at the violent arm movement of the throw, or I fluffed the aim. Only once did I strike a fish; a glancing blow that dislodged four scales that still danced in the muddy turbulence long after the fish's escape.

Switching to a hand line, I caught three small piranhas and we scorched them on a fire and picked the flesh off the charred carcasses. It did nothing to reduce the feeling of emptiness. Heather sprawled on the rocks and went to sleep, and after turning over the damp books and clothing I lay down too and put my head on the hammock sack. Give it fifteen minutes more, I thought, and we'll be off. I didn't feel inclined to read any more of her diary. The opportunity was there but I knew what she thought of me now. She might dump me when we got home, might she? Well she might find that I gave her the boot first. Ungrateful little hussy.

Over three hours later I awoke with a pounding headache and dancing lights flashing in my skull. My lips had cracked and sealed to each other, and it felt as if one of those great raspy ox tongues had been transplanted into my mouth. Heather was still sleeping, but when I tried to wake her, only a tiny croak got through the dried-up badlands of my throat. Patches of skin that had missed out on the earlier application of sunscreen were red and painful to the touch, and it was lucky that we'd still been dressed in long trousers and T-shirts.

Splashing around in the margins of the rapid trying to rehydrate myself, I saw a familiar dark shape flash through the fast water and disappear under a rock. Reaching in after it, I felt its textured flank, gripped it and yanked it out, managing to keep my hold even though its pectoral fin had painfully pinched my fingers. An armoured shad at last. Just shows how a little hunger can overcome squeamishness and timidity.

I encouraged Heather to give it another try, and she too caught one on the second attempt. We then walked the margins of the rapid and seized four more.

Served with melted butter and black pepper, these fish would command the highest prices in the restaurants of the West. The flesh is flaky and succulent even when poached in a pan of river water and sprinkled with a pinch of salt, and we picked and sucked every scrap from the crannies of their armour. That felt better.

I was stifling the urge to give a satisfied belch, feeling Heather had been provoked enough by my laddishness for the morning, when she let rip a real snorter herself.

'Oh please. That's so uncouth. At the very least ask to be excused from the dinner table first,' I chided.

'Sorry, it slipped out,' she said sarcastically.

With only half a day remaining, we paddled southwards, treating three rapids much more circumspectly than the day before: even carrying the canoe around one in a failure of nerve. We'd learnt our lesson for the moment. Long stretches of calm water separated these rapids, a wide silver highway between walls of unchanging green. Torsos shiny with omnipresent perspiration (well, my torso at least), we dipped, dipped and dipped our paddles in a rhythm that made the jungle wall pass by at jogging speed, but it wasn't long before ungrateful little thoughts began to bubble up through the blankness of my skull. Newly released from the tyranny of rainforest trails and unnavigable trickles, it seemed absurd to find myself bored with the monotony of the open river. Every stage of the journey had had its quota of tedium, and this was no exception.

'Shall we sleep in Surinam or French Guiana tonight?' asked Heather in our first exchange for three hours, and an obvious attempt at peacemaking. I'd been glowering at her back and wasn't feeling very well disposed towards her. I might accept the olive branch or I might snap it over my knee.

'French Guiana,' I answered curtly, killing any jocularity in the exchange. We lapsed into silence again, finally camping on the right bank an hour later and finding more white man's rubbish: 12-bore cartridge boxes, two empty cans of corned beef, and a spool that had held nylon fishing line. Perhaps this part of southern French Guiana wasn't as closed to outsiders as we'd been led to believe.

To escape the rather frigid atmosphere I walked down to the rocky foreshore to place some night lines. I now had the excuse that I was engaged in some essential activity; a wily Jeremiah Johnson sort of dude, constantly seeking food for the table. That suited me pretty well because I'd never needed an excuse to go fishing before. I baited four lines and dropped them in the shallower margins where the biggest fish wouldn't come and smash them in the night, and hung a pebble-filled tin can to the bushes to act as an alarm signal.

Smaller fish might be the optimum size to catch on unattended lines, but there were whoppers out there, including the mysterious and dreaded *aimara*. Pinching a section of rope from the length that supported the tarpaulin, I spliced a wire trace and a big hook on to the end of it, tied the other end around a tree, tossed the baited hook into the deep water, and settled back with a book to wait.

It was getting a bit too dark to see the page comfortably when the rope suddenly jerked tight and thrummed with the strain. It sawed through the water from one side to the other, creating an arc of spray, while sediment and debris boiled up from the riverbed. Instead of leaving the tree to take the strain I grabbed the rope, but was swung off my feet by another sideways rush like a competitor in a collapsing tug-of-war. I tried again, but as soon as the fish felt increased pressure it gave unstoppable spurts of acceleration and I fell over once more.

Best let it tire itself out. The tree would hold it, even though a ring had been gouged in the bark by rope burn. I itched to call Heather down to share in the excitement, but all was quiet in the camp behind me and I suspected she'd gone to her hammock already. I'd surprise her soon enough when I got this beast to the shore.

Every time the fish paused to rest, I tweaked on the rope and it moved off again, gradually exhausting itself, and soon I could begin to haul it in. Not that it consented calmly to that. After retrieving a couple of yards it would force me to let them out again by yanking it painfully through my hands. I was staggered by the weight and power: if I'd hooked it with a rod I'd have been dragged off, waterskiing behind it.

Fifteen minutes later I was winning. Hand over hand I hauled in the rope that slowly mounted in coils at my feet, managing to halt any attempts at a rush by digging my heels in. Once, a huge tail fin broke the surface, giving me an idea of the size of my catch, and later the broad back porpoised up, confirming that I'd hooked a fish of a lifetime. About 4 feet long I estimated, and well over a hundred pounds. The last stage of the fight was a noisy affair, with the fish flapping and writhing in the shallows, sending up gouts of water. Finally it rolled on its side and I pulled it half on to the rocks, whiskery mouth gaping and gills flapping. My whiskery mouth was hanging open too, and my shirt stuck to my body with sweat and spray.

And at that very moment the hook pulled free.

It tore away from the white fleshy softness of the inner lip and whipped past my ear, still dangling segments of the piranha bait, and tangled in the shrubbery behind me. The fish was too beaten to react immediately, but I had to do something. Should I get a club and bludgeon it to death? A bit brutal, and there was nothing to use out on these rocks. I hopped up and down in uncertainty. The fish was so dauntingly large.

'Heather! Come and give us a hand,' I shouted, hooking my hand into a sharp-edged giant gill and tugging forward. The fish slid a foot, but then slapped its tail on the water with such a smack that I nervously jerked my hand away.

'What?' came a sleepy and ill-tempered voice from the jungle.

'Give us a hand. Quick!'

Swinging its head slowly from side to side, the catfish was gradually reversing back into the water, so I leapt into the shallows and for want of any better idea, more or less lay on it like a wrestler trying to force a submission. It had a section of bony scales on the back but its flanks were smooth and slick. Its fins were bony too, and possibly tipped with spikes that could trap my fingers against the body, so I handled it tentatively, trying to get my hands in its gills and roll it back on to the rocks. But I was tired and the fish was gaining confidence; it sensed freedom and was moving more strongly now. Violent thrashes and waggings of its great head flung me to one side, so I seized the base of the tail, much as one would a salmon, but the girth was too large to grip and a succession of explosive slaps intimidated me from making any further attempts to restrain it.

I was sitting in water up to my chest staring at where the fish had been when Heather came down the bank.

'What is it?'

'It's too late now.'

'What is? Are those your sleeping clothes you're swimming in? Why the hell didn't you strip off first?'

'I've just lost an absolutely colossal fish,' I said, still numbed by the loss, but shaking with the thrill of the hunt.

'Oh yeah?'

'About five feet long I reckon.' My hands left my side and ended up stuck out at full stretch as I tried to do justice to the fish's dimensions. Heather looked sceptical at this parody of 'the one that got away'.

'Didn't you hear it splashing?' I asked.

'I heard you swimming.'

'No, that wasn't me. I've only just got in the water. I jumped on its back when the hook pulled out, but it threw me off and escaped!'

She was already turning away.

'Whatever. I'm going back to bed. You're going to have a cold night without any dry warm clothing, aren't you? Goodnight.'

Bloody cow, I thought. She doesn't even believe me. Miserable old killjoy. Oh well, I'd seen it for myself, had it half on the bank, and the memory of that struggle would remain forever. Shame though. In my new role as cunning hunter-gatherer, 100 pounds of fish would have scored me some points. I would also have loved a photo to flash at those friends who still think that a wet afternoon down by the polluted canal trying to catch a quarter-pound roach is a suitable activity for a grown man.

Heather was right about one thing. I did have a cold night. Hungry too. When the tin can finally rattled on the bush I got up and pulled in a fish of about 6 pounds that we cooked and ate there and then in the darkness.

The rapids were often marked on our map with their Indian names. Wataou Tilili, Pakira Emeni, Conotopata, Couli Couli, and most were easy, allowing us to paddle straight through. Even so, we managed to capsize again. Carelessness, stupidity and tiredness played their part, but teamwork wasn't helped by an unwillingness to talk to each other. The glide near the right bank had seemed the obvious choice, until a submerged boulder, whose telltale turbulence was masked by a frothy channel rounding an island and joining the mainstream nearby, was suddenly beneath us, punching up one side of the canoe. If we'd sat still, all might have been well. It was our surprised sway away from it that tipped us over.

So we bobbed along in fast calm water, bickering at each other. There'd only been one rock and we'd hit it. I blamed Heather and she blamed me. At least no sacks floated alongside this time. All our possessions were tied to the canoe, so when we pulled it up on a sandbank ten minutes later nothing was lost.

We passed the sites of old Indian villages, abandoned so long before that no structures survived and the jungle had sent out tendrils to infiltrate the modest clearings and bring them back into its embrace. We knew it couldn't be long before we met someone, and kept our shorts on to maintain the minimum of modesty. It might sound an unnecessary preoccupation when any Indian we met might be naked too, but few tribes leave the genitals totally uncovered. Some wear loincloths, others tie the foreskin painfully against the belly, and women wear aprons or tanga thongs.

I remembered an embarrassing encounter on a previous expedition when I'd been carrying a sack around a rapid, stark naked and unprepared, and found two canoe-loads of Indian men, women and children preparing to portage the other way. It would have been tough enough at any time to go through the greetings, to smile manically, patting shoulders, but when they were all fully clothed in Western cast-offs I felt at an uncomfortable disadvantage.

Underneath faded T-shirts the women wore ill-fitting bras that compressed their breasts into unlikely shapes, and I could see the interference here of some North American Protestant zealot. Nakedness was a sin, they'd been taught, and here was another white man, perhaps not looking so very different from the missionary, letting it all hang out, not even having the modesty to lassoo it with a piece of cord. Never had so many eyes peered at my crotch for so long, and it was at least half an hour before I could slink away and search for my trousers.

Being trespassers in forbidden territory, we were apprehensive about our first contact with the Wayana. They'd have every right to turn us back, probably not understanding that by doing so they'd be condemning two incompetents to death. The French authorities might reprimand us, or make us leave the country immediately, but they wouldn't send us back over the Tumucumaque to Brazil. But the French were down in Maripasoula, and the Indians presumably had the right to police their own territory as they saw fit.

So when we saw some thatched roofs peeking over the high clay bank we propelled the canoe ashore with reluctance. That thin veneer of sociability and confidence had worn very thin in our long time alone together, and interacting with these people was going to require heaps of bonhomie and jocularity to compensate for our lack of language. We'd accepted our silences as normal for so long that it was going to be tough switching abruptly to full extrovert mode.

We climbed the mud steps like a couple ascending the scaffold, and emerged on a sun-baked clearing with six huts. No one had seen us coming; the air was soon going to be filled with the startled cries of children.

But no. The huts were still intact, sections of logs were placed in groups where people had sat around the charcoal of past fires, but the place was deserted. A trailing leguminous plant had begun to encroach upon the well-trodden earth, but that was the only indication that this village had been abandoned.

We explored timidly, sneaking some oranges and cashew fruit off the trees like children in a farmer's orchard, expecting to get caught in the act. One hut had a wooden box placed over newly disturbed earth in the floor and we resisted the temptation to peek inside. We've since learnt that Wayana dead are normally cremated and the ashes buried in their hut. If the chief dies, or if several people die soon after each other – denoting the work of evil spirits – the village is abandoned.

We didn't know that then, but although it was late and the huts would have supported our hammocks perfectly, we paddled a mile away before making camp in the forest. A wise decision, it turned out.

While breakfasting on traira bouillabaisse, an alien sound stilled the chomping of our jaws and those fussy little probes with the tongue that searched out the fish bones in each mouthful and shunted them forward to the lips. The Queen Mother wouldn't last long out here; she manages to choke on trout and salmon bones every year, even after a platoon of bone-disposal experts have searched the dish for hazards. These ones were Y-shaped, designed to pitchfork into the trachea, or catch a snake behind the head and pin it to the ground.

We each regurgitated a half-explored lump of fish so that we could talk.

'Outboard motor,' said Heather, as she finally recognised the distant buzz.

'More than one?' I ventured.

'Could be.'

Our camp was buried in the trees, the canoe almost invisible beneath low branches. Only the smoke from our fire would give us away. We peered through a screen of leaves as ten minutes later three large canoes passed by in midstream over 100 yards away. Faces framed by long black hair were turned our way, but the motors never faltered.

'I'm glad we're not camped in that abandoned village, aren't you?' said Heather as we returned to our seats.

'I'm sure we'd have been committing some enormous social gaffe if we had,' I agreed. 'I wonder where they're heading. They seemed to be carrying a lot of stuff.'

A couple of hours later we met two more canoes, and though we steered to pass within comfortable hailing distance, the occupants merely returned our waves and kept going. Men and women wore bright red loincloths and the canoes were traditional dugouts, only the powerful outboard motors seemed out of place. Again, we could see the centre of the canoe was piled high with a cargo covered with banana leaves.

Half an hour later another appeared, and then another, and still we hadn't exchanged a word with anyone. It seemed that no one regarded us as worthy of closer examination. When an eighth canoe appeared ahead we'd had enough, and positioned ourselves within 10 yards of their course. Even then, only a shouted, 'Bonjour! Où est-ce que vous allez?' in appalling French forced one man to reluctantly reply in something incomprehensible. We shook our heads and he repeated the word, adding 'Oelamari', and then they were gone. No smiles, no curiosity, but we now knew they were heading up the Oelamari River that we'd passed the day before.

Shortly afterwards we saw a village ahead on the right bank that had canoes on the foreshore and people gathering on the high bank to watch our approach. A shelf of rock that jutted into the current made us keep near the opposite bank, and we'd decided to give them a wave and keep on going when some women made unmistakable gestures of invitation and urged us to stop. We veered across some choppy shallows, zigzagged through the hazards and slipped the canoe through the impossible gap between two large dugouts to glide up on the sand with a hiss.

'Gave them a little demonstration of the forgotten art of paddling, didn't we?' I muttered as we stepped ashore, smiles firmly in place, while skeletal dogs lunged at our bare legs.

We were greeted warmly, but the language problem was insurmountable. Our attempts at French were met with blank stares, but that might have been the case in Calais too. An old woman pinched the hairs on my chest and said something droll, and I joined in the laughter with manic enthusiasm. Men tapped and kicked the fabric of our canoe like a bunch of dealers at a car auction, puckering their lips and muttering. One powerful young man with a handsome haughty face and shoulder-length hair, a bit like an Italian playboy in fact, came disconcertingly close and barked something. I smiled a puppy dog smile, eager to please, and he barked it again. He was probably telling me to get that stupid grin off my face, but I hazarded a guess, waved my hand upstream and said, 'Brazil, Brazil, Brésil,' five or ten times for good measure. He grunted and turned away, probably pondering why, if he asked me 'What do you want?' I should reply that I wanted a neighbouring country.

Heather was facing a similar barrage of interrogation from the womenfolk that might well have included, 'Those slim hips are mighty pretty, but wait until childbirth', 'Got any recipes from your country?' or 'Is that husband of yours as good in the sack as he looks?'

But the mention of Brazil had a positive effect on our communication. A woman said 'Ouaremapaan?' and we were launched into an interlude of enlightenment, able to nod and toss in 'Mapaoni', at which they nodded too. We were making progress, and a crowd led us up the hill to where a bunch of dignified men were tucking into a pot of fish stew, determined to remain cool and unexcited by the arrival of white aliens, but offering us a slab of manioc pancake and gesturing at the communal dish, which we fell upon with glee. We found slivers of onion, a tingle of chilli and the tang of lime juice. It needed all our control to remember our manners and not slip into an orgy of slurping that would finish the lot.

By repeating the names Brazil, Ouaremapaan, Mapaoni and Jari we made up for some of our conversational weakness, and prompted a lot of animated discussion between them. One man asked something several times before we twigged what he meant. He said 'Malocco Potay', and the difference between that and the Brazilian pronunciation 'Molocopochee', stopped us recognising Molocopote immediately. Our heads went into a paroxysm of excited nodding.

Pointing to his chest he said something, then pointed at two other men who also tapped themselves on the chest.

'They might have lived there in the past,' hazarded Heather.

This was hard work. Beads of sweat tickled my shoulder blades, and cheek muscles threatened cramp from such marathon smiling.

After that luncheon we all strolled down to the river to wash hands and cool off, and an excited yell heralded the approach of a thin, shambling, naked figure who was homing in on those welcoming signals I must give off, audible only to lunatics and drunks. This youth seized my arm in his mole-grip claw, and drooled happily between unnerving barks and attempts to pull on the waistband of my shorts and peek inside.

My periods spent in such Amerindian villages have confirmed that I'd make a lousy anthropologist. Watching the men hunt and fish, or the skilful way the women weave baskets or make pots is interesting, and it's fun playing with the children, but after a week trying out the intoxicants I'm ready to move on. I'll put up with any number of privations when pursuing silly expedition objectives, but I find Amerindian village life pretty grim, despite the warmth of the welcome. The diet of manioc in all its stodgy guises, half-cooked meat still covered with scorched hairs, the skeletal dogs, the menagerie of bedraggled monkeys and parrots, the way the hunters are sometimes immune to the suffering of their prey, the smoke-filled huts that are worse than any public bar, the burrowing chiggers and biting bugs…

Most of all I need my privacy, a legacy from years at crowded boarding schools I suppose, with days punctuated by ringing bells. I don't really like people calling round our house without telephoning first, so you can imagine what an Amerindian village is like for such a withdrawn misery. People breeze in and out of your hut without a by-your-leave and then squat for hours in the corner, observing you unblinkingly. They root around your possessions, smoke all your cigarettes and follow you doggedly into the bush when it must be obvious you're off for a crap. I sometimes climbed trees to snatch the opportunity for a quiet read, but soon the branches would be sagging with the entire male population of the village.

Our experiences in this Wayana community were further exposing our inadequacies. My new friend was certainly one red bead short of a necklace, and he clung to me amiably like a two-toed sloth to a cecropia tree, yipping contentedly into my ear, but I've had worse encounters on the London Underground. It made conversation a little difficult.

Another young man addressed me several times, but I smiled apologetically saying, *'Je ne comprends pas. Parlez-vous français?'* wondering why he was looking increasingly disgruntled. Then I finally heard his pained protestation that he was already speaking in French, before he turned on his heel and stomped off. Oh dear, another gaffe.

Chasing him with my ten-stone burden, who by now had undone the drawstring of my shorts and was plucking fistfuls of hair from my belly, I did my best to make amends. Having him to interpret would make life much easier, and I penetrated his curious accent enough to learn that he'd worked with government expeditions to the interior, one of the few opportunities of paid employment available to the men. Heather managed to string a few coherent

French phrases together, but my attempts emerged as a Euro-mix of Portuguese, Spanish, French and English that the young man, already convinced I was a boorish idiot, received with disdain.

I glanced at the river and saw a strange apparition paddling powerfully to our rescue. He too wore a red loincloth, had necklaces and bracelets of red and blue beads and little bands of material around his biceps, but his hair was ginger and his skin pale and freckly. In fact, he'd obviously gone so native that he'd foresworn sun protection and our first instinct was to rush over with a T-shirt, hat and some factor 25, so parboiled was his torso.

This was Thierry; he spoke excellent English and he arrived at just the right moment when the villagers were tiring of us. Less tolerant Amazon tribes would have clubbed us to death in disappointment at our poor entertainment value, then started pickling our heads and shrinking them into little tennis balls of wizened features and sun-bleached hair, but the Wayana just looked bored. An anthropologist, Thierry had spent two years with the tribe, and he was able to interpret between us and a handful of villagers who still thought we might have something of interest to say.

Gradually everyone retired to their hammocks for a siesta, leaving the mad dog whites out on the unshaded riverbank chatting rather manically in the way of people who have spent too long deprived of company. Heather and I said more to Thierry in the next two hours than we had said to each other in the last two weeks.

'Doesn't anybody paddle round here any more?' was one of my first questions.

'Hell, no. Only poor white trash do that these days.'

As the Wayana live on the border between Surinam and French Guiana, both countries try to woo them with gifts, but the Indians play them quite skilfully, demanding useful and expensive items like good outboard motors and shotguns.

'Makes them a bit dependent on petrol supplies but luckily they've got Cognat to defend them.'

'Who?'

'Haven't you heard of André Cognat? Been out here since 1961. He's quite famous in France, written a book called *I Chose to be an Indian* or something like that, and he's become a bit of a father figure and protector to the Wayana. Maybe he goes too far sometimes, but he's able to defend their interests and interpret the implications of government policy. I'm not sure he'll be very happy that you're here, actually,' he added. 'I had a lot of trouble with him in the beginning. He tried to get me thrown out, but I'd found a village chief who let me stay. You'll pass his village of Antecume-Pata two hours downstream – Antecume being his Wayana name. Whether you stop or not is up to you, but he'll hear that you've arrived, so if you intend hanging around for a while you'd better clear it with him.'

It emerged that we'd just missed a major fishing festival when channels of the low water river are dammed and fish are poisoned with the sap of a vine. The laden canoes that had passed us were carrying some of the catch back to villages in Surinam.

'It's a great sight,' Thierry enthused. 'Dozens of fish float gasping to the surface, including great big catfish, but its actually not as destructive as it sounds. There are some species which the people don't eat, and these are left behind and recover completely from the effects of the poison.'

We followed him to the edge of the clearing where racks of fish were being kippered and preserved above smoking fires. 'I think they might go out once more, so perhaps you'll see it for yourselves.'

Every few months the men would journey into the unpopulated regions on long hunting trips. What we'd assumed to be white man's rubbish had been left behind by these Indian parties.

As the village returned to life we were shown a hut where we could hang our hammocks, and a woman said we must stay around for a big dance in five days time.

'I don't think I can manage five more days here,' Heather whispered and I agreed, but we nodded enthusiastically at the invitation anyhow. Most of the village followed us down to our canoe, and I naively assumed they were going to help us carry our gear up the slope, but they squatted down with an air of expectation. It needed Thierry to explain what should have been obvious.

'They are hoping you might have some presents,' he prompted gently.

This is a matter we never give enough thought to during our expedition planning. 'Presents for the Indians' is scribbled on our shopping list, but down at the bottom, to be considered last. Consequently we are always ill-prepared for these moments when people jostle eagerly for the material wonders of the developed world. Whatever we'd brought would have been disappointing to a tribe who already had 25-h.p. outboard motors and French 12-bore shotguns, but our pathetic bag of red and blue beads, fish hooks and monofilament line, disposable cigarette lighters and postcards of the Clifton Suspension Bridge in our hometown of Bristol, looked positively insulting. To make it worse I forgot protocol and didn't offer the choicest rubbish to the chief first, and he huffily pushed his way forward and snatched it from me. In fact the chief turned out to be a different individual from the old man we'd been ingratiating ourselves to since we arrived in the assumption that *he* was chief. Gaffe upon gaffe. Anthropologists, I salute you.

In case you're thinking of going to Wayana country yourselves, bundles of red cloth, red T-shirts, blankets, tobacco, torches, pots and pans, knives, good machetes and fishing rods with fixed-spool reels like the one we had lost are all considered acceptable tributes. We couldn't have carried stuff like that all the way from Brazil.

At least I was spared the embarrassment of presenting the 6-inch nails that Peter and I had carried up the Mapaoni. These, we'd been assured, were highly prized, to be hammered flat between rocks and turned into spear tips and the like. Trying to explain the use of a rusty clump of nails to this sophisticated lot would have needed the skill of a Blue Peter presenter.

Seeing their disappointment we searched around for any items that we could live without until we reached Maripasoula. We handed over a torch, two biros, a kilo of salt and a penknife. Hardly enough for us to be hoisted upon their shoulders and carried to our hut while the women ululated with joy and raised dust beneath their dancing heels. We carried our own luggage up the slope.

After nightfall we were invited to join a group of men who were supping from calabashes of *cachiri*, a mildly alcoholic brew whose fermentation I knew was aided by the womenfolk chewing manioc mash and spitting it into the pot. It would take more than that to put me off an alcoholic drink, and anyway, I reasoned, it was only saliva, and I'd never been squeamish about women's saliva before. The *cachiri* had a lumpy consistency, more soup than drink, but it was refreshing and I took a good slurp every time it came back to me. The men around us became more and more animated, cackling at each other's jokes, listening to the chief telling some hunting tale I guessed (because he mimicked an animal on all fours at one point), making little '*aaaeeeiii*'s of wonder, clucking their teeth, sighing and grunting with each development of the story. I obviously couldn't understand a word, and Thierry was too far away to ask for a translation, but the sky was sharp with stars, our group was gently lit from fires in the shelters, and these men were such natural storytellers and perfect listeners that it didn't matter somehow.

Suddenly one of the men turned his head sharply to one side and a jet of vomit blasted from his mouth and splashed to the ground 4 feet away. Again, I've seen worse on the London

Underground but it was the reaction of the others that surprised me. The conversation didn't falter for a second, and the man wiped his mouth with the back of a hand and took a good swig next time the calabash returned. Thierry caught my eye and winked. Australians would love it here.

The trouble was that I'd drunk about 6 pints of the stuff and couldn't feel any intoxication at all, but my belly had swollen into a tight little paunch that felt uncomfortably bloated. I looked at my fellow drinkers with envy. They were having a really good piss up, the conversation was convivial, they stood on wobbly legs, their eyes had reddened, and one by one they'd had a good spew. We Europeans sat prim and sober, almost silent. I swallowed another pint of *cachiri*, until there seemed no space left in my stomach. I imagined the level halfway up my throat, and my bladder was equally taut and painful. Shifting on my stool I tried to work out where it was acceptable to piss, but the movement caused a sudden churning in my guts and with barely time for the thought, 'I'm going to be sick', I jerked round to the clear ground behind and my jaws were wrenched open by a hot lava gush that bashed and bounced little lumps off my teeth, reamed my throat, and almost broke the distance record of the village. The only mistake I made was not to pinch my nostrils shut to stop painful chunks trying to exit through my nose.

The relief was immense. Through watering eyes I noticed that the men were laughing and raining slaps on my shoulders, crying 'Wahaay! Nice one my son!' or words to that effect. I might bring lousy presents, be a dull conversationalist and be socially inadequate, but I could puke like a man. If only people had been so understanding when I was a student. When the calabash returned I took a polite swig, but would need a few more days in Wayana society before I could build up to serial bulimia.

Slipping away from the group, Heather and I headed for the fringe of the clearing where I flattened some saplings with a high-pressure blast of urine, and she caused some serious gully erosion that the unwary would fall into if they walked this way in the dark. Feeling agreeably purged we then crept to our hammocks under a thatch that rustled with the movement of rats, snakes or both.

If the dance in five days time had been one of the *marakés*, or initiation rites, we wouldn't have missed it for anything, but it turned out to be the end of the period of mourning for the dead chief of the abandoned village we'd passed two days before. People were going to daub their bodies red with crushed berries, dance all night and sink a few pints of *cachiri*, but, with respect to the chief, it didn't sound quite exciting enough to wait around for.

The *maraké* is administered at puberty. More than a hundred ants or wasps are collected and somehow placed in a wicker frame with their heads on one side and their abdomens on the other. Quite how you catch the wasps and manhandle them through the weave without undergoing a test of your own I don't know. After a session of all night dancing the initiates are given a big slug of *cachiri* and then brought into the ceremonial hut for their transition to adulthood. The shaman repeatedly presses the squirming mass of abdomens against the unfortunate's body, passing down the outer thighs, up the inner, against the chest and finally the forehead and cheeks. The victim is supposed to make no sound and stand still if he or she is to be considered ready for adult society. And to think I used to consider the British public school a tough preparation for adulthood. Wayana submit themselves to the *maraké* at intervals throughout their lives and it's a powerful way of preserving the group's cultural identity.

Many of the villagers pretended to be sorry when we announced we were leaving the next day. My inability to hold my drink had earned me a little respect, and they'd forgiven our bad manners and miserliness. Feeling more relaxed, we'd also stopped behaving like manic weirdos and adopted the calm respectful approach that the Wayana prefer. Thierry was taking us to see the last of the poison fishing, and then we'd make our way down to Maripasoula, after calling in on André Cognat and explaining our presence in his fiefdom.

On the previous day, men and boys had waded several hundred yards up a cul-de-sac inlet of the river, beating the surface and driving fish ahead of them. Then a barricade of sticks had been thrust into the riverbed to block the escape, and a canoe placed behind the sticks to catch any that might try to vault the barrier. Now most of the males from Thierry's village paddled with us to the spot, excited, chanting, assuring us with gestures that the catch was going to be huge, and some of the fish enormous. It looked promising: the enclosed area, about the size of an Olympic swimming pool, was agitated by the movement of the trapped shoal, and five fish that had attempted to jump the barrier lay dead in the canoe.

Bundles of forest liana, sundried to a rusty brown, were placed on rocks in the shallows and beaten with clubs until the fibres separated to a pulpy mass, releasing a soapy white froth. Five or six men beat several bundles each for half an hour before the first fatality rolled to the surface, then other fish began to leap as they felt the numbing toxins. Some managed to clear both fence and canoe to safety, and secretly I cheered them on. The killing began. Everyone lunged into the shallows, loosing arrows, lashing out with clubs and stabbing harpoons with trident-barbed tips at the dark shapes that rolled gasping into sight. Stab, a shake to drop them into baskets or the empty canoe, then stab again, like litter collectors in a rubbish-strewn city park. The children squealed with excitement, threatening our bare legs with their hasty arrows, poking at two stingrays that lashed viciously with their tails.

Hoping for catfish like the one I'd lost three days before, I was a little disappointed in this collection, where a 15-pounder was a good specimen, but the chase was exhilarating and chaotic as we each pursued our chosen victim through the melee. The Indians seemed happy with the result: 200 fish that they threaded on slender vines to carry back to the smoking racks.

We spent the night in the communal hut before we said farewell to the village and continued south. Thierry planned to accompany the next party that crossed over the Tumucumaque to Brazil; not to the Jari, but to the river Paru where a handful of Wayana still live among the other tribes in the Tumucumaque Reserve. We gave him the aerial navigation chart that showed the course of the respective rivers. We felt regretful and embarrassed that there were no presents left for the people of his adopted village.

Thierry's warnings about André Cognat's protectiveness had been repeated by several of the Indians. One young man had told us that we must go and see André 'immediately' and ask permission to stay.

'If he says no,' Thierry translated, 'you must leave and not stop paddling or sleep until you are out of Wayana land!'

Antecume-Pata consisted of ten families in as many huts. Tying the canoe between two others we were greeted with falsetto cries of 'Palasisi! Palasisi!' from the children, presumably the local term for white man. But when we asked for André, we were told he was away, down in Anapaike.

This was the largest Wayana settlement on the Surinamese side of the river, and by all accounts a salutary lesson in the wisdom of keeping the Wayana apart from 'civilisation'. While the French have forbidden the presence of missionaries on their territory, the Surinamese and Brazilians have allowed the Protestant Summer School of Linguistics to work aggressively among the Wayana in a three-pronged attack: from Anapaike on the Litani, from Parumó on the upper Tapanahoni and from Aldeia Boa on the Paru in Brazil.

These evangelist missionaries disapprove of the taking of more than one wife, of drinking *cachiri*, of smoking tobacco, of dancing or performing the *maraké*; in short, of everything that the Wayana hold dear. Every time I hear of an evangelist missionary being killed by Indians, my only surprise is that they aren't all killed on sight. I once watched an old National Geographic film about a bunch of missionaries meeting an uncontacted tribe, and it moved me to tears of pity and rage. The Indians approached timidly, wide-eyed, fingering their weapons, poised to fight or flee, and the big gringos flashed their perfect American teeth and patted the tiny natives on the head. It brought to mind Eve and the serpent: innocence manipulated and trust betrayed. In a later interview the expedition leader was asked what his first words were to the Indian chief.

'I've come to tell you about the Lord Jesus Christ!' ranted the man predictably, but if he'd been truly honest he should have seized the poor warrior by the shoulder and announced, 'Now you've had it. Nothing's ever going to be the same again, and you're going to end up as confused wretches in Western cast-offs. If only you'd clubbed us on sight.'

We paddled away from Antecume, and soon afterwards met a white couple out in an aluminium canoe pushed by a small outboard. The man had a fishing rod with a lurid spinner attached, and told us he was off after *aimara*. From his description of the ferocious, leaping fight that ensued when you caught one, I doubted even more that this was the local name for traira. At first we thought the man was André Cognat, but he introduced himself as Jean-Paul, the local teacher. His wife was less forthcoming in her greeting.

'André wears the *kalimbé*,' he signalled at his waist to represent a loincloth, 'not jeans like me. You have to look twice to see that he isn't a Wayana.'

By now I'd been six or seven weeks without a cigarette and could sometimes go ten minutes without even missing them, but when he pulled out a pack and offered me one, my hand reached gratefully forward with a will of its own, only to be slapped on the wrist by Heather.

'*Il ne fume pas,*' she told the French couple, who regarded me with pity. 'Honestly John! You've given up, remember? The first little test you get and you crumble. Just say no!'

'Have you seen Cognat yet?' the woman asked.

'Not yet. He wasn't home.'

'You shouldn't be here, you know.'

'So we've been told, but we didn't know that when we left Brazil,' I lied.

'You could have brought diseases with you. Have you had malaria on your journey, or any other illness?'

'No. We're healthy.'

'The restrictions are here to protect these people,' she added coldly. 'If everyone flaunted them they'd be wiped out in no time.'

She was absolutely right, and Jean-Paul broke the ensuing awkwardness by asking us about the Tumucumaque and life on the other side of the border. We learnt that he'd been living with the Wayana for more than ten years in the village of Touanké, and was providing the children with literacy in French to help them with a difficult future.

Half an hour after leaving them we found the river widening into a lagoon, overlooked by a large village that was probably Touanké. People called to us from the shore, but having no offerings to give them we merely waved and paddled on. The shouts increased in urgency, and among them we could hear one calling '*Messieurs! Arrêtez-vous!*' but we ignored it until a canoe raced out to intercept us and we shipped our paddles and awaited their arrival in resignation.

The two occupants were in their mid teens, but what they lacked in years they made up for in officiousness.

'What are you doing here?'

'Just passing through.'

'You shouldn't be here.'

'We're sorry.'

'You must go back.'

'Back to Brazil?'

'You've come from Brazil?'

'Yes.'

'You shouldn't have.'

'We're sorry.'

'Go back!'

'No way.'

And so it went on for half an hour as the canoes lazily pirouetted around each other in the current.

'*Au revoir*,' we announced at one point, but the helmsman started the motor and blocked our departure.

'Listen you little creeps,' I said in English, patience exhausted. 'Just get out of our way.'

'What? What?'

'You're too young for this job,' I said in French. 'Go and get an adult to speak to us.'

Hearts and minds, eh? That really poured oil on troubled waters.

'You must accompany us to the village, and we'll radio Maripasoula for a gendarme to come and arrest you!'

'What's the point of that if we're on our way to Maripasoula anyway? In fact, if you'd left us alone we'd probably be there by now. We're going.'

'No you're not!'

'Yes we are!' We started paddling while they zigzagged around trying to block our escape, and we only made it worse by getting an attack of the giggles that grew in intensity with each glance at their apoplectic faces. Paddling was out of the question now because hands were needed to clutch midriffs that ached with merriment, and guffaws and snorts echoed across the lagoon.

'You won't find it funny when the police arrest you!' one shouted.

'I'm going to get my shotgun!' cried the other. 'You'll have to come with us then.'

Suddenly I thought of a new tactic to break this impasse. 'I don't think Jean-Paul will be very pleased at the poor welcome his friends have received,' I said in a lugubrious tone, wiping my streaming eyes with a shirt-tail.

'You know Jean-Paul?'

'Of course. We're good friends.'

'I went to school with him,' added Heather for good measure, and very implausibly given their difference in ages.

Immediately the youths backed away. 'You should have told us you knew Jean-Paul,' one muttered, all bravado gone, moving the canoe out of our way. 'We were only doing our job.'

Feeling almost sorry for them, we shook hands and then wasted no time putting plenty of clear blue water between us and Touanké before our buddy Jean-Paul returned from his fishing trip.

Anapaike was the antithesis of a Wayana village; an artificial community of two hundred inhabitants, established by the missionaries to better control the population but too large to be self-sufficient in food. Most of the young people wore Western dress and sported dark glasses. Michael Jackson played from transistor radios. There was an air of listless boredom about the place, in contrast to the companionable periods of leisure that broke the many daily tasks of a healthy Amerindian community. Presumably there would be no game to hunt within easy reach of Anapaike, so the inhabitants relied on hand-outs of food, and inactivity had driven many men to alcoholism as mild *cachiri* was replaced by local rum that the Wayana couldn't handle. There'd also been several cases of suicide among the young, denoting a desperation unknown before.

As we walked through the dusty streets in our search for Cognat, several people challenged our right to be there, but we brazened it out with our new friendship for Jean-Paul. André Cognat had escaped us again. He had moved on somewhere else. I suspect we might have passed him in the maze of channels between the small islands. Oh well. That was all the excuse we needed to head back to our canoe and continue on our way. Anapaike was dispiriting, and we weren't desperate to meet Cognat and get a scolding, but at least he'd hear that we'd tried. We could now push on to Maripasoula and journey's end.

We knew that we'd regret not staying longer in those first Wayana villages, and so we do now that the memory of our anthropological inadequacies has faded. It was only after we got hold of a copy of Cognat's book, *J'ai choisi d'être Indien*, back in England that we came to regret missing him too. In it he tells how he first arrived in Guyane in 1961 after leaving his job in a Lyons steelworks, nearly drowning when his canoe capsized on the Maroni. Befriended by the Wayana, he has stayed ever since.

The picture we gathered of Cognat from Thierry and others, of an authoritarian figure and an overprotective guardian, might be true, but he was also an adventurer and a free spirit. He too had crossed the Tumucumaque on forays with the Wayana, from the Oyapok to the Cuc (a tributary of the Jari), to the Mapaoni via the route we had just taken, and from the Jari to the Paru overland. Impressive achievements. He'd even spent a month at Molocopote before it was abandoned by the Wayana. He also mentions Raymond Maufrais in his book, and evidently regarded him as a kindred spirit:

> In spite of my tiredness [he was on Maufrais' route to the Tamouri when he wrote this] I reckon that I'm living the greatest adventure of my life: walking barefoot, dressed in a mere scrap of fabric, my skin tanning, my feet and hands toughening; and above all living a full life, free and primitive, that everyone would like to try if only for a short while. I think too of Raymond, who also experienced unforgettable adventures, who preferred this primitive life to the humdrum routine of the city. He knew the risks, but he accepted them. I'd like him to know how much I admire and respect his ideals (many of which I share), and which

alas, led him to his death. But what a lesson in purity,
humility and courage he gave us!

André Cognat has helped the Wayana maintain their way of life
in the face of increasing pressures, and since the 1960s he's been
employing his French anti-clericalism to counter the falsehoods
promulgated by the missionaries. He was at Molocopote when
chief Molocco was persuaded to leave Brazil and take his people
to Anapaike by an emissary of the evangelists who threatened
punishment by floods and thunderbolts if he didn't comply. In
1968 Cognat advised the Wayana not to take French citizenship,
a decision that can be criticised for leaving them foreigners on
their own lands, but which was motivated by a desire to resist
government manipulation. He was also responsible for the
establishment of Jean-Paul's school and a health service.

I think once we'd convinced him that we weren't a threat to his
adoptive people we'd have got on famously. It was a great shame
that we missed him.

The Litani tumbles into the confluence with the Maroni down
a long staircase of rapids between forested islets. Thierry said it
was tricky but just canoeable if one chose the correct channels,
so we asked directions from a man who was crouched on a rock
scaling a fish. He gave us the sort of long-winded instructions that
I always get from pedestrians when I stop the car to ask the way,
made even more unintelligible in this case by having very little
language in common. Waving his arms, he stressed 'left, left' then
'right', then 'left' again, and even 'centre' for a bit. His gestures
drew boulders in the air, described trees of a singular appearance
to a Wayana, but just a tree to us. He clicked his tongue and trilled
lots of 'aaaeeeiii's to denote dodgy bits, counted something on
the stubby fingers of one hand and made some hasty paddling
motions. At one point he seized my upper arm and implored, 'Pas
gauche! Très dangereux!' and made signs of tumbling bodies,

mouths gasping for air. It was a mesmerising performance and we nodded sagely and set off no wiser, only to hear a shout and see him gesticulating frantically to the left. We hadn't even got the first part right it seemed.

'Let's camp, and deal with this in the morning,' Heather suggested once out of sight, so we chose a pretty island dominated by a tree that suspended a fringe of seed pods shaped like crescent moons almost to the water. Alone again after three days with company we luxuriated in our solitude, returning to our little world of coffee, diaries, books and… hunger. That morning we'd helped to catch a couple of hundred fish but hadn't had the sense to keep a couple for our supper.

CHAPTER THIRTEEN

What a mess we made of getting through our last rapids; finding all the unnavigable sections with unerring skill and twice getting stuck on little islands with mayhem all around and risky paddles and traverses to reach safety. After wading through deepening channels, lowering the canoe on the rope, portaging everything over rocky shallows, it was late afternoon before the Litani eventually spat us out contemptuously into the Maroni, just leaving time to shoot two more rapids before camping.

At least we had food. Because we'd been on the sort of channels never visited by more competent Indian boatmen, the fish were easy to catch and we'd grilled four armoured shad for lunch and grabbed eight more for our evening feast. This might be the last night out in the wilds and it was a fitting dinner to end on, although somewhat lacking in starters, side dishes or desserts.

The final two Wayana villages of Aloike and Elae were in this area, outside the restricted zone and consequently visited by groups of tourists. We wouldn't be stopping. From now on we'd be in Bush Negro country. These are the descendents of slaves who escaped the colonial plantations in the seventeenth and eighteenth centuries and sought refuge in the forest. That they should have adapted to tropical rainforest is not surprising, as many had been dragged from such regions in West Africa; more surprising is that people from territories as far apart as Senegal and Angola could create new tribal groups that incorporated such diversity.

Inevitably, as the runaways pushed inland to distance themselves from the coastal plantations, they encroached on Indian land and bloody fighting ensued. The blacks also took alien diseases upstream, causing a crash in the Indian population. But that was all a long time ago, and the Indians now have their territory on the upper rivers and the Bush Negroes on the middle and lower. White people haven't risen much in the latter's esteem, and that's quite understandable given their history, kept alive by storytellers from generation to generation.

We covered the last 20 miles in less than five hours, paddling powerfully on a slack current under a cruel sun on a river that was 200 yards wide. Many villages and the huts of homesteaders occupied clearings on the banks, and our canoe was but one of many as we neared Maripasoula.

We also passed a couple of gold prospectors' dredgers, the pumps and compressors clattering in a blue smoke haze. If it wasn't for the restrictions in the south of the country, French Guiana would presumably have prospectors exploring every creek, especially the Brazilian *garimpeiros* who don't give a fig for international boundaries if there's gold about.

It was a Saturday, a good time to arrive in a town that had been growing in stature over the past weeks. It might look an insignificant dot on the map, but it was the administrative centre for central French Guiana; it had a biweekly flight to the capital, a hospital, post office, police station, hotel and school. Maripasoula was evidently a place of importance, and it would certainly have a selection of bars and restaurants to choose from. We could step straight from our canoe into the Good Life, from asceticism to hedonism, from sobriety to inebriation, from jungle savagery to urban sophistication, from... well, you get the message.

So when we saw a collection of canoes dragged up on the foreshore in front of a handful of dilapidated buildings we scrutinised the scene carefully. Not much was going on. A group of Bush Negro women were assembling around a large dugout, noisy with shouts and laughter, carrying produce. Two men shovelled building sand from another canoe onto a pile on the shore, while others unloaded cinder blocks. Two goats grazed the scant patches of green, and a pack of thin dogs followed a bitch on heat with that single-mindedness of many males on a Saturday night.

'What do you reckon?' I asked.

'Maripasoula must be near,' Heather answered, 'but this isn't it. Probably one of the suburbs.'

I agreed. 'In this climate they'd position the cafe terraces on the highest sections of the riverbank to catch the breeze, wouldn't they? There's nothing up there.'

No Martini umbrellas or white tables under awnings, no neon signs to flash into life at dusk. We paddled on, still searching, desperate to hold on to our dream of a tropical Shangri La, and eventually hailed an old man and asked him how much further we had to go.

'You're going the wrong way!' he said with inappropriate glee, chuckling through a waterpipe of phlegm. 'It's three miles up there. You'll have to go all the way back, against the current!' He bashed his forehead with the heel of his hand to illustrate our stupidity. Boy, was he going to have a tale to tell when he got home. 'That way! Turn around, Monsieur et Madame Blanc!'

When we pulled up on the sand, 20 yards from the other canoes, the scene hadn't changed much. One dugout had departed but another was filling with passengers, the dogs had disappeared and the goats had advanced 20 yards. Nobody paid us the slightest notice. In Brazil a crowd would have gathered, but here everyone studiously minded their own business. Our appearance might have had something to do with it. We'd kept healthy but had slimmed down to an exhausted, rangy stringiness that accentuated our bushed-out eyes. I had an unsavoury beard that was much darker than my sun-bleached hair, Heather's curls had knotted into impenetrable clumps, and our clothing was faded by sun and sweat to a stained pastel.

I've finished expeditions in much worse shape, as have many explorers in the Amazon. 'After so long a voyage,' wrote Richard Spruce, 'I was much fallen in flesh.' Henri Coudreau reached the Wai-Wai tribe after a tough journey up the Trombetas in 1884. He slept for thirty hours and a kindly old chief said to him, 'You are not old, and yet your hair is white and your eyes are ill. Go home to your land. The paths of the savannah and forest are not good for white men.' William Curtis Farabee, having lost 48 pounds in weight during a malarial eight months in the interior of Guyana, was told by a grocer whose shop he entered, 'You have made a mistake. The man who buys old rags and bones is next door.'

'I'll go and find the town centre,' I told Heather, 'then we'll know how far we've got to carry our stuff to the hotel.' The dream hadn't died. It was wobbling and buffeted by doubt, but still attainable. This was just the waterfront of Maripasoula; the *centre-ville* was over the hill.

Meeting a collection of people out in the dusty streets, I asked them for the hub of the metropolis, but they either failed to understand or chose not to. Finally one young girl giggled nervously and waved inland over the hill. Aha! I thought, we were right, and I stepped out with new energy, expecting the dust to soon turn to tarmac under my feet. Maybe I should have brought some French money to get on a bus or hail a taxi?

Half an hour later I seemed to have left development behind and entered a patch of secondary forest, and a man who cycled by with a shotgun slung across his shoulder pointed back the way I'd come. So far I'd found nothing more exciting than a handful of houses roofed with corrugated iron and shaded by mango trees.

French Guiana is one of those peculiarly French creations; not a colony, but an overseas department with the same status as Languedoc or Normandy. Quite what France gets out of it now that the penal colony is closed, is hard to fathom. At least in the good old days between 1852 and 1938, 80,000 criminals had been removed from the mainland with the certainty that 70,000 of them would die before completing their sentences. The British Conservative Party must be wishing they could recreate such a place for the present day. Now the whole population of Guyane only totals 100,000, making it the second least populated country in the world after Mongolia.

Thanks to generous state handouts it has the highest standard of living but the lowest level of productivity in South America, and three-quarters of salaried workers are employed by the government. Even though the cost of living is half that of Paris, social welfare payments are indexed to the Parisian scale, and the average inhabitant receives more foreign aid per capita than any country on earth. The popular clamour for independence must be faint indeed.

Another curious statistic from this curious land: no country in the world has more unmarried middle-aged men and women; half the inhabitants between forty-five and fifty have never married. Read into that what you will.

After it was awarded to the French by the Treaty of Breda in 1667, France struggled to hold on to Guyane, facing attacks from the British and the Dutch. In order to stamp its possession on the unpromising swampy coast, the French mounted a huge settlement programme in 1763 when fourteen thousand Frenchmen arrived in a gigantic flotilla. They seem to have been misled about their destination – some bringing ice skates. They landed in the middle of the rainy season without food or clean drinking water, and thousands died before the government evacuated the survivors two years later. This fiasco probably showed them Guyane's potential as a penal colony.

A more recent attempt at settlement came in 1975, when the government called for 30,000 Frenchmen to emigrate to a new life in the sun. Thirty-six thousand pioneers applied; all but thirty were rejected because they lacked the minimum financial requirements, or were too old, young or infirm.

So the population remains a mix of Bush Negro, Amerindian, Chinese, Lebanese, Indonesian, Haitian and Brazilian. There have been some unusual success stories. A priest led a thousand H'mong Indochinese tribesmen from a refugee camp in Thailand to French Guiana and they've made a flourishing agricultural settlement 60 miles from Cayenne. The greatest concentration of whites is at the European Space Station at Kourou, which occasionally launches rocketloads of satellites to explode and create unusual firework displays for the locals. Actually the space station is sited in Guyane because of its proximity to the equator. The gravitational pull is apparently weaker, and less fuel is required for take-off. Hardly any fuel is required when the whole thing goes *bang* only a mile from the ground.

It took a Brazilian to break the news to me about Maripasoula. 'There's no town centre, because this isn't a town,' he told me compassionately. 'Wish it was, but building one would be too much hard work for these lazy bastards. This is just a village.'

Wilson was a gold prospector on one of the dredgers we'd seen, come to Maripasoula for the weekend, and he took me to a shack where seven other Brazilians lived in cheerful chaos. I guiltily accepted a beer knowing that Heather was still out in the scorching sun, but one deep swallow swept such sentiments away. A delicious effervescence ran mischievous fingers down my throat, and a forgotten iciness constricted the sinuses and made my brow ache. The men laughed at my obvious pleasure and got me another. It made a fitting symmetry that our trip was beginning and ending in the enjoyable company of Brazilian gold prospectors.

They had some pent-up grievances to vent about the inhabitants of Maripasoula and interrupted each other in their eagerness. Their boss was a local politician who knowingly employed them illegally, made them provide their own food out on the dredger, and paid them a much lower percentage for any gold found than they would receive in Brazil.

'Whenever we complain he threatens to send us back to Brazil without our money, but I think it's time we just downed tools because he wouldn't find anyone who would do our work among these lazy shits.'

'Here everyone wants to be in charge, because to them being in charge means sitting in the shade shouting orders,' added another.

Nothing had changed. In 1950 Raymond Maufrais met a prospector from St Lucia who made similar complaints:

What would Guyane be without us? Who'd work the seams if we didn't? The Guianese are all policemen or customs officials. They don't do a damn thing for their country.

Raymond had passed through several gold prospecting villages on his way to the Tumucumaque, and wasn't complimentary about the miners:

In Brazil the diamond-hunters and other prospectors are unscrupulous toughs who take a canoe, a gun, a pick, a shovel, and a wash-trough, and start off, not caring about food or shelter, into the hinterland. They penetrate ever deeper, shoot up the untamed Indians, live the life of nomads: they're real adventurers.

In contrast:

... the miners of Guyane are like white-collar workers, in that most of them are established family men with a great fondness for their village, their friends, their settled habits. Adventure for its own sake, risk, chance, famine, the forest — all these terrify them, and they linger on in stagnation. If I'd wanted the feeling of adventure I'd have been more likely to find it among the miners of Lille. These people here are just a pack of navvies.

Raymond had been stuck in Maripasoula for nearly three weeks and that might explain the unusual sourness of his tone.

In the end I had to interrupt the Brazilians, promising to meet up again later, and go and rescue my wife from the riverbank. I'd learnt that there was only one hotel in town, and one restaurant, both owned by the same woman.

'We'd invite you to stay here,' Wilson said, 'but as you see we're already living in space for four.'

I took Heather one of their beers and after she'd finished enthusing about its sublime qualities we packed up the canoe.

'See that woman over there, the big one with the green headdress?' she asked, indicating the crowd of Bush Negroes that now sat in one of the large canoes ready for departure.

I nodded.

'Well while you were away, I separated some items that we wouldn't be needing any more, and as she was sitting nearby I walked over and held out the frying pan, making gestures that she could have it.' She giggled. 'You know it was a bit sooty and not looking its best...' In fact it was encrusted with carbon and the sort of congealed fat that accumulates over four months with no washing-up liquid and no hot water. '... but there was still no need for her to be so snooty about it. She held it fastidiously at arm's length, and looked at me as if I'd handed her a warm dog turd or something. Not a word of thanks, no smile, just a look that said, "Is that the best you can do you pathetic, grubby piece of white trash?"' She laughed again. 'It was really embarrassing. She still accepted it though, I noticed, and stowed it in her bundles. What the hell was she expecting? The Le Creuset cast-iron casserole set with teak handles and copper bottoms?'

Having carted our gear from the river to the hotel, we sprawled on hard beds in an unaired stuffiness watching cockroaches peeking at us from the cracks around the shower tray, and little lizards scampering up the flaking distemper.

However hard an expedition might have been, I always feel strangely deflated and sad when I reach the destination. However eagerly I might have anticipated the escape from jungle life, re-entry to civilisation is always an anticlimax. For a start the reality could never live up to the feverish expectation, and 'civilisation' is a laughable term for the average Amazonian frontier community full of poverty and disease. The last hours of paddling had passed us through a shocking hinterland of devastation. The reality of rainforest destruction had been forgotten in the months travelling through unsullied primary forest, but now suddenly it was all around – fires, chainsaws, sawmills, cattle ranches, homesteaders – all nibbling, nibbling, nibbling at the forest edge.

Even the expectation of a decent dinner in Maripasoula couldn't halt nostalgia for our forest camps. We'd been locked in a treadmill of our own making by choosing an extreme goal and pursuing it doggedly through its many joyless stages. We'd barely had time to appreciate our surroundings or savour the experience, especially with dwindling food supplies forcing the pace. We hadn't wanted to try and emulate Raymond's attempts at living off the land. Now we wished we'd taken it a bit easier on the Litani or at the Indian villages instead of rushing down to this.

It was 8 p.m. when we emerged on to the street, freshly showered and dressed in clothes that had collected spots of black mould and a sour scent of mildew from months of storage in plastic bags. First stop was a shop-cum-bar where we sat down to a palpable lack of welcome and a ten-minute quarantine before an enormously fat woman consented to shuffle over in a clatter of flip-flops to see what might have brought us there.

'Two rum punches please,' I said in mutilated French.

Her round shoulders shrugged almost imperceptibly and an eyebrow rose 2 millimetres under a wig of such syntheticity that I could see the hairs on my arms bending towards its static field. She had evidently reached that stage of exhaustion beyond speech.

'Two rum punches.'

She sagged until her breasts came to rest on her stomach and her carthorse arse swayed outwards until it was blocking the road outside. If ever an artist needed to illustrate the Seven Deadly Sins, here would be the perfect model for Sloth. Her lunch seemed to have been left on her blouse to keep for later. She just stood there in a listless languor while flies strolled over her cheeks unnoticed. I stared at her bulk in fascination. The way her ham-like forearms met her hands: instead of a wrist she just had a crease, a bottomless fold where she probably kept her cigarettes and lighter.

'Try again,' Heather prompted.

'Two rums, understand? Rum? Ron? Rhum? Tafia?'

Success. She finally spoke in a surprisingly squeaky voice, 'I don't understand American.'

'Neither do we. Rum, please.'

'Why don't you wipe the table, while you're at it?' added Heather, gesturing at pools of drink that had caramelised with age into a future amber, in whose depths you could see trapped insects that no longer inhabit the earth.

She swore something unintelligible and shuffled off, thighs chafing, lowering herself into a settee with a twang of protesting springwork and turned her moon face back to a satellite TV programme.

'Fat slag,' said Heather with venom. 'You get her to understand the word "rum", and I'll teach her the word "punch"!'

I laughed, and walking over to a shelf, helped myself to a half-empty bottle of rum and two glasses and went back to the table. The woman and her friends glared but said nothing.

'Cheers!' We toasted each other, and then raised our glasses mockingly in their direction. 'To civilisation!'

'At least you get a cheery welcome at Brazilian towns, even if they are dumps.'

The rum was a little fiery for our inexperienced palates so Heather went to fetch a Coke from the fridge.

'I have a sneaking feeling they're going to overcharge us when we come to pay.'

They tried.

'Forty francs,' she demanded from the sofa on our third attempt, refusing to turn her gaze from the dubbed antics of Sergeant Bilko.

I took thirty out of my wallet and left the notes on our table, figuring it would be a few days before she summoned the energy to go over and collect it.

'Did you remember to leave a tip?' Heather asked as she took my arm and we strolled down the street past shadowy figures on verandas who seemed not to hear our greetings. The alcohol had worked its magic and we laughed unconcerned, determined not to let anything spoil our evening.

'Feeling peckish?' she asked.

'Starving.'

'Now try not to eat too much,' she advised. 'You know how ill you've made yourself in the past – especially that time with Peter.'

After our hungry weeks at Molocopote waiting for a flight out, Peter and I had rather overdone it when we arrived in Santarém. We had many hungry weeks and a lost Christmas to catch up on. First stop was a supermarket where we bought bread, cheese, crackers, chocolate, fruit, mayonnaise and jam, and made sandwiches with a sickly combination of fillings. That evening, our shrunken stomachs already protesting, we went to a *'rodizio'* eat-all-the-meat-you-can-handle restaurant and had the staff peeking out of the kitchen door in admiration.

We waddled back to the hotel like a couple of women in their third trimester, and lay on our beds groaning in agony.

'This is no good,' gasped Pete an hour later, stumbling over to the toilet and sticking a finger down his throat.

He wiped the sweat off his face and rinsed his mouth out.

'Ah, that's better. What a relief! You should try it.'

I did, and he was right. I brushed my teeth and on my way back to the bed I paused by the laden table.

'You know, I think I've now got room for a little cheese and crackers.'

The restaurant at Maripasoula was a great improvement on the rest of the town, the owner even gracing us with a tiny smile as she told us the dishes of the day. There was soup, followed by a meat dish composed of some jungle fauna that we suspected might be tapir, and a chocolate dessert. A couple of very cold Heinekens filled the interval before a soup arrived that contained more vegetables than we'd eaten in fifteen weeks, and crusty baguettes that we smeared with pats of butter. The meat lay in tender chunks among a rich sauce with mashed potato, fried bananas and haricots verts. There were extra dishes of rice and black beans that were refilled whenever we emptied them, which was often.

Wine was beyond our budget so we had more beers, and soon the unfriendly world outside was almost forgotten. Like two characters spotlit on a stage, surrounded by darkness, we concentrated on the food, the drink and each other. Nothing else mattered. We toasted the crossing of the Tumucumaque, and I noted Heather's newly-washed hair, how her face had thinned, exposing new bone structure, while her blue eyes sparkled from her Maroni River tan. She looked good, with a body taut from toil. My gaze was drawn to the outline of her breasts. I'd seen them naked and unfettered for weeks without much interest but now the glimpse of a nipple through the thin cotton of her blouse caused a forgotten stirring in my groin. Allelujah, life was returning. I told her she was beautiful and she laughed in embarrassment.

'You wouldn't look so bad yourself if you took that horrible beard off.'

'As soon as I find a razor.'

We held each other's gaze.

'I don't think you liked me so much a week or two ago,' she said teasingly.

'I didn't. I couldn't bear your company any longer,' I admitted.

'Neither could I. In fact, you really gave me the creeps.'

I know, I thought, I read about it in your diary. I fleetingly thought of confessing, but decided against it. It would lead to a row and spoil the evening. That afternoon in the hotel room I'd leafed through my own diary and come across the following entry written while we were still on the Mapaoni, after a grim day:

'Bloody Heather's useless at practical things. She can't tie a decent knot. She can't scale or fillet a fish. She won't learn to fire a shotgun. She doesn't like sticking her hand up a dead bird's arse and pulling out the guts (who does?). The list goes on and on. What am I doing bringing her out here? Did she really want to come? Wouldn't I rather be with a mate? Are we even suited? I'm amazed that we've been married for three years and together for six – we're chalk and cheese. Can it last?

Today I've seen it all – pigheadedness, pride, prickliness, sulkiness, ineptness – the works. Give me strength!'

Imagine if she'd sneaked a look at my diary and read that. What are diaries for if you can't have a bitch in them? Anyway she'd been right; I had been a bit flaky out there.

'Really?' I prompted now. 'In what way was I creepy?'

'You started to act as if you were cracking up. You know you did, you admitted as much the other day – fussy, obsessive, maddening.'

The other day! It already seemed months ago. All the worries of the days on dry land in the Tumucumaque had started to diminish once I'd got back on my natural habitat of the rivers.

'Sorry about that,' I said. 'I feel masterful again now. Next time let's opt for a canoeing expedition pure and simple, with no hiking and trail cutting and watershed crossing. My nerves wouldn't stand it. That was one dumb plan.' We laughed.

'Aren't you glad you've done it at last?' she asked.

'Sure I am, and even more relieved that it didn't end in another failure.'

'Did you think last time was such a failure?'

'Not really, no. All right, we didn't succeed in doing what we'd set out to do, but I was satisfied that we'd given it a good shot and not given up too easily. We'd been scuppered by malaria and circumstances out of our control. Actually, now that I've seen the Tumucumaque, I'm really relieved that Pete and I weren't confident enough of our position to start hacking our way into the hills.'

'We must send him a postcard and rub his nose in it a little.'

'Yeah. I'll attribute our success to the tougher companion I had with me this time.'

'Right.'

The owner appeared at our side, bringing the desserts: slabs of creamy chocolate cake lying in lakes of condensed milk. We started to eat eagerly... and then my evening began to fall apart.

In the space of three minutes I went from feeling marvellous to feeling very ill indeed. Heather's voice seemed to have been snatched away as if borne on a gale, and was now too faint to hear. My vision wobbled, doubled, swung from exaggerated technicolour to drab monochrome. Clammy sweat erupted on my face but my hand seemed too heavy to wipe it away.

'Are you all right?' Heather mouthed in concern.

'I feel awful,' I gasped.

I needed air. I had to get out into the street. Lurching to my feet, knocking the chair over, I headed for the door on shaky legs. The floor seemed a long way down, as if I'd grown a few feet in height. I sank down on a patch of grass outside, too miserable for pride.

Everyone probably thought I was off for a Wayana-style spew, but I wasn't sick; just dizzy and shaky with my senses shortcircuiting.

It might have been the shock to my system of rich buttery sauces, additives and the chemicals in beer and rum after months free from toxins and impurities. I'd been poisoned. Maybe the cook had slipped something into my soup, I thought deliriously, to get rid of this white intruder whose presence awoke grievances centuries old? I was making a bit of a spectacle of myself, sprawled in such a well-lit spot on the threshold of the restaurant, so I crawled to the shadows and lay in the dirt, drifting in and out of consciousness. I hadn't felt so ill since my malaria attacks of the past. What the hell was happening?

Heather brought me water, then returned to eat her dessert, brought me more, then finished my dessert and paid the bill. She helped me back to the hotel room where I sprawled over the bed, still clothed, the room spinning wildly, my body shaking in spasms. I prayed to be sick, craving the relief, but when I stuck a finger down my throat and vomited I felt no better.

'It's going to be cheap getting you drunk from now on!' joked Heather as she covered me with a blanket.

'It wasn't the drink!' I protested feebly. It seemed important to get her to believe me. 'I didn't have that much, did I?'

'Well, I feel quite drunk and I only had one rum, you had two.'

'It takes more than two rums and four tiny cans of weak Heineken to get me pissed,' I boasted pathetically. 'Something's poisoned me. It's like my body's gone into shock. It might have been something in the drink, but it wasn't the alcohol...'

'If you say so.' She sat on the bed and wiped my face with a cloth. 'Go to sleep now, you'll feel better in the morning. Maybe you've got sunstroke? We spent a lot of time out in it today.'

By morning I was more or less back to normal, just tired after a night of alternating shivers and sweats, with my temperature hovering around 103 degrees. We shuffled over to the restaurant for coffee, where the owner's unsympathetic attitude made it clear that I'd disgraced myself.

'We've got a financial problem,' Heather told me. 'Last night's bill for the meal was over forty pounds.'

'What!'

'Yeah, forty pounds, and we only had fifty pounds in French francs to start with, and we haven't paid the hotel bill yet.'

Our airless cell at the hotel cost an exorbitant £30 a night, but when we asked the owner if we could change money in Maripasoula, she shook her head.

'Go and get the shotgun,' Heather ordered.

'What?' I said, cradling my aching head in my hands. 'Hold her up? Isn't that a bit extreme?'

'No, stupid, to see if she'll buy it.'

The hotel owner examined its rusty length carefully, squinting down the barrel, testing its firing mechanism.

'No,' she decided. 'I'd never be able to sell it.'

'Of course you would, it just needs a bit of a clean with emery paper and oil.'

'It's not the condition that's a problem, it's the calibre. Nobody wants a small gun like this. I don't think you can even buy twenty gauge cartridges in Guyane. Everyone wants twelve bores.'

I bet they do, I thought. Even the Indians probably have braces of Purdeys with hand-engraved stocks.

When we found the airline agent and reserved seats for Cayenne, we were told of a Lebanese trader who would change our remaining $700 at an appalling rate. That was all we had left. After paying for the plane tickets and excess baggage there was barely enough left to pay the hotel and one meal a day until our departure. Such frugality was beyond us. We ate three times a day, sticking it on the bill to settle later. The owner would have to take the shotgun whether she liked it or not.

We spent an evening with the Brazilians whose warmth was much needed in this frosty village, taking rum and some unidentified meat that we'd bought from a street trader. Neighbours watched us disapprovingly from over the back fence while the barbeque belched white smoke.

'Capybara?' I guessed, sinking my teeth into a kebab. The others chewed, eyes distant, letting their taste buds investigate like a bunch of wine tasters.

'Maybe,' said one.

'No way! This is deer.'

'Oh come on! Deer meat is more fibrous, less gamey. It could be puma.'

'Puma?' coughed Heather, her jaws slowing.

'It's not puma, you idiot,' argued the oldest of the prospectors, the bow-legged, sinewy Milton, skin like an expensive briefcase. The others listened respectfully. Milton had eaten everything.

'This is anteater,' he pronounced, sweeping challenging eyes over the gathering. Maybe it was.

As mainland South America's only First World colony, French Guiana should be a model for rainforest conservation and sustainable development. Instead there are no established national parks and few controls over the activites of hunters that go well beyond the feeding of a family or village. Most of the restaurants, even in the capital, seem to specialise in exotic jungle fauna, and teams of Indians are supplied with portable freezers, generators, spotlights, and high-powered rifles to travel to the interior and furnish the towns with game. While so engaged they also collect skins and furs, or parrots and toucans for export, and pretty feathers to be made into tourist trinkets. The French army, using Guyane as a training ground, might be usefully employed enforcing wildlife regulations, but instead allows its troops to bag trophies to take home.

'In Brazil and elsewhere, rainforest destruction is driven by the harsh demands of poverty and economics,' argues environmental journalist Damien Lewis. 'Yet in French Guiana population pressure for new land is negligible, and as the lure of affluence draws people to coastal towns, the interior is becoming depopulated.'

Milton asked us many questions about our journey, and the overland crossing of the Tumucumaque.

'I've done a few hops from river to river like that myself in Brazil,' he said. 'From the Jatapú to the Nhamundá, from the Juruena to the Aripuana. It's tough leaving the river behind isn't it?'

'Did you carry your canoe across?' I asked.

'God no!' he laughed. 'How can you get a canoe thirty miles overland?'

'We've got a canoe that folds up and weighs twenty-five kilos.'

He chuckled. 'You gringos, you and your fancy gadgets! I was on an expedition once with some gringo scientists on a river in the Mato Grosso, and the stuff they had! One man had some foamy soap in an aerosol, and when he wanted to shave… psssst!' he gestured with a giggle, 'all this white stuff came out and grew in his hand! Another had a bed he filled with air every night, and another a fishing rod that telescoped into itself and could fit in a sack. One woman would only wash in hot water. We had to heat up saucepans for her to pour over her head. Can you imagine?' His pixie face screwed up in happy cackles, and he shook his head in wonder.

'So how long did it take you to cross those thirty miles from one river to another?' I asked to steer him away from further catalogues of gringo eccentricities.

'Oh, a couple of days, three perhaps.'

'Then you went back for your gear?'

'No, we carried that with us.'

'All of it?'

'Anything we couldn't carry between us got left behind. As long as you've got a sack of manioc flour, a shotgun, fishing line and hooks, an axe, machete, hammock and pick and shovel, you can go anywhere, don't you find?'

'Oh yeah. Sure.'

'Takes a few days to hollow out a new canoe and then off you go. New river, new gold, new adventures.' He finished rolling a cigarette and reached into the fire for a smouldering stick to light it with. I watched him enviously as he dragged the smoke down deep.

'Twenty-five years I've been a *garimpeiro*. Now I work the dredgers, but when I was younger I liked to prospect new finds, sneak into Indian land, cross into Guyana and Venezuela, keep moving, always hoping for the big one.'

'Ever find it?'

'Not really. Made a lot of money once or twice, enough to buy a nice house that I have in Rio for my old age, but it never lasted. If I'd stayed and worked at the stakes for longer I'd have made much more, but after six months shovelling gravel around in one place I'd leave it to my partners and go off exploring again. I get bored easily.'

'Must be quite a life you've had.'

'No complaints. I've been my own boss and that's the main ingredient for happiness in this life.'

We concentrated on eating for a few minutes.

'Maybe I'll go back to Brazil by the route you took,' he announced. 'Up the Litani, over to the Mapaoni and down the Jari to the Amazon. Sounds better than going round the coast to St Georges and Macapá. Save me a bus fare.'

'The Indians might stop you.'

'I don't think so. I like Indians and know how to win them over. So you leave the Ouaremapaan and cross to the Mapaoni, right?'

'Yeah, it's about fifteen miles and lots of hills.'

'About two or three days then?'

I hesitated.

'How long did it take you?' he asked, squinting against the smoke of his cigarette. 'Six weeks,' I replied.

'What?' he howled. 'How long?'

'Six weeks.'

'Fifteen miles in six weeks! What happened? Were you captured by Indians?'

'We had a lot of stuff, including the canoe. We didn't know where we were going, we got a bit lost...'

'Six weeks! I don't believe it!'

'It's true.'

I never really got much sense out of Milton after that. He returned again and again to the subject, his incredulity and mirth fuelled by slugs of rum, slapping his thighs, chuckling and hooting new witticisms.

'Fifteen miles in six weeks! That ant down there could do it faster! Hey, watch out, that snail wants to overtake! Beep beep! Tortoise coming! Ha ha ha!'

The next morning when we said goodbye as they boarded a canoe to return to their dredger, he tried to apologise. We assured him that he hadn't caused us any offence, but he insisted.

'It wasn't until I got to my hammock that I thought what it must have been like to spend six weeks in the bush,' he said. 'That's a long time to be away from a river. You must have had a hard time.'

We shrugged and he gave us each a hug, pressing his face against my chest and muttering that I was too damn tall to embrace properly. Then his impishness returned.

'Still bloody slow though!' he cackled. Then he made one last observation, astute and slightly uncomfortable.

'I expect when you get home you'll write a book about it all, won't you? We spend years in the forest and you gringos come for a couple of months and immediately you're explorers. Someone should come and write my story. I'd do it myself if I knew how to write.'

Before we could get on the flight to Cayenne there was one item of unfinished business: the absence in our passports of any stamp authorising our stay in French Guiana. We were illegal immigrants and it was time to go and surrender at the police post.

The two white gendarmes in the suffocating office must have done something terribly wrong back home to be sent to Maripasoula; perhaps accepted bribes, shot an innocent bystander or slept with the Commissioner's wife. This was Devil's Island without the sea breeze.

We explained our predicament, having to indicate our entry point on a large map of Guyane that hung on the wall.

'We can do nothing here,' said the senior officer. 'We have no authority to handle immigration. When you get to Cayenne airport go to the Immigration Department and surrender yourselves.'

'Will we be in trouble?' Heather asked sweetly.

'Of course you'll be in trouble! You've entered the country illegally via a prohibited route and travelled through a controlled Amerindian area! I think you're in pretty deep shit.'

Next morning we packed up our gear and strolled over to the restaurant for breakfast, preparing ourselves for yet more trouble when the time came to settle our bill. So nervous were we that the already unaffordable sum was inflated with extra *cafés au lait* and toast.

Finally we sidled over to the counter and asked for the total bill for accommodation and meals, and the amount made me give a little hysterical gulp that caused the woman to glance up with suspicion. The shortfall was about F2,000.

'Madam,' I said, 'regretfully we don't have enough money to pay this bill, but we do have some valuable items that I'm sure you'll agree will more than make up the difference.' And like a tinker I opened a sack and proceeded to pull out an embarrassing poverty of delights.

She let out an angry cry when she saw the little shotgun again, the fifty cartridges, two machetes, the antimalaria drugs, the 150 quinine tablets, and the other contents of our medical kit. She told us to get our filthy hammocks and blankets off her clean bar, and asked what the hell she was supposed to do with two paddles.

'How about a tent?'

'Who do you think uses a tent in Maripasoula?' she snorted, and we couldn't come up with an answer to that.

The argument went on for nearly an hour, but I don't think she was too disappointed with the deal. I've seen quinine tablets sell in Brazil for a dollar each, and a shotgun of any calibre is better than no shotgun at all. At least she didn't call for the gendarmes, and ask for us to be thrown in the debtor's prison. The little tease even wagged her finger at me and called me *'mechant'*, and once or twice I think I saw her suppress a smile.

All the other passengers taking the flight on the little turbo-prop to Cayenne the next morning had small suitcases and modest hand luggage. Not the Harrisons. We had to scrounge a lift in the airline pick-up to get our sacks and paraphernalia to the airport, and although the driver was alone in the cab he made us ride in the back to get covered with fine red dust. I could see that Maripasoula was going to be sorry to lose these English big spenders.

The plane was late so we sat in the shade of a hangar and watched a military plane unload a bunch of Foreign Legionnaires, all cropped hair, tattoos and muscle.

'One day they might be hardened and trained enough to make it into the Tumucumaque and climb one of those peaks without using helicopters,' Heather suggested.

'I doubt it. They'd need a chopper just to carry the soft drinks, wine, and cement to write their names in.'

'We saw no sign that they'd been anywhere near the trail for forty years or more, did we? Obviously just too risky for that bunch of wimps.'

Her mention of wimps reminded me of her diary and the reference to my uncertain future in her affections. 'At least they won't have to try and keep a relationship together while they're at it,' I commented unsubtly.

'What?'

'It's quite a test of a marriage to do a jungle trip together, isn't it?'

'What's brought this on?' she asked suspiciously.

'I'm just saying that we were pretty tested out there, that we saw each other at our worst, and yet we're still talking to each other. That must mean something.'

'I guess so.'

I was hoping for more, so blundered on. 'At one stage you thought we didn't have a future together, didn't you?'

'I don't think I ever said that.' Her eyes had narrowed thoughtfully.

'Maybe not in so many words,' I said quickly, 'but that was the impression I got. Do you still feel that way?'

'I got really sick of you, sure. I saw a side of you that I hadn't seen before, and I didn't like it much. You seem to have reverted more or less to your old self now, thank God, but it came as a shock.'

'Those spooky old hills got to me.'

'At least we got out of them alive. Anyway, you felt the same, didn't you? I remember you saying that you couldn't understand how we'd stayed together so long – that we were totally incompatible, and that you wished you had done this expedition with a mate! Imagine how good that made me feel!'

'Did I say that?'

'Yes you did.' The sound of engines put into reverse thrust made us glance at the airfield. 'Look, that's our plane. Better make sure our sacks get loaded safely.'

I walked behind her to the little departure shed, lost in thought. I'd never voiced those feelings, had I? I didn't think so. No I definitely hadn't. Which meant... could she have? There wasn't any other explanation. Why, the little...! All the preaching I'd had from the moral high ground about reading Mark's diary!

'Got the paperwork?' Heather asked, turning towards me. 'Why've you got that grin on your face?'

'No reason, sweetheart. No reason at all.'

We'd asked the gendarmes for a letter to confirm that we'd done our best to legalise our position in Maripasoula, and handed it to a moustachioed little immigration official when we arrived in Cayenne the next day. He looked at it, scratched his head and disappeared into a door marked 'Chief of Immigration', emerging five minutes later to usher us inside.

'What do you mean by disregarding all our regulations in this way?' said the Chief without preamble. 'Do you think they are of such little importance that you can say "Pah!" and ignore them all? Wander casually around our territory without presenting yourself at a border control? Be illegal immigrants for a month, maybe longer?' He stood up and paced to and fro. 'And travelling through an area closed to everyone except the Indians!' He glared at us contemptuously. 'You just breeze in and do as you damn well please, but all these restrictions are made for very good reasons. To protect the Indians from disease. To stop idiotic adventurers killing themselves in the forest, like a young French guy did many years ago.'

'Do you mean Raymond Maufrais?' I interrupted.

'Oh you've heard of him have you? A barmy hothead who thought that life in the forest was easy, and got himself killed for his stupidity.'

I felt the urge to jump to Raymond's defence. Having come close to losing our way and perishing in the Tumucumaque, our admiration and sympathy for him had grown. He deserved better than that dismissive insult.

But the man had moved on in a tirade so reminiscent of a headmaster's dressing down that I had to fight the urge to giggle.

Out of the corner of my eye I could see Heather's cheek muscles bunching and looked quickly away. Doing our best to look contrite, ashamed, humbled, we hung our heads and shuffled our feet.

'Do you know the powers I have?' he asked. 'Do you?'

We shook our heads.

'I could put you in prison. I could send you back to Brazil by plane. I could fine you very heavily. That would spoil your reckless little adventure wouldn't it?'

We nodded.

'Give me your passports!'

We handed them over, and the sight of them seemed to enrage him even further. He swore and raised his eyes to the ceiling.

'You mean to tell me you're British?' he shouted.

We nodded. Had he been reading our tabloid newspapers with their insulting tirades against our European neighbours?

'I thought you were American. Why the bloody hell have you been wasting my time?'

We stared at him in confusion. 'Don't you understand the difference? You still travelled through the Indian area without authorisation, but there's not much I can do about that now. But as for the rest...' Seeing us still gawping, he impatiently explained. 'You're British citizens, you're on French territory and border controls have been relaxed within the European Union. You don't need your passports stamped!'

With that he dropped back into his chair, seized a pile of paperwork and waved us dismissively towards the door.

'Now get out of my sight.'

POSTSCRIPT

It usually proves to be a mistake to return to places that you've loved.

The restaurant's still there but the chef has changed. That idyllic beach now has three huge hotels instead of the shacks where you slept and ate before. The little village you grew up in has become a town that sprawls through the fields where you played. The fishing hole that had those large trout is now in private hands.

And so it is when I return to the Amazon. Manaus has lost its romance (maybe it never had it; I was probably just seeing it with bush-crazed eyes). The rivers I canoed in the Mato Grosso are now fringed with ranches and farms instead of virgin forest.

And Brazil is booming. With a growing international market for its food and raw materials, Brazil's future looks assured. It can still expand its acreage of agricultural and pastoral land by clearing forest. Exports of beef, soya and timber have increased massively year on year.

There are two new threats to the remaining forest. The recent completion of the Interoceanic Highway from the Brazilian state of Acre to the Peruvian coast has finally given Brazil access to ports on the Pacific Ocean. This will inevitably lead to more destruction as produce is sucked from western Amazonia (and the largely intact rainforests of Peru) to the insatiable markets of China.

Secondly, there are plans to build a string of hydroelectric dams along many Amazon tributaries. The largest of these – Belo Monte on the Xingu River – will be the third largest in the world. All of them will displace people, drown virgin forest and interrupt fish migration.

And yet there has been one item of excellent news from this part of the world; and in the region travelled in this book.

On 23 August 2002 the Brazilian government announced the creation of the Tumucumaque Mountains National Park along the border with Surinam and French Guiana. Totalling 38,874 square kilometres this will be the world's largest tropical forest park – larger than Belgium.

When put together with the adjoining Guiana Amazonian Park in French Guiana, the total protected area totals 59,174 square kilometres.

It seemed probable that the creation of the new park would give Molocopote airstrip (where this book began) a new role. It could become a base for scientists while they study the region and catalogue the species that live here. Later, when the park is opened to limited tourism it could make a perfect site for an ecolodge.

However, until the national park gets the staff to enforce its protected status, the government thought that the airstrip was just attracting the wrong sort. Drug smugglers, gold prospectors, foreign canoeists and the like. So in February 2010, a group of federal policemen used 1,700 kilograms of dynamite to blow craters in the runway of Molocopote, and the nearby Anotae and Cruzado airstrips, rendering them unusable.

So actually I could probably return to the much-loved Mapaoni River one day and find it even more beautiful than I remembered. You can't say that very often.

The fact that we wouldn't be allowed to paddle freely through the area as we did in the past, is a small price to pay, I guess.

John Harrison
April 2011

BIBLIOGRAPHY

Barros Prado, Eduardo *The Lure of the Amazon* (1959, The Adventurers' Club)

Caufield, Catherine *In The Rainforest* (1984, Picador)

Cognat, André *J'ai choisi d'être Indien* (1989, L'Harmattan)

Cowell, Adrian *The Decade of Destruction* (1990, Headway)

Davis, Wade *One River* (1997, Touchstone Books)

Donner, Florinda *Shabono* (1984, Paladin)

Fleming, Peter *Brazilian Adventure* (1933, Jonathan Cape)

Goulding, Michael *Amazon: The Flooded Forest* (1989, BBC Books)

Guppy, Nicholas *A Young Man's Journey* (1973, John Murray)

Guppy, Nicholas *Wai-Wai* (1958, John Murray)

Harrison, John *Up The Creek: An Amazon Adventure* (1986, Bradt Publications)

Hemming, John and Ratter, James *Maracá: Rainforest Island* (1993, Macmillan)

Jordan, Martin and Tanis *Out of Chingford* (1988, Muller)

Kane, Joe *Running the Amazon* (1989, Pan)

Manciet, Yves *Land of Tomorrow: An Amazon Journey* (1964, Oliver and Boyd)

Maufrais, Raymond *Journey Without Return* (1953, William Kimber)

Maufrais, Raymond *L'appel de l'aventure: Collected Writings* (1991, Editions Caribeenes)

Maziere, Francis *Journey Into Legend* (1955, William Kimber)

Monbiot, George *Amazon Watershed* (1992, Abacus)

O'Hanlon, Redmond *In Trouble Again* (1988, Penguin)

Perry, Richard *The World of the Jaguar* (1970, David and Charles)

Popescu, Petru *Amazon Beaming* (1991, Penguin)

Schulz-Kampfhenkel, Otto *Riddle of Hell's Jungle* (1940, Hurst and Blackett)

Shoumatoff, Alex *In Southern Light* (1988, Corgi)

Shoumatoff, Alex *The Rivers Amazon* (1987, Century)

Starkell, Don *Paddle to the Amazon* (1989, Futura)

Swan, Michael *The Marches of El Dorado* (1958, Jonathan Cape)

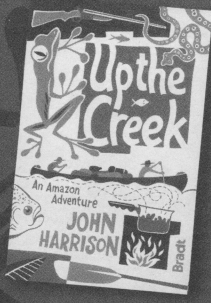

THE
GRINGO
Trail
A DARKLY COMIC road trip
through SOUTH AMERICA
ANDES
MARK
MANN
'dog-eared copies are sure to be falling out of backpacks in airports the world over'
FHM

THE GRINGO TRAIL

A DARKLY COMIC ROAD TRIP THROUGH SOUTH AMERICA

Mark Mann

ISBN: 978-1-84953-063-7   Paperback   £8.99

'Mark Mann plunges us into the drugs culture of the Gringo Trail'
WANDERLUST

... there I was in the middle of Bogotá, coked up to my eyeballs, in a hallway holding two machetes, while some drunk Colombians argued about whether or not to blow up a bar with a live hand grenade...

Asia has the Hippie Trail.
South America has the Gringo Trail.

Mark Mann and his girlfriend Melissa set off to explore the ancient monuments, mountains and rainforests of South America. But for their friend Mark, South America meant only one thing: drugs.

Sad, funny and shocking, *The Gringo Trail* is an *On the Road* for the Lonely Planet generation – a darkly comic road-trip and a revealing journey through South America's turbulent history.

LOST
IN THE
JUNGLE

A HARROWING
TRUE STORY OF
ADVENTURE
AND
SURVIVAL

YOSSI GHINSBERG

LOST IN THE JUNGLE
A HARROWING TRUE STORY OF
ADVENTURE AND SURVIVAL

Yossi Ghinsberg

ISBN: 978-1-84024-672-8   Paperback   £8.99

'Every so often an inspirational tale pops up that is simply better or more frightening than anything Hollywood can create. Lost in the Jungle... is one of those'   THE SUNDAY EXPRESS

I heard the rustle again, too close and too real to ignore. I clutched the flashlight, stuck my head out of the mosquito net... and found myself face-to-face with a jaguar.

Four travellers meet in Bolivia and set off into the Amazon rainforest on an expedition to find a hidden tribe and explore places tourists only dream of seeing. But what begins as the adventure of a lifetime quickly becomes a struggle for survival when they get lost in the wilds of the jungle.

The group splits up after disagreements, and Yossi and his friend try to find their own way back without a guide. But when a terrible rafting accident separates them, Yossi is forced to survive for weeks alone in one of the most unpredictable environments on the planet. Stranded without a knife, map or survival training, he must improvise shelter and forage for wild fruit to survive. As his skin begins to rot from his feet during raging storms and he loses all sense of direction, he wonders if he will make it back alive.

It's a story of friendship and of the teachings of the forest, and a terrifying true account that you won't be able to put down.

Have you enjoyed this book?
If so, why not write a review on your favourite website?
Thanks very much for buying this Summersdale book.

www.summersdale.com